www.PT-157.com

First Edition: March 2012
Second Release: August 2012
Commemorative release: March 2013
2014 Edition: Summer 2014

ISBN-13: 978-0615579122 (Carney Publications)

ISBN-10: 0615579124

Cover design by Bridgeman H. Carney

Front cover image:

(inset photo) PT-157 - July 9, 1943, underway out of Rendova Harbor, Renard Entrance in back of them, on July 9, 1943. Photo by U.S. Marine Sgt. Jerry Sarno

Rear cover images:

Left: MTB Log Report the the PT=157 rescued the crew of the PT-109
Center top: Map of locations in the area the PT-157 operated
Top Right: Lt (jg) William F. Liebenow and TM 1/C Welford H. West
Bottom Right: The crew of the PT-157 (July 9, 1943) and Commander Robert B. Kelly on July 9, 1943 in Rendova Harbor. Photo by Marine Sgt. Jerry Sarno.
Bottom Center: Section of page from PT-157 deck log the night they rescued Lt. John F. Kennedy and crew of the PT-109
Center left: Asiatic-Pacific Campaign ribbon
Center right: Silver Star Medal with ribbon

Also by Bridgeman H. Carney:

PT-157: A Scale Model Builder's Notebook -- A Carney Publication

The John Wayne movie, "They Were Expendable", introduced America to Motor Torpedo boats. John Kennedy's PT-109 story made them a national obsession. Recently, I was fortunate enough to receive a pre-publication copy of *First–Up, Chronicles of the PT-157.*

Bridge Carney has spent months (no … years) getting to know the surviving sailors of PT-157 and countless hours interviewing them. As his research gave him a good level of Squadron Nine expertise, he could ask "Bud" and "West" very specific questions and thus "the Skipper" and the "Torpedoman" fill in the countless details that only they knew and that make their stories so real. And since they are both in their nineties –or at least soon to be--first-hand accounts from the early squadrons are very rare and could soon be lost forever.

Bridge showed his mastery for detail with his first book *PT-157: A Scale Model Builder's Notebook.* For both books, he completed exhaustive research into the original documents available at the National Archives.

Bridge initially convinced me about his model making and research skills in *PT-157*. I am now overwhelmed by his narrative ability. This book has it all. Bridge is not interested in a "Washington and the Cherry tree" type story. In *First –Up,* we have an unvarnished account of what it was really like to "be there". The real-story does as much to honor the veterans as that of both John Wayne and John Kennedy.

Nathaniel Smith

Nathaniel Smith
2nd Generation of PT-154 and PT-154 historian

FOREWORD

FIRST-UP is a must read for the PT boat enthusiast and everyone interested in a slice of World War II history. Bridgeman Carney has been able to prod the memories of both Welford West and myself and merge them with the reports from the naval archives into a readable chronicle.

FIRST-UP is justly dedicated to the memory of Sam Koury, our Radioman, who was killed in action.

William F. Liebenow, Skipper of the PT-157
- December 21, 2011

Until now most everyone who knew of the PT-157 and its role to rescue Lt. J. F. Kennedy and the crew of the 109 would ask me only about that mission. And yes, that's understandable; but there was so much more during the summer of 1943.

At my age now and looking back nearly 70-years, this recounting from the last two of us from the 157 that summer can tell more of our story for current and future generations. The timeframe of this chronicle is during the most intense days for RON-9, the 157 and me. In the assembling of this book there were moments when I found myself back on the boat like it was yesterday. While recounting the details to Bridge, I often found my heart racing and my palms sweaty as I went back to the moments of these patrols and missions. Today I still give thanks that my prayers to survive, what I thought on several occasions would be my last moments, were heard.

I greatly appreciate that this book could bring some of those moments to light and give the readers a more complete perspective of what we were asked to do and what we did. To them I say, here is our story.

Welford H. West, Torpedoman 1/C of the PT-157
- January 5, 2012

FIRST-UP:

Chronicles of the PT-157

Rendova and Lever Harbor
June 28, 1943 – September 1, 1943

By

Bridgeman H. Carney

with

William F. 'Bud' Liebenow

Welford H. West

'We were just doing our job'

*A frequent sentiment said by William 'Bud' Liebenow and Welford West
in the course of the hundreds of conversations between us.*

This is the story of the job they did.

- *Bridgeman H. Carney*

SAM R. KOURY

DEDICATION

——— ◦ ———

To all the personnel involved with the PTs who went to the front lines in boats that turned the heads of its admirals and generals and commanded the attention of a formidable enemy nation.

To the crew of the PT-157 whose unique combination of experience and skills forged a team that brought it through its patrols on the darkest of nights to help our nation see the continued daylight of freedom.

And to Radioman Sam R. Koury of Leesville Louisiana who is the only crewman of the PT-157, from those included in this book, to be killed in the line of duty. Sam was killed on deck September 11, 1943 by enemy shore fire. His death is still the most difficult memory to his crewmates some seventy years later.

Sam, and the other 305 PT Crewmen who died in the Solomons, still keep vigil on our freedom.

It is with great honor to use Sam's lasting image from that summer of 1943 to express appreciation to all those who went to do their duty and to those who went on the 'Last Patrol' all too soon.

Memorial Day Weekend 2013 – on the 70th anniversary of the missions of the PT-157 in the summer of 1943. Skipper William F. 'Bud' Liebenow (left), Torpedoman (and frequently as helmsman) Welford H. West (right) and Bridgeman Carney. [photo courtesy: Roy Forbes]

Welford West passed on March 25, 2014. He was preceded in death by his wife of 57 years Rita West and survived by two sons, Dennis and Glenn West, daughter Brenda Toole grandchildren Bobby West, Denise West, Mathew Toole, Adam Toole, Angela Murchison, Rebecca Kowalski; and eight great grandchildren….and after having spoken to the Author and the Skipper one last time.

ACKNOWLEDGEMENTS

My warmest thanks to the many sources of information contained in this volume.

The National Archives and Research Administration [NARA] of the United States continues to be the protector of the PT log books, PT's Daily Action Reports and photos that are contained herein. I express my deep appreciation to both Nathaniel Smith, whose own research in connection with the PT-154 on which his father [Hamlin Dunlap Smith] was the Skipper, for the photo versions of many of the NARA documents and for his maps which helped me create the maps in First-Up. And also to Nathaniel Patch at the National Archives, for his research of additional documents that helped complete the documentation foundation of this chronicle, and PhotoResearch for securing the photos from NARA that have been used in the book.

I should note the trio of tools for publishing and distribution of books today. They are Microsoft WORD for formatting (this entire book was done in WORD; although I did have a few challenges to overcome), the internet which allows us to research and communicate immediately and to CreateSpace/Amazon which publish and sell books in a way which allows authors bring new titles to life in a very simple process. Both this book and my previous publication, *PT-157: A Scale Model Builder's Notebook*, were produced using this set of tools.

Thank you to Peter DeWilde, son of the PT-157's Quartermaster [Waldo DeWilde], for providing a number of the photos that his father had assembled in the early 1960s.

Of special note are the interview contributions of Mosquito Fleet Exhibit founder Frank Andruss, with audio tapes from many years ago of the 157's Skipper, William Liebenow, and Alex Johnson's 2001 correspondences, also with Liebenow, and as well as crewmen Ted Aust and Raymond Macht.

For Dick Washichek's PT-157 diagrams, made specifically for this book, and who is one of the bigger keepers of the PT flame, my sincere thanks…. and for this and all the significant contributions he makes daily to the remaining PT veterans, historians, model makers and enthusiasts.

My appreciation to Victor Chun, author of "American PTs of World War II" and now his recently released Version II of this same book, for encouragement and ideas in the making of this book.

To my father, William F. Carney Jr. who taught me history, and the people that made it.

My special gratitude to Lucy Tyler Liebenow and daughter Sue Liebenow for their help in the proofing of 'First-Up'.

And of course to Bud Liebenow and Welford West for recalling the details of the missions and patrols and their patience as I ask my seemingly endless questions over the nearly one-hundred conversations during the past two years.

aces 'n' eights

Nickname of the PT-157

Nickname chosen by crewman [Leon] Harry Armstrong while the PT-157 was in crew training in Panama. He painted the logo on the front of the chart house while the crew was ashore. The names, and image, stuck. The image (show below) is a tight close-up zoom and its location is on the front of the chart house as can be see on the cover photo and (same photo) on page 47.

The 'aces 'n' eights refers to the dead-man's hand as it was, legend says, the five card poker hand held by Wild Bill Hickok when he was murdered in a saloon in Deadwood, South Dakota.

Liebenow and West have said they had been asked numerous times about the cards shown on the 157 and the order they were in. Neither recalls, although both know the story of the dead man's hand which is two aces and two 8's and a fifth card which history has never been sure. However, after having found a much clearer photo of the 157 underway in the US National Archives, the author was able to zoom in and provide the answer to the nearly 70-year old question.

The cards read (top-right-to-bottom-left)
8-spades, 8-hearts, 7-spades, Ace-hearts, Ace-spades

The PT-157

July – August 1943

Model by Bridgeman Carney

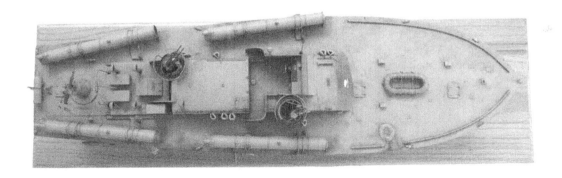

Overall model length: 33" (83.8cm)
Weight: 7lbs-11.5oz (3.5kg)
Scale: ~ 1:30

REFERENCE MATERIALS

Table of Contents

THIS BOOK'S ORGANIZATION

Eyewitness Recounting: Eyewitness recounting by both the PT-157's Skipper, William F. 'Bud' Liebenow, and torpedoman, Welford West are the real substance and cause in writing this book. These details are not found in any document and yet are the glue by which we can piece the personal daily 'as-it-was' occurrences of the days and nights in the summer of 1943. These invaluable recollections tell us what it was like on many of the more difficult and memorable patrols and missions of the 157. In addition there are the recollections from interviews of Liebenow and crewmen, Ted Aust and Raymond Macht, from correspondences provided by PT historians Frank Andruss and Alex Johnson to the author.

The telling of the PT-157's chronicle also relies on documentation references (Appendices 'B' and 'C'). The foundation is set by the Daily Action Reports generated by the MTB Commander and the PT-157's own Deck Log Book. Supplemental documents in Appendices 'D' and 'E' give additional insight as to Commander Kelly's actions to add 20mm Oerlikon guns in the forward turret of all his PTs of Squadron-9 (note that squadrons were called 'RON' for short at the time so this is RON-9) and later his outlook of how the PTs are faring against the Japanese barges. And finally, through the book are photographs of people and scenes of the crew of the 157 and things they would have seen. This blend then becomes a great and necessary combination of the sequence, details and first-hand eyewitnesses to this PT history.

PT-157 Time line (Appendix A, Page 79): For quick reference, a brief time line of the PT-157's patrols/missions.

The Deck Logs (Appendix B, Page 83): Generally gives us timing of the patrols (time they left for patrol and time they return). They are a good cross check to the Daily Action Reports but their best value is on the few occasions such as when the 157 moves out of the theater, such as moving from Rendova back to Tulagi for rearming of torpedoes and repairs to its engines, as those details do not exist in any other reports.

The PT-157's Deck Logs were provided to the author by the National Archives and by Nathaniel Smith for the period of time covered in this book.

The MTB Daily Action Reports (Appendix C, Page 101): Gives us the daily locations of all the PTs at Rendova and Lever Harbor, where they patrolled (if they were on patrol that night) and the action that occurred. This is important as the PT Deck Logs purposely lack in the listing of actions such as if they fired torpedoes, enemy interceptions and so on so as to not have such detail available to the enemy in the event of capture. The 157's log does, however, in a number of instances, note if they were bombed upon by aircraft.

Additional documentation is contained in two additional Appendix Sections from Commander Kelly (the Commander of RON-9):

- Commander Kelly's review to U.S. Naval command on the efforts of the PTs in barge fighting during August of 1943 (Appendix D, Page 163).
- Commander Kelly's memo requesting and reporting on the use of 20mm Oerlikon guns in the forward turret and how that worked out once in the Pacific (Appendix E, Page 173)

Photographs: As much as possible only photographs that were directly connected to things the crew of the 157 would have seen are included. A few photos are shots that have not been seen for nearly 50-years or possibly have never been published before. With most of the photos you will see a reference to 'NARA' and a number such as [NARA 80-G-13091]. This refers to the U.S. National Archives and Records Administration catalog number under which it is stored in their filing system.

A few Points about PTs

This section of *FIRST-UP* provides a background regarding a few aspects about PTs that for those not too familiar with the 'ELCO PT-103' production series of PT boats; of which the PT-157 was included. These are helpful to know, as they were part of the Skipper's and crew's knowledge at the time, before reading through the actual 157's patrols and missions and documentation sections.

THE PT'S TORPEDO STRATEGY

The signature profile of the early PTs was, of course, the four deck-mounted torpedo tubes. Their appearance was certainly a threat and gave a certain armed-to-the-teeth-and-ready-to-fight appearance at a time when the US needed to show resolve to the enemy...and to the folks back home. The Japanese respected that these PTs could indeed sink their ships. A torpedo is a torpedo, so the Japanese had to alter their strategies and defend against them. The days of the open seas would no longer be possible for them. That is exactly what the PTs, as our *first responders* to use more current terminology, were meant to do immediately following Pearl Harbor.

The job of the PTs in the Solomons was the interdiction (interception) of Japanese ships and barges carrying soldiers and supplies. It was the continuous flow of these resources down the New Georgia Sound, known as 'the Slot', that posed the immediate threat; and had to be stopped. Many of the water passages around islands that bordered 'The Slot' however were not suitable for large ships and even the shallow draft PTs could, and some did, hit sand, or worse coral reefs, which could badly rip the bottoms of the boats which in most cases caused them to be abandoned and then destroyed to prevent capture by the enemy.

With the limited number of the enemy's capital ship targets and the shallow waters, the PTs in the Solomons, as it turns out, rarely got to use torpedoes. But the torpedoes presence was an ever present threat to the enemy who, should they decide to send bigger ships into the nest of PTs, would likely take losses. Losing a large steel ship by an attack from a small wood frame/hulled PT was not a good risk/reward calculation to the Japanese...and one they avoided when possible. If they had known the problems of the PTs torpedoes the effectiveness of the PT fleet would have been greatly reduced.

TORPEDO ISSUES

So what was it like to actually be on PTs during the period of time that the torpedo issues were making themselves known? Aside from the technical problems with the 'fish' (navy slang for a torpedo) itself there was risk of exposing your location when you did get it off and in the water.

The inside of the tubes was wiped with an oil based lubricant so as to help slide the torpedo in the tube when loading and secondly seal in the gases that 'pushed' the torpedo out and move the [heavy] torpedo with less friction. Each time a torpedo was fired the inside of the tube had to be wiped down to remove the black power residue from the firing shell. This required a [small] crewman to physically crawl through the tube with rags and oil to clean and re-lube the tube before reloading. Given the tightness of the tube, the heat of the days in the Solomons and cleaning material vapors, this was not pleasant work. Welford West said one time he noticed more than the usual vapors coming out of the tube that was being cleaned and realized the sailor inside the tube had been using gasoline as the cleaning agent and had pretty well passed out from those fumes. West had to scramble inside the tube to retrieve the sailor who made it out OK.

The maintaining of the torpedo tube was trivial compared to the one that could cost a PT and its crew their lives. PTs were night fighters and the launching of torpedoes required that they be at close range to ensure the accuracy of the torpedo's launch which was based most times on the dead reckoning of pointing the PT toward the target. It was the surprise element the PTs needed.

The concern by crews each time a torpedo was fired was the possibility of 'flashing'. All too frequently when the shell that fired the torpedo out of its tube went off, it would also ignite the oil lubricant in the tube. The results of the subsequent flash would greatly endanger the PT and crew as it identified their location to the enemy ships and thus became a bulls-eye at which to shoot. The second affect was the Japanese response to the flash, knowing torpedoes had just been launched, was to alter their course to avoid the torpedo's (or torpedoes') path. So not only would you come under heavy enemy fire but the odds of hitting a ship with the torpedo were greatly diminished.

The torpedo tubes of the early PTs used the 21" (diameter) Mark VIII torpedo. The Mark VIII was a post World War I design and in the first half of World War II there were numerous complaints about these torpedoes not hitting their target or not exploding when they did. Eventually, after numerous complaints from the field, there was a litany of identified issues with the Mark VIII. This included that the Mark VIII ran about 11-feet lower in the water causing them to pass right under their intended target. Many spent torpedoes were later found floating in the water or having run up on the beach of some nearby island.

The PT squadron Commanders, such as Commander Robert Kelly of RON-9, were getting the complaints from their Skippers and trying to push it up through the upper Navy echelon to take notice and provide a solution*. In the PT Action Report of August 5, 1943 (By Lt. Commander T. G. Warfield) to the Commander-in-Chief, U.S. Fleet is the **Comments and Recommendations** section of the report below that highlights the frustration and what was being said at the time:

MOTOR TORPEDO BOATS, RENDOVA
5 August 1943.
MTBR/A16-3
Serial 0034
Declassified (8 SEP 59)

From: The Commander.
To: The Commander-in-Chief, U.S. Fleet.
Via: Official Channels.

7. COMMENTS AND RECOMMENDATIONS:

(a) …..

(b) …..

(c) …..

(d) The Mark VIII torpedo again manifested its want of capacity to inflict real damage. Enemy destroyers kept going after certain hits had been scored. Intelligence reports that 5 unexploded torpedoes are on the shore of Kolombangara Island.

(e) Flashes and burning in the tubes on firing not only give target opportunity to avoid but disclose PT positions. Not enough interest is being taken in this matter behind the firing line.

T. G. WARFIELD.

<end of Action Report>

---

* For an excellent, comprehensive review on this subject there are many publications and on-line resources. This web page has an excellent recap: http://pt-king.gdinc.com/Torpedo.html

In the Fall of 1943 the Navy began to remove the PT's tubes and replace them with a hanging rack system that would hold the 22.4" (diameter) Mark XIII aerial torpedoes; the same type used by naval dive bombers. New PTs coming out of production also were being fitted with the hanging rack system. That also removed a good deal of weight of the tubes themselves giving the PTs a bit more speed and maneuverability.

PTs OVER THE WAVES...*SLOW DOWN*!

PTs are most often portrayed as flying over the water at high speeds. Those photos were good for recruitment and gave the hidden message that 'speed wins'. [Note: *Even the cover photo of this book has the 157 running at top speed out of Rendova however we will see this was a unique and rare event*]. The PT-157 was clocked, while on training exercises in Panama loaded with four torpedoes, at 52-knots (that's 60-mph) so this 80-ft boat was *very* capable of speed!

In firing torpedoes the PTs would run at about 27-28 knots (about 30-mph). You can't, and wouldn't, fire torpedoes at any higher speed or you would end ahead of the torpedo itself.

Actual experience shows a different picture. In talking to Liebenow and West and in Action Reports it is noted that running at high speeds, day or night, created a boat wake that easily showed the enemy your location.

In the PT's routine of night fighting, a sizeable wake could catch any moonlight and reveal its presence and position. For these reasons the more active PT patrol nights were due to the high activity of the Japanese who chose nights with little or no moonlight so as to hide their wakes as well. Secondly, the PT's three propellers churning the water in high speed travel at night could also kick up a luminescence trail due to the micro-life in the water. What better way to paint an arrow to your location for your enemies to follow than to have two glowing lines of your wake converging on your boat!

In moving a PT in daylight hours, which was rare, the skippers knew to keep it slow and cut engines at the sound of aircraft. Without a wake, the PTs, which had been repainted to camouflage themselves and not reflect daylight/moonlight light, were hard to detect.

These lessons were also followed by the Japanese as well. Often PTs noted the slow speeds of the larger enemy ships which were also avoiding making wakes and kicking up luminescent trails.

Admiral Bulkeley, who was the first Commander of PTs and was responsible for the actions to get General Douglas MacArthur out of Corregidor by use of PTs, wrote in his memoir, **At Close Quarters,** that the perfect PT attack has the PTs running slowly with silent engines, by using the PTs unique flapper/exhaust system, moving quietly into position, firing torpedoes and then moving slowly and quietly away without detection.

It is not until the PTs engage in barge fighting that they fully utilize the high speed and quick maneuver to capability as they made their hit and run tactics against the well defended, coast hugging barges of the Japanese.

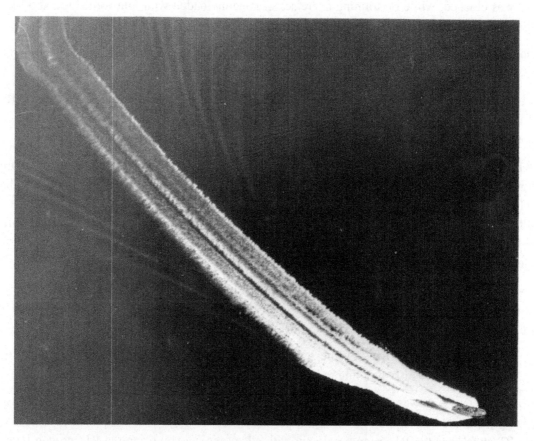

A PT (lower right) is making both a beautiful *and dangerous* wake
[NARA 80-G-13091]

CONFIGURATION OF THE ELCO PT-103 SERIES

The PT-157 was produced by the ELCO Corporation in Bayonne New Jersey. The 157 is from the series of PTs produced called the PT-103 series. The configuration of the 103 series was constantly changing, based on the changing requirements at the front lines, improvements in engineering, production and parts.

For RON-9's PTs, their Commander (R.B. Kelly) had anticipated the need for heavier firepower and therefore, apparently using some of his fame as one of those that brought General Douglas MacArthur out from certain capture at Corregidor earlier in the war, had arranged an 'experiment' to outfit his PT Squadron with 20mm Oerlikon in place of the twin 50-cal guns, in the starboard [front] turret (memos to his request and the results of its use are in Appendix 173)

On the following two pages (pages 8, 9) is a profile and deck drawings of the PT-157 and its configuration as it was in the summer of 1943.

Not shown is the 157's 37MM deck cannon. In mid-August the 157 as one of the first two PTs of RON-9 to have a 37MM 'jury-rigged' to its deck as one of a number of trial-and-error attempts to find solutions for attacking enemy barges.

A Special thank you...

The drawings on the next two pages were prepared for this book by noted PT historian, webmaster for the http://www.PTBOATS.ORG; Dick Washichek. In 2009 Dick found microfilm rolls of the original ELCO blueprints in the National Archives. It had been believed that all the blueprints had been lost in a fire at ELCO in the 1960's. The 'find' of these microfilm rolls and his subsequent transferring into digital format, and making them available to us, has been a real treasure to PT aficionados. Mr. Washichek is also the creator of a library of PT boat posters which may be viewed and purchased, as well as the PT blueprints, at the PTBOATS website or at http://www.gdinc.com/ptgallery.html

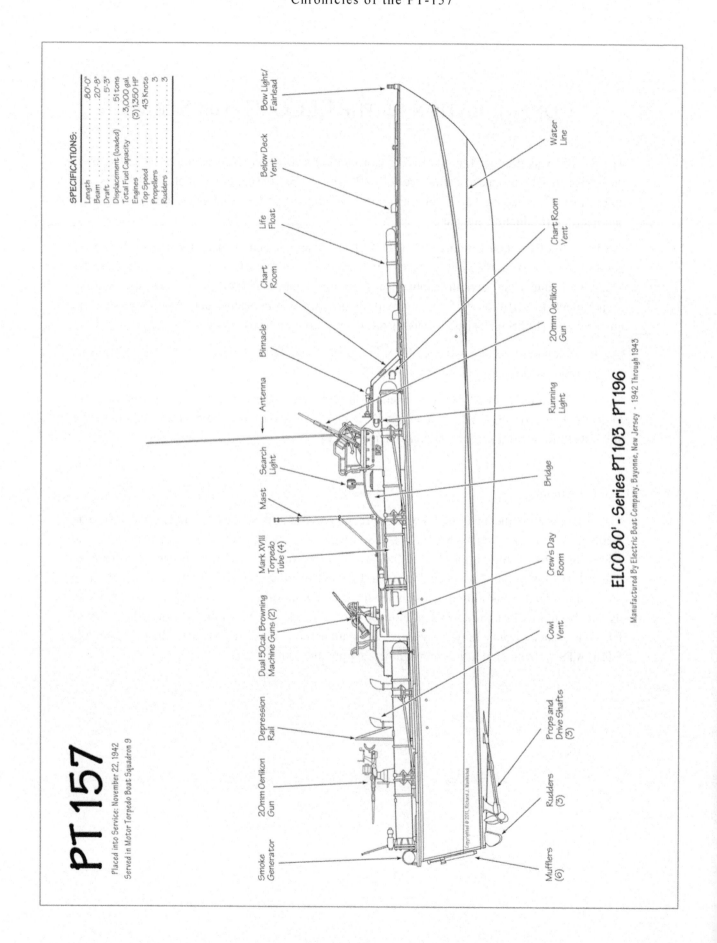

PT 157

Placed into Service: November 22, 1942

Served in Motor Torpedo Boat Squadron 9

SPECIFICATIONS:

Length . . . . 80'-0"
Beam . . . . 20'-8"
Draft . . . . 5'-3"
Displacement (loaded) . . . . . 51 tons
Total Fuel Capacity . . . . . 3,000 gal.
Engines . . . . (3) 1,350 HP
Top Speed . . . . 43 Knots
Propellers 3
Rudders 3

Bow Light/ Fairlead

Below Deck Vent

Water Line

Life Float

Chart Room

Chart Room Vent

Binnacle

20mm Oerlikon Gun

Antenna

Search Light

Running Light

Mast

Bridge

Mark XVIII Torpedo Tube (4)

Crew's Day Room

Dual 50cal. Browning Machine Guns (2)

Cowl Vent

Depression Rail

Props and Drive Shafts (3)

20mm Oerlikon Gun

Rudders (3)

Smoke Generator

Mufflers (6)

ELCO 80' - Series PT 103 - PT 196

Manufactured By Electric Boat Company, Bayonne, New Jersey - 1942 Through 1943

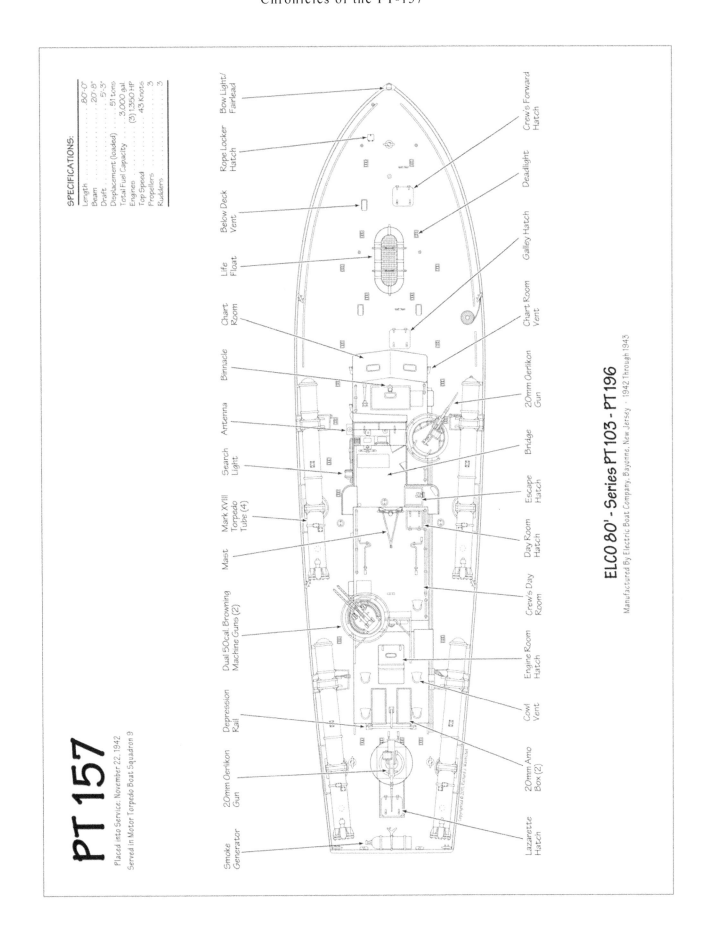

PT 157

Placed into Service. November 22, 1942

Served in Motor Torpedo Boat Squadron 9

SPECIFICATIONS:

Length	80'-0"
Beam	20'-8"
Draft	5'-3"
Displacement (loaded)	51 tons
Total Fuel Capacity	3,000 gal
Engines	(3) 1,350 HP
Top Speed	43 Knots
Propellers	3
Rudders	3

Bow Light/ Fairlead

Crew's Forward Hatch

Rope Locker Hatch

Deadlight

Below Deck Vent

Galley Hatch

Life Float

Chart Room

Chart Room Vent

Binnacle

20mm Oerlikon Gun

Antenna

Search Light

Bridge

Escape Hatch

Mark XVIII Torpedo Tube (4)

Day Room Hatch

Mast

Crew's Day Room

Dual 50cal. Browning Machine Guns (2)

Engine Room Hatch

Depression Rail

Cowl Vent

20mm Oerlikon Gun

20mm Amo Box (2)

Smoke Generator

Lazarette Hatch

ELCO 80' - Series PT 103 - PT 196

Manufactured By Electric Boat Company, Bayonne, New Jersey - 1942 Through 1943

CREW OF THE PT-157
JULY-AUGUST 1943

PT-157's Deck Log (above)

William F. 'Bud' Liebenow	Boat Captain
John W. Ruff	Executive Officer
Dan J. Jamieson, Jr.	Motor Mechanic 1/C
Sam R. Koury	Radioman 3/C
Welford H. West	Torpedoman 1/C
Raymond A. Macht	Gunner's Mate 3/C
Waldo DeWilde	Quartermaster 3/C
Stanley 'Red' Kendall	SC 3/C
Theodore Aust	Motor Mechanic 3/C
Leon H. 'Spit' Armstrong	F 1/C
Robert Shaw *	Motor Mechanic 1/C
James S. Smith	Seaman 1/C
Harold C. Goodmote	Seaman 1/C

* Shaw was transferred before the PT-157 moved up to Rendova

PT-157 crew photo with Cmdr. Kelly (center, in fatigues with collared shirt) taken July 9, 1943 in Rendova Harbor. Photographer Marine Sgt. Sarno is standing on the deck of an adjacent PT as all the PTs moored in harbor as they have not yet any dock to which to tie up to. [NARA 80-G-52794]

From left to right…..

Uncertain but possibly Q/M Robert C. Link (visiting from PT-161)
Harold C. Goodmote
Waldo DeWilde
Dan J. Jamieson, Jr.
Welford H. West
John W. Ruff
Robert Kelly (RON-9 Commander)
William F. 'Bud' Liebenow
Raymond A. Macht
Sam R. Koury
Theodore Aust
James S.'Smitty' Smith
Leon H. 'Spit' Armstrong
Stanley 'Red' Kendall (in the turret)

LIEBENOW AND WEST

FIRST-UP
Chronicles of the PT-157

William F. (Bud) Liebenow Jr. had graduated from college and was teaching in Fredericksburg, Virginia, at 21-years old when he signed up for service the day after Pearl Harbor. 'Bud' entered active service as a U.S. Navy Seaman 2/C. At Notre Dame he received 4-weeks of Naval indoctrination followed by 12-weeks of midshipmen school at Northwestern University in Chicago, 4-weeks of torpedo school in Newport, Rhode Island and finally 8-weeks of PT boat Operation in Melville, Rhode Island.

At the end of 1943 Bud was assigned to the war in Europe under legendary PT Commander John Bulkeley to assist the OSS for drop-off/pick-up of agents along the German held French Coast. He was then assigned Skipper of the PT-199 in the Atlantic. On D-Day the PT-199 pulled over 60 crewmen from water around the sinking USS Corry that had been hit by German shore fire.

Liebenow was awarded a Silver Star relating to two specific missions which occurred in the summer of 1943 in the Pacific and a Bronze Star for his service in the Atlantic.

Welford H. West. After having served in the U.S. Merchant Marines for one year, West joined the U. S. Navy in November 1942. Prior to this, West worked on torpedoes at the U.S. Naval Munitions facility in nearby Yorktown, Virginia. When he entered the Navy he carried a letter of recommendation from the Yorktown facility's Commander Roach, and was given the rank of Petty Office 3rd Class while in boot camp.

Welford had grown up in the tidewater area of Virginia, and helped his father who was a local oyster fisherman. Combined with West's seaman training in the Merchant Marines, he would provide critical advantages to the PT-157 in knowledge of sea and boat operations as we'll see on the missions. For example, he knew how to run a lead line and could stand on the bow of the 157 calling out the depth readings to Skipper Liebenow or scan the water ahead for 'shallows' created by sandbars or coral or see 'coconut logs' well before others spotted them. These logs could severely damage a PT's prop and/or prop shafts especially when navigating into shore for personnel drop-offs/pick-ups such the PT-157 frequently did.

Although his formal crew position was as torpedo man of the 157, he frequently was the helmsman and when not at the helm at the antennae mast as lookout. He also operated the smoke generator and later manned the 157's first .38-cal gun when it was installed. West served almost 18-months on the 157 which was twice as long as was the general rule due to the wear and tear on his body riding PTs for that length of time. After leaving the 157, Welford was an instructor at the torpedo training school in Melville, Rhode Island.

13

The CREW of the PT-157...

Liebenow quickly learned to trust West in the operations of the boat. West was experienced on the water and knew how to handle a boat and that provided advantages to the 157. West had great confidence in Liebenow for ability to keep a level head during pressure situations.

Overall the PT-157 crew had some advantages that, on the surface, were not so obvious but certainly contributed to the 157's success on their missions and patrols. Here are some found along the way.

Liebenow, *Boat Captain*: A college graduate before entering the USNR (not so common before WWII). He was involved with sports (including high school football, on the offense, and the very personal contact sport of boxing).

After reviewing their more notable missions, and West's comments about how Liebenow responded in tight situations, Liebenow seems to have blended his educated thinking and boxing reflexes.

The education gave him logic of decision making. How should I approach situation X, Y or Z. What sequence makes sense for this given situation? His education had now added the processes by which he could deduce the best approach.

The boxing experience seems to give him unique advantages added to his educated, logical thinking. PT fighting was a combination of defend & attack; and sometimes at the same time. Cover with the left and jab with the right. You're in a ring, in a fight and fight you must to win. Even more so as this was war. As a boxer will tell you, fear is something that robs your reflexive and decision abilities. You may have fear, but you have to learn to replace it with a response reflex.

A college educated thinker with boxer reflexes. He had both and in critical moments and used them.

The following are but brief bios of those mentioned in the course of my interviews and discussions.

West, *Torpedo man*: In his youth worked with his father on fishing boats off Virginia, so was well acquainted with the sea and boat handling in all conditions. Later West worked in a nearby torpedo factory (Yorktown, VA) so was very familiar with torpedoes. In the year before the US entered World War II he also spent a year in the Merchant Marine. That put him in the action of the war as the merchant marines transported materials to Europe under the Lend-Lease plan and so he was already in harm's way before Pearl Harbor. It also provided him with more formal training in seamanship skills.

When West entered the Navy he had a letter from the torpedo company about his knowledge in torpedoes so he was given rank of Petty Officer while still in boot camp!

Koury, *Radioman*: Worked on the railroad before the war on the telegraph and so Koury knew Morse code and how to operate the key. He was the best Morse code key man in RON-9 according to Liebenow and West and, much like a musician who can turn notes on a page into music on an instrument, could 'hear' incoming messages just by listening to the dots and dashes as they were coming in.

Macht, *Rear turret gunner (twin 50-cal)*: Ray worked for a construction company prior to the war. After finishing Class A ordinance school in San Diego, he and 19 other students were selected to go to PT boats. Ray had never heard of a PT boat until that moment. Although the smallest man on the boat, that has advantages. As a turret gunner you are in a cramped space and need to be agile to move the turret assembly quickly by using your body. Mach's size also seems to have been a possible reason why he was in the dingy to row the wounded crewmen of the PT-109 from shore the short distance to the PT-157. He was certainly strong enough to row and his size allowed for maximum space for the wounded sailors in the small dingy.

Smith, *Forward turret gunner (20mm Oerlikon)*: ('Smitty'). The forward turret is an important location on PTs as it is the forward eyes as PTs move forward. You can see his intensity when underway as in the close-up in photo of him on page 24. Welford West best remember Smitty's actions on the night of August 15/16 (page 64) and breaking a rule to fire on a menacing Japanese plane that was strafing them. Notable of Smith habits was his desire to shower during any rainstorm as we'll also see on page 24.

Jamieson, *Motormac*: The oldest crewman at over 40-years old. He had worked on engines all his life. He knew engines repairs and operation and had forearms arms that were oversized from years of engine work. Liebenow said his forearms were large, like Popeye's in the old cartoons. West said the 157 never missed a patrol due to engine issues. Jamieson will work sheer magic when he brings the center engine back to life after it was heavily damaged in the 'Squeeze Play' patrol of July 2/3.

Aust, *Motormac*: [in his own words taken from interview with Alex Johnson in 2001] "Fresh from AMM school in Jacksonville, Fla., being in the top 10 of my class, I had the honor of choosing my next assignment. Nineteen years old, AMM3/c, eager and fired up with patriotism and enthusiasm, I, along with 21 other guys, chose PTs. Bulkeley and MacArthur were the current heroes of the Pacific, and we were young and impressionable…. on completion of school, I was sent to the Brooklyn Navy Yard where I was assigned to Squadron 9 and PT-157 being built in Bayonne, NJ. The crew at that time consisted of 8 men and 1 officer, the Skipper. Ens William Frederick Liebenow, III. He proved to be the finest officer in our squadron."

DeWilde, *Quartermaster*: Waldo was 38 years old in 1943 so again this was another crewman who had lived some life and brought maturity to the crew. Like Liebenow he was a college graduate, very smart according to Liebenow and West. He was ideal for keeping of the 157's log.

Liebenow related a story that when the crew was in Panama their Squadron Commander, Robert Kelly, came on board for his first official inspection of the boat. Kelly went all over the entire boat and seemingly could not find anything that was out of place. As a commander Kelly knew it was good naval management technique to always find *something* out of order so just as Kelly was about to leave the boat, with the crew standing in line at attention, he looked up at the flags flying on the PT's mast yardarm and said 'replace that frayed flag!'. Waldo turned his head (breaking the required look-straight-ahead when at attention) and looked at Kelly and said 'OK' to which Kelly exploded and asked Liebenow if his crew knew how to address an officer and then instructed Liebenow to drill his team for the rest of the afternoon on how to address and officer! The crew knew that Kelly had to complain about something and got a good chuckle out of this whole event…even 70-years later.

Liebenow says some 68-years later now "I had a great crew!". Welford says the same. The bonding of the crew started right at the beginning. The 157's MotorMac Aust wrote the following in remembrance during their days of crew training in boat handling while in Panama before being shipped out to the Pacific….

> "Well, we hadn't been paid in quite awhile, so we pooled our money. $6-$7 between us. Too bad. 'Lieb ' was getting on his dress uniform and looked in the crew's quarters said, 'what's wrong with you guys?'. 'Not enough money to buy two rounds'(said Aust), so he [Liebenow] digs out a $20 bill and says, 'Here, use this', and he starts taking off his dress whites. 'What the hell is this?' I said. 'You have my money', Lieb says. So, we split the $20 with him, and we all went out and had some fun."

Liebenow said the crewmen did their jobs and did them well on their own without having to be managed. This was a sentiment that seemed shared by crewmembers according to their descendents. While researching for this book I located some of the children of some of the other crewmen. In my discussions they all said their fathers talked throughout their lives with great pride about their time on the 157.

To note, RON-9's Cmdr. Robert B. Kelly was close to Liebenow and the crew of the 157. That seemed to happen right off. Liebenow and Kelly got along very well and he seemed to call on the 157 as the 'go to' boat on many of the non-routine missions.

TWO TYPES OF OFFICERS

In talking to our two eyewitnesses and another crewman, who served later on the 157, there seemed to be two flavors of PT officers. The individual officer's 'flavor', meaning the manner in which they interacted with their crew, would frequently be based on their prior naval experience.

The PTs were a very non-traditional type officer assignment. There was little room for 'Brass Officers' and standard naval Academy protocol. However these are U.S Naval boats which have many Annapolis trained Skippers so the adjustments to command on PTs are interesting challenges.

One mode followed the traditional protocols of naval-officers-to-crew relationship, which came from the hundreds of years of mostly US and British naval experience. These officers usually had been officers before the war and many were Annapolis graduates. They acted on orders from their superior and they in turn gave orders to their subordinates. They tended to separate themselves a bit from deck sailors and followed a chain-of-communication-command. In an interview with the 157's Ray Macht, when asked about a Skipper from another PT, he commented in passing, "Pessolano was an Academy man and most thought him to be strict." showing his own general connection that Annapolis officers have a different approach to their crew. Pessolano did eventually transfer out of PTs and back into the big boats[1].

The second type of officer received basic training *after* Pearl Harbor and were anxious to get into the fight; that's why they joined. They mixed with their crewman frequently; on and off duty.

Liebenow's style fell into the second mode obviously. He ate with the crew, did not expect to be saluted by the crew and didn't push any aspect of the uniform a crewman would/should wear (while at the combat areas.) The actions of Liebenow where he mixed with the crew as noted (on page 15) was another example. He wore shorts and a tee-shirt…and wore the same one for weeks on end. He did not have a problem with a superior officer talking directly and individually to his crew which Cmdr. Kelly also did on many occasions.

Liebenow's approach certainly suited the crew. Liebenow and West certainly feel they got a great draw when these crews were assembled by Kelly back in New York and Melville. In response Liebenow got a crew that performed very well as a unit. In addition to the recollections from Liebenow and West about their time on the 157, comments the author received from the son of the PT's forward turret gunner (James Smith) the daughter of the rear turret gunner (Raymond Mach) and the son of the Quartermaster (Waldo DeWilde) all said that their fathers talked throughout their lives with great pride of the experiences they had during their service on the 157. So for the 157, the non-traditional approach proved to get the most from that crew…and it worked.

It was a bit more challenging for the 157's Executive Officer, Lt-jg John Ruff, who was more the traditional command type. Ruff outranked Liebenow (Liebenow was an Ensign), but Liebenow was the assigned Skipper and a Skipper commands the boat!

Lt-jg Ruff had come aboard the 157 after the 157 crew had been formed and bonded with Ensign Liebenow, and Kelly was not prone to make changes in his boat command, and so Liebenow was promoted (by Kelly) to Lt-jg. Throughout Ruff's service as the 157's Exec Officer, and even more so later as the 157's Skipper, Ruff's relationship with the crew was distant and aloof. The changeover from Liebenow's non-traditional style to Ruff's traditional style was difficult. [*It wasn't until Kelly, who got the word of the problem, added a new Executive Officer, Stan Marshall, that things on the 157 calmed down*].

[1] Lt.(jg) Michael Richard Pessolano transferred out of PTs to regular Navy and died in the sinking of the U.S.S. Indianapolis

Liebenow was fortunate that RON-9's Executive Officer was Lt. Hank Brantingham and Brantingham's Commander was RON-9 Commander Robert. B. Kelly. Both Brantingham and Kelly, who were involved with the rescue of Douglas MacArthur out of Corregidor using PTs, wore traditional officers uniforms and both were U.S Naval Academy (Annapolis) graduates but their operating mode was not traditional; same as Liebenow's. As long as this chain of command was in place things were fine.

Things did get a bit more challenging for Liebenow and crew in the summer of '43, when late in July Commander Kelly was off scouting for a new base (later to be Lever Harbor), and RON-9 was temporarily under the *direct* command of Lt. Commander T. G. Warfield....*very much a navy traditionalist.* Lieb, as Liebenow was called by everyone, was very relieved when the 157 moves to PT Base Lever Harbor and was again under Commander Kelly.

KELLY

RON-9 Commander Robert B. Kelly's tall 6-4 size and his underweight make it easy to pick him out of photos. By 1943 Kelly already had a noted service history with PTs, including having commanded one of the PTs under John Bulkeley that evacuated General Douglas MacArthur and staff from Corregidor.

'Commander Kelly on-board the 157'. Commander Kelly is looking almost relaxed (a rare thing for Kelly according to Liebenow). The photo was located in the National Archives (NARA) and mistakenly refers to Kelly being on the 'his' boat, the PT-153. However Kelly had no personal boat and the 153 is actually grounded on reef, along with the 158, at the moment this photo was taken. We know this is the PT-157 as that is PT-157's MotorMac Dan Jamieson's face on the right edge of the frame. A close look (of the digital version of this photo) shows the helmeted solder says "Mansfield' above the pocket and was apparently part of the Combat Photographer's Unit. A note was sent by the author to NARA requesting corrections be made to this photo's caption. [NARA 80-G-52599]

Kelly is well respected by the PTs crews and some officers; but not all of the officers. Commander Robert B. Kelly was an Annapolis graduate, which one might assume would make him most likely to follow traditional naval protocol (i.e. that is seaman are seaman, and officers are officers and rarely do they mix). Kelly however had no hesitation, and routinely would carry on conversations with crewmen from any of his PTs…which, as just discussed in the previous section, would not sit well with the traditional command style PT Skippers. The 157's rear turret gunner, Raymond Macht summed it this way, "Commander Kelly was a very good squadron Commander. I can't speak for the officers, but the enlisted people liked him."

Kelly also stood his ground even against the likes of the legendary Medal of Honor recipient and PT Commander Bulkeley. Aust recalls a conversation he overheard shortly after arriving at Russell Islands "and patrolled there for awhile. Two boats stripped their bottoms on a reef ... props, struts, and rudders. Repairs were made in Tulagi after Kelley and Bulkeley had a big argument; you could hear them half a mile away. I don't know who had the vilest vocabulary, but they both did well!"

Kelly wore the official Navy fatigues despite the heat, humidity (and lack of change of clothes). Visually he was a Navy traditionalist but personally operated without the invisible lines of communications protocol associated with a traditional officer. Most every night Kelly would patrol with any of his PTs subjecting himself to all the same dangers as any PT crewman. In some ways he was a throw back to the leadership of the Civil War, or like a George Patton with his Third Army in Europe against the Germans; lead from the front.

However Kelly knew how to work the Navy from the inside as well. He used that knowledge, and possibly some of his notoriety, when he convinced the Navy brass to outfit his newly minted RON-9 PTs with 20mm guns in the forward turret in place of the standard twin 50-cals. He did this under the guise as an *experiment* to see if 20mm would be more effective. He knew however they would need the extra punch of the 20mm Oerlikons to counter the Japanese ships and barges firepower and defenses when firing at close quarters. He also knew you can't just change the already approved design of the PTs coming off the production line so he devised this *experiment* to get his changes and no doubt did some name dropping to assist him. A series of memos from the period are in Appendix F on page 173 if you wish to read more of Kelly's proposal and reported results with the 20mm experiment. [Thank you to Nathaniel Smith for his research on this subject (which he had done sometime before this book was even considered) at the National Archive and Records Administration]

Kelly assigned Liebenow to the 157 right after a minor situation came to Kelly's attention. Back in New York Harbor, as each new PT was being released from ELCO to the Navy just across the water in Bayonne, New Jersey, the Commander (in this case Kelly) would assign a boat to its newly minted Skipper. On a rather windy day the Skipper of one of the new PTs was having difficulty getting his new PT to come along side the dock with the whipping winds upsetting his approach. Liebenow had positioned himself on the dock to receive the PT's bow line and tie up the boat when he saw the PT Skipper's growing frustration fighting the winds while docking the boat. Liebenow then leaped onto the PT's bow and, with the Skipper's appreciation, Liebenow parked the boat nicely along side the dock where the crew then tied the boat down. Kelly heard of Liebenow's actions and assigned him the very next boat released by ELCO.

On June 30th, after arriving at Rendova, Kelly did get into some hot water when he torpedoed the US Navy Attack Transport APA-4 USS McCawley which had been unloading supplies to Rendova before coming under Japanese aerial attack during the day. Later, on a near moon-less night, the PTs were told there would be no US ships in the zone (Blanche Channel) in which Kelly was patrolling. Kelly took the McCawley to be a slow moving Japanese destroyer when actually the McCawley was in tow after having been hit by

Japanese planes hours before. As the McCawley was pretty much a loss due to the hits by the Japanese planes and no personnel were hurt in the incident, this passed quietly as a misfortune of war. The Navy brass addressed the communications problems between the PTs and regular Navy as best they could, however, it would still have occasional breakdowns in the days to come. As for Kelly, the incident did likely become a roadblock to his advancement to Admiral.

Liebenow had no qualms at all with Kelly's non-traditional style. In fact he, and West, embraced it fully.

Only once, Liebenow said, did Kelly give him a written order; handwritten at that. That order occurred when all the PTs were still in Panama and Kelly chose the 157 to escort the President of Panama around on the boat in a sort of dog-and-pony show of the PT's capabilities. That event was apparently important enough that Kelly felt he had to put it in writing.

What Kelly wanted from Liebenow was Liebenow's level head in tight situations. Liebenow recently said one of the moments he remembers was the first time the PT-157 came under attack by enemy fighters. Kelly happened to be on-board. Liebenow directed actions and maneuvers to avert the planes attack until the plane finally left them. At that point he said to the crew "relax, it's all over". Kelly gave him a firm 'great job!' while they were standing at the bridge. To have received that comment from Kelly, a guy who himself had already seen so much in the war, was in his own words 'a great moment' for him.

This insight comes from Ted Aust. "I do know one thing, our crew would do anything and go anywhere for our "Skipper" [Liebenow]. As for our squadron commander [Kelly], he is one of the few men I've ever known who seemed to have no fear. One night, on patrol, he was standing in front of the cockpit sucking on a dead pipe, and a bunch of barges opened fire on us. You could hear the 'plitth' of bullets going through the plywood and canvas "protecting us". Kelley said – 'God-damn! they're getting pretty close.' But he didn't duck. All 6'3", or so, of him remained erect. I guess that's a rare gift???"

Given what the author has heard from Liebenow, West and Ted Aust's comment, it is very likely Kelly saw much of himself and his own style in Liebenow's abilities.

FIRST-UP
Chronicles of the PT-157

OFF-PATROL HOURS

When not on patrol the PTs crews had time (and more time) on their hands. There is no place to go but ashore on the small Lumbari Island, which is where Kelly and the other officers' tents were located. You could also use the shore based toilet 'facilities' (which beat the routine of grabbing the flagstaff on the back of the PT while underway and relieving yourself).

Liebenow (right) training/sparring with Yeomen Joe Loveless. Location: Likely Base Tulagi

When in Tulagi Liebenow was 'volunteered' by Commander Kelly. Liebenow had done some amateur boxing before the war. Kelly decided Liebenow's experience would help the impromptu Navy boxing team in the match against the Marines. The Navy team went over to Guadalcanal (in another boat other then the 157). It wasn't until the writing of this book that West heard about this boxing match and certainly, and correctly, assumed Liebenow won his match. His boxing reflexes will be seen again in details we will hear about in the upcoming patrols and missions.

When leaving the PT base at Tulagi for Rendova, the 157 stops for the night at PT Base Russells. The crew got to watch 'Lost Horizon'; which was the only movie they will get to see for quite a while, and the only movie Liebenow ever saw while in the Pacific.

Once at Rendova, the crews stay on the boat all the time. Mostly they sleep, eat and clean and check their weapons and the motormacs check the engines. They ate meals on board prepared by their cooks in the PT's galley. One of the pastimes for the crews was to ride up near the incoming Army supply barges and 'liberate' food and water for themselves as the Navy had not planned on sending ships to restock the PTs; they were again on their own. The supplies liberated during these sorties were shared among other PTs. Sometimes you gave and sometimes you received.

The skippers ate on board their boats as well, but slept in tents on Lumbari Island. These were larger tents with 3 to 4 skippers in a tent. This made it convenient when Kelly was ready to roll out the night's patrol assignments or, in case of an emergency scramble, quickly assemble all skippers. William (Bill) Battle and Lt. John F. Kennedy of the 109 were Liebenow's tent mates after their arrival in Rendova in late July.

Liebenow and West said what everyone sought the most was sleep. This was a high priority. While on PT patrols half the crew would sleep for four hours and the other half would crew the boat. After four hours this was reversed so there was no long night's sleep during patrols. Liebenow, unlike other crew members, would generally not sleep at all during the entire patrol, because Commander Kelly told him that was the way it was and his sleep was even more significant.

James 'Smitty' Smith, the 157's forward turret 20-mm gunner, had a habit when the rains came down heavy. Smitty would immediately grab some soap, strip off his clothes while standing on deck and take a shower. Liebenow recalls going into hysterics when Smitty did this one time and at the moment when he was totally lathered the rain suddenly stopped. Smitty swore up a blue storm and after coming to the realization that he had used his ration of fresh water and no more rain was coming had to jump off the boat to rinse himself off. That wasn't a preferred way to rinse off as it left dry salt water grit on you, and considering you didn't know what was in the water around the boat when sitting in harbor.

PTs needed refueling their 100-octane gasoline fuel tanks after most every patrol or mission. Gasoline liquid doesn't burn until it is mixed with air and the thought of an enemy tracer round going into a half full fuel tank was itself a motivation to keep the tanks full. Pumping the 100-octane fuel at a forward base such as Rendova was

The 157's Gunners Mate (forward turret) James 'Smitty' Smith

done by hand pumps from 55-gallon drums (until a dock with a motorized pump was built in late July). The drums arrived on the LST boats that were carrying in supplies for the Army and Marines on Rendova. They were heavy and had to be positioned for hand pumping, and hand pumping was a tiring task with each crewman having to contribute to the pumping activity. On July 5th, for example, they put in 450 gallons according to the log book. That's about 8 drums to pump. The only thing going for the hand pumping duty was that there was little else to do. No distractions at Rendova. Going onto Rendova Island itself wasn't really an option. It had just been inhabited by Japanese soldiers and you didn't want to be the one to find out they were not all gone. You can see some drums on deck in the photo on page 25 .

Two crewmen on a RON-9 PT in Rendova in July 1943 cleaning 50-cal guns. Note to the 50-cal gun just in front of the foredeck hatch. This might narrow down which PT this is however it is not the 157 and the author has been unable to identify the RON-9 PT and the crewman. In the background is Lumbari Island in Rendova Harbor. [NARA 80-G-52591]

Cleaning the deck guns was an essential routine. Given the hot, humid environment keeping the guns in ready state through constant dismantling, as seen in the photo above, usually was considered a grunt type job but being stuck on the PT 24-hours a day it became yet another diversion.

Writing letters home, the Skippers rotated on censor duty and would have to censor all outgoing mail. The mail you received (courtesy of Army supply ships and LCTs) would be a month to three months old by the time you got it. Liebenow said that although it didn't happen to anyone on the 157 a couple of guys in RON-9 got 'Dear John' letters and that was really tough. Being so far, so isolated from home and having no way to quickly respond back home made this a hard situation.

In Ted Aust's remembrances, the 157s were not big on card playing. They did talk to each other alot; about anything and everything…which says something about the comfort they had with each other.

In an unusual event while at Lever Harbor, Kelly gathered the RON-9 officers on a nearby beach one day. Placed out in the water was a series of empty 55-gallon drums floating on the water at approximate distances of 50, 75 and 100-yards out. Kelly produced a bazooka and said he wanted the officers to practice firing the bazooka at the drums. Whether he meant this as some form of training, entertainment or whether he wanted to see how effective the crewmen could be firing bazookas from a PT (as he was wrestling with ideas as to how to better attack the Japanese barges) is unclear. Maybe, and likely, it was all three. When it came to Liebenow's turn with the bazooka, Kelly challenged him to hit the farthest drum out in the water. He hit it spot on. From that time forward, Liebenow recalls, PTs going out were to take bazookas with them. However, there were not enough for all boats so those going out each night got them from those that were not. If more boats went out than there were bazookas, some went without. In the end there were no times during the summer of '43 when they were ever used against the enemy.

Aside from the water around the boats when sitting in the harbor, the waters of the Pacific south sea isles were very clear says West. West recalls that on a clear, sunny day and when the sea was flat, you could look straight down 50 feet and see things on the bottom with crystal clarity. You could spend a few moments in Paradise ….and forget you were sitting on a PT in the middle of a war.

As night fell they would often find Tokyo Rose on the ship's radio. The show played great music, same as that played on the top hits radio shows in America. They tried to ignore the specific announcements and taunts to American units that their positions were known to them, or that their wives and girl friends were home having a good time with the '4F' guys who had not joined the war effort. Shortly after the 18 Japanese bombers attacked the PT boats in Rendova Harbor (August 1 in which PT 117 and 161 were the only two PTs hit and sunk) Tokyo Rose announced that *all* the boats in Rendova Harbor had been sunk. *That showed the Rendova based PT crews, and the nearby US troops on Rendova Island, that Rose's music was far better than the accuracy of her 'victory' announcements.*

TRACKING PT-157'S MOVEMENTS

The two primary documentation trails used in compiling the 157's daily movements were the PT-157's log book and the MTB Daily Action Reports of RON-9 that were (usually) generated within 24-hours of the previous night's patrols and other activities.

The PT-157's Deck Log Book

To follow the PT-157 through the summer of '43 at Rendova, the first of the log pages of the 157 were provided to me by Nathaniel Smith, son of Hamlin Dunlop Smith who was the Skipper of the PT-154, also of RON-9 at Rendova, and later additional pages provide by the United State National Archives with the assistance of NARA Archivist Nathaniel Patch.

The 157's log book was not heavy in details although enough to confirm its location each night, the time of certain events, how much fuel it took on the next morning and anything that was out of the ordinary. After having read a few pages of the PT-157's log books you notice that those log entries contained the same style of content as found in the 154's; also provided to the author by Nathaniel Smith.

Liebenow says that his Quartermaster, Waldo DeWilde, was in charge of entering the daily log information. Some of these entries, especially those around the rescue of Lt. John F. Kennedy and his surviving crew on August 7, 1943, become the only real-time account of the events of that night.

DeWilde's daily regimen included putting the following at the end of nearly every log page entry…

"Made daily inspection of magazines and all other daily inspections required by current security orders. Conditions normal."

…and this exact same phrase can be found in log books of other PTs. Their Quartermaster training must have therefore included what points to put in a log book and a strong requirement to include the phrase above. Note that DeWilde, and other log books from other PTs, avoided putting in information that you would not want read if you were captured. There are occasional references to Daily Actions Reports that do describe the details of torpedo firings and hits on enemy ships.

Liebenow didn't recall having written in nor looked at the daily page entries during his time on the 157. After having looked at the log book pages recently, Liebenow notes that the first page is his actual signature. He said he has always joined the 'W' and the 'F' of the first initials of his name. Looking at the subsequent pages it is apparent that from that point forward, where the 'W' and 'F' are not joined and the 'F' is a cursive 'F' that Waldo made daily entries and simply signed that off for Liebenow's signature.

The Daily RON-9 'MTB Action Reports'

To supplement the PT-157 log book information, copies of the Action Reports written at the time for 'MOTOR TORPEDO BOATS, RENDOVA' and the later "MOTOR TORPEDO BOATS, LEVER HARBOR AND MOTOR TORPEDO BOATS SQUADRON NINE' were secured from the United States National Archive both by Nathaniel Smith and directly by the author. Only the pages applicable to the 157's actions are included.

By having the 157's original log book entries and the Action Reports we can crosscheck locations, dates and movements of the PT-157, and develop maps of patrol locations and then fill in with the eyewitness accounts from both Liebenow and West to complete our picture of life and times aboard the PT-157.

REFERENCE MAPS

The following pages contain a series of relevant maps for the PT-157, other PTs of RON-9 and other various RONs with the author's marking overlaid on Google satellite maps. The water areas have been made black; which is appropriate as that is what water was to the PTs who fought mostly always at night. The maps are progressively more detailed as they zoom closer in to key areas.

You can see that when the PT-157 is at Rendova the action begins on the western and northwestern side of Kolombangara Island, a Japanese stronghold with 10,000 troops, and then shifts to the southern and eastern side of the island when they are based out of Lever Harbor

Each map has both geographic locations (land and sea) and positions of the PT-157's patrol and/or mission locations detailed on daily activity review starting on page 40. A circle with a letter denotes a PT base (i.e. (A)). A circle with a number (i.e. (5)) denotes a patrol/mission run from Rendova. A number with a square (i.e. [19]) designates a patrol/mission run from Lever Harbor.

Each map is labeled at the bottom as 'Map **Oak X**' where 'X' is the number of the map. The use of 'Oak' is not really necessary for the book, however it was the chosen call sign for RON-9 PTs in radio communications. We'll use it here in the spirit of the subject.

Map Oak 1: (top of page 30) Overall view of the Solomons. The two circled locations show PT Bases at Tulagi and Russells Islands. The dashed lines show the routes taken by RON-9 when they went to/from the main PT Base of Tulagi/Russells Islands to/from Rendova and the trip from Russells Islands to Lever Harbor. There are area references to Map Oak 2 and Map Oak 6 for the next level of details.

Map Oak 2: (bottom of page 30) Still at a high level: New Georgia, Rendova and Kolombangara Islands. The only patrol location is number 3, Segi Point, which is arrived at by the same route from Rendova as if going to/from Russells Islands. The more significant value of this map is to show the area locations of Map Oak 3, 4 & 5.

Map Oak 3: (top of page 31) This is the closest map to show the locations of Rendova Harbor and Lever Harbor and the areas in between which are the areas of most activity for the PT-157 in July/August 1943

Map Oak 4: (bottom of page 31) All the locations shown, except for number 19, are for patrols/missions out of PT Base Rendova.

Map Oak 5: (top of page 32 This is a close in view of the Rendova and Munda Airfield. The distance between the two is only about 6 miles.

Map Oak 6: (bottom of page 32). The map shows the two most northern reaches of the 157, with Liebenow as Skipper, working out of Lever Harbor. Location 15 is shown as a dashed line representing the picket line the PTs created from Bako Point of Vella LaVella Island to 5–miles east.

Map on page 33: Based on this being a U.S. Navy map and the arrowed points on the map, this was apparently for showing key points the Navy protected as entry points while the US Army and Marines marched in from the backside to take Munda Airfield which was originally held by the Japanese.

Map on Page 34: Locations pertinent to showing the PT-109 events had been overlaid on this map showing many other area locations. This map is more helpful to find the names of locations as they were known at the time of the US military activity in 1943.

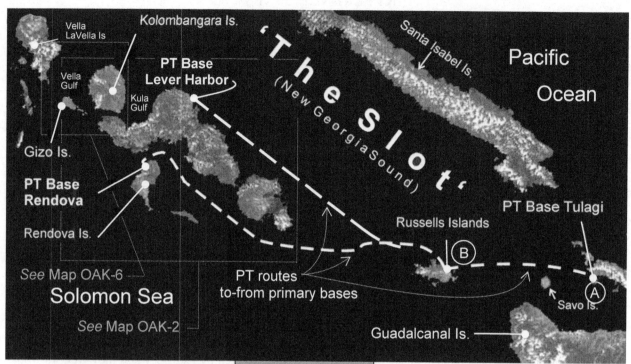

Map **OAK-1**

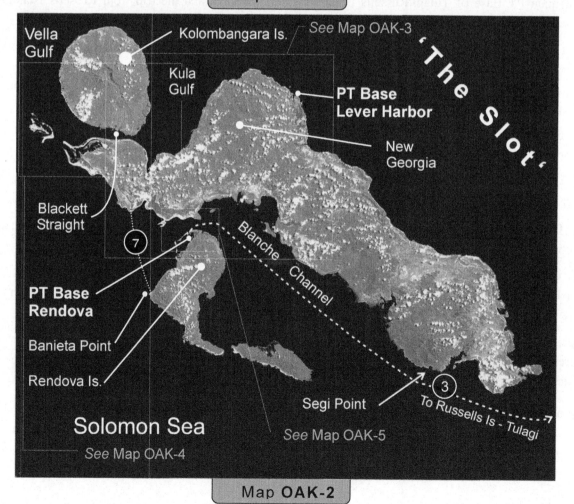

Map **OAK-2**

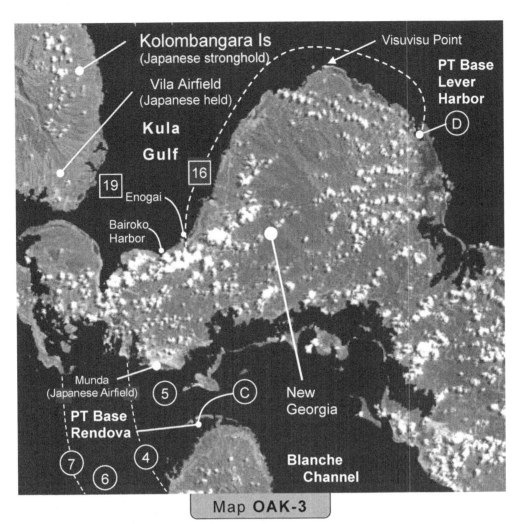

Kolombangara Is
(Japanese stronghold)

Vila Airfield
(Japanese held)

Visuvisu Point

PT Base
Lever
Harbor

(D)

Kula

Gulf

[16]

[19] Enogai

Bairoko
Harbor

New
Georgia

Munda
(Japanese Airfield)

(5)

(C)

**PT Base
Rendova**

(7)

(6)

(4)

**Blanche
Channel**

Map **OAK-3**

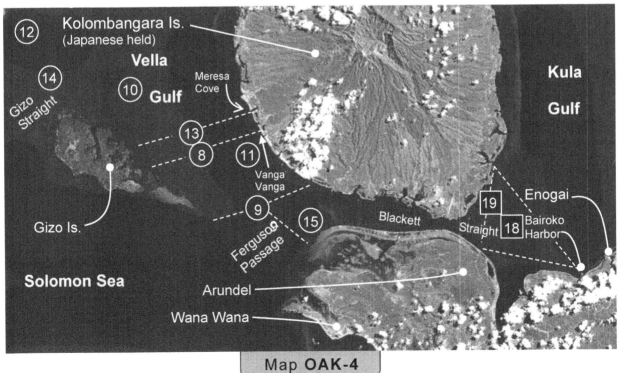

(12) Kolombangara Is.
(Japanese held)

Vella

(14)

(10) **Gulf**

Gizo
Straight

Meresa
Cove

Kula

Gulf

(13)

(8)

(11)

Vanga
Vanga

(9)

(15)

Blackett

Gizo Is.

[19]

Enogai

Straight [18]

Bairoko
Harbor

Solomon Sea

Ferguson
Passage

Arundel

Wana Wana

Map **OAK-4**

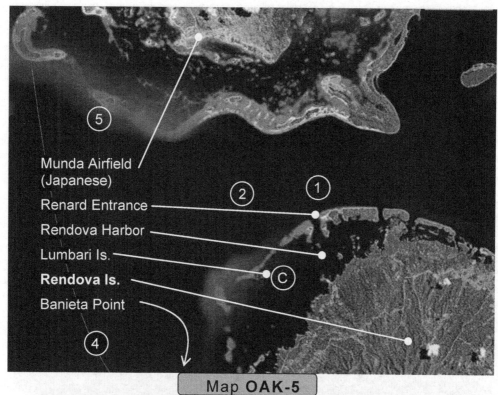

⑤

Munda Airfield
(Japanese)

Renard Entrance

Rendova Harbor

Lumbari Is.

Rendova Is.

Banieta Point

②

①

Ⓒ

④

Map **OAK-5**

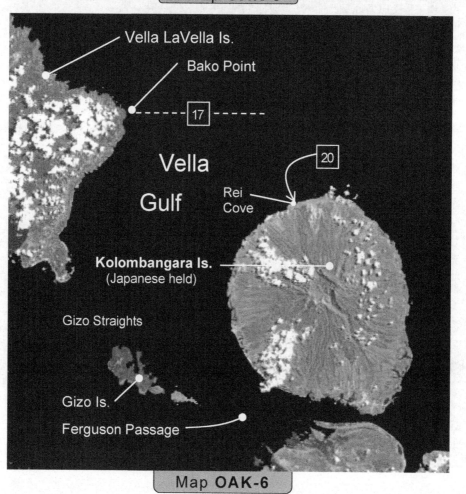

Vella LaVella Is.

Bako Point

17

Vella

Gulf

20

Rei
Cove

Kolombangara Is.
(Japanese held)

Gizo Straights

Gizo Is.

Ferguson Passage

Map **OAK-6**

U.S. Navy Map
Source: U.S. NARA

Undated origin but estimated the Fall of 1943 as the
Munda Airfield is shown in U.S. hands however
Vila Airfield still held by the Japanese.

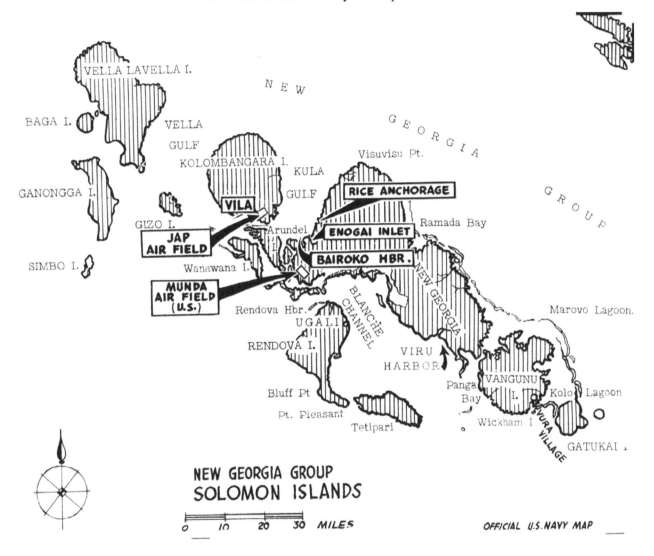

NEW GEORGIA GROUP
SOLOMON ISLANDS

0   10   20   30   MILES

OFFICIAL U.S. NAVY MAP

U.S. Navy Reference Map
Undated, source: U.S. NARA

Original map appears to have locations added to show the PT-109
and crew movements of August 1-2 to August 7-8 1943. The author's
assumption is that these were likely added as an aid to those interested in the
PT-109 story as its Skipper, John F. Kennedy, rises in political fame and
eventually runs for, and is elected as,
President of the United States.

RON-9 IS 'FIRST-UP': ON TO RENDOVA

June 28, 1943, After meeting light enemy resistance, Rendova Island is taken by the U.S. Army and Marines as part of the four key objectives in the launch of New Georgia campaign called OPERATION TOE NAILS.

"Landing operations on Rendova Island, Solomon Islands, 30 June 1943. Attacking at the break of day in a heavy rainstorm, the first Americans ashore huddle behind tree trunks and any other cover they can find. [ARA FILE #: 080-G-52573---WAR & CONFLICT BOOK #: 1176--- original filename is HD-SN-99-02835.JPEG]"

GETTING TO RENDOVA

June 1943: The PT-157 and its crew have been in the Solomons at Naval Base Tulagi since April. They arrived after spending 3 months in Panama training in tactics, getting acclimated to maneuvering the ELCO 80' PT boat and practicing target shooting with the various deck guns and torpedo launching. With the exception of a few officers, most all personnel on the PTs had come straight from civilian life and had little or no knowledge of the sea, and how boats behave on the sea. Like so many at the beginning of World War II, they learn a little now during training and lot more in combat.

The Japanese had been at war already for nearly 6 years and were already seasoned. The U.S. is in a catch-up mode.

Along with working at their new, trained positions, they also had to learn to coordinate their movements as a team with fellow PT boats. Each crew member, in time, was to learn other crew members' jobs. West said there was a general goal in PT training: if only one man is alive, he must be able to bring back the boat.

On patrols PTs would often work in a side-by-side line formation, much as a line of football players strung across a field, waiting to intercept the enemy; which in the Solomons were enemy boats trying to come through their lines. They would learn to depend on each other as they might need to cover each other with gunfire or smoke to make good an escape if discovered.

PT boats were part of the U.S Naval Commands early response to give a message to the Japanese that 'we are here'. Much like the Doolittle raids in April of 42, the victory value was a strategic and emotional lift to US military and the folks back home. With the Pacific Fleet still being rebuilt following Pearl Harbor, the PTs were a part of the response message to the Japanese that the days of their unimpeded expansion in the Pacific were coming to a close.

In June of '43 the Battle of Guadalcanal was pretty much over and the PT RONs (reminder: RON is short form for 'squadron') who had arrived ahead of RON-9, had already set the tone and reputation in the minds of the Japanese. These mahogany hulled PTs were much smaller than destroyers and battleships, however, they had two advantages which changed the game: speed and torpedoes. And anything that carries a torpedo must be taken seriously.

The first PT crews at Tulagi had told RON-9 crewmen how on the first attacks on the Japanese ships, which was at night of course, the Japanese had fired their guns defensively skyward thinking that the growling engine sounds they heard were those of American aircraft. They soon realized the growl was *not* coming from the sky but the water, and quickly learned these new 'devil boats', the nickname Japanese would soon call the PTs, carried torpedoes. Forever more the Japanese destroyers could not ignore these boats darting about them in the night; to ignore them could invite a death blow at any time.

Before leaving Tulagi, Liebenow's crewmen and the other RON-9 crews were sent to the large food supplies warehouse and loaded up with 2-weeks of K-ration, C-ration and Spam. This will be all they have for food for the foreseeable future. They are working on the assumption that there will be nothing where they are going. Aust said "the 157 was so heavy - our bilges were stuffed - that we drew 3-1/2 feet instead of 2-3/4 feet and couldn't keep up. Kelley kept hollering, "157! Move it up!" "We're at full speed, sir," we'd answer. (Three weeks later, we were eating three meals a day, other boats only two and Kelley moved aboard to get some decent chow.) However, he called us "Liebenow and his 40 thieves". We did eat well, but I still lost 40 pounds."

Liebenow was assigned the Stores Officer for RON-9 by Kelly shortly before leaving Tulagi. Liebenow wasn't sure what a Stores Officer was, really, but when handed a list of needed provisions by Kelly he understood he was to get whatever was on the list. Liebenow approached one of the Quartermaster clerks near the docked supply ships and handed over his list to the clerk. Somewhat to his dismay *all* the requested items (and maybe a bit more) were provided! He did know one thing about supplies, you rarely get all that you ask for! He looked up at the Officer in charge and Liebenow was shocked…half way around the world on this island few know the name of, he has run into one of his neighbors and friends since childhood in Fredericksburg Virginia! Capt. Manley Wright (US Army) is in charge of the supplies. This was the same Manley Wright that gave Liebenow his paper route for the Richmond Times Dispatch when Manley, who was a few years older, had moved on to another job. This was an amazing cross of paths in this far away land. After talking for a while, Wright hands Liebenow a box and inside are three bottles of Scotch Whiskey and a note saying they are compliments of Captain Manley Wright. Later Liebenow, not a drinker really, gives the bottle to Kelly, also not a drinker; so where that rare bounty ended up is not known.

June 28: Liebenow looks out over the bow of the 157 as he heads out of base Tulagi which has been their home port for some time now. The 157 and the other 9 boats of RON-9 (PTs 151 and 152 had been transferred to RON-12 in May) plus PTs 117 and 118 (which apparently had been reassigned from RON-6 and put under RON-9's operational command for the time being) are moving out. They are 'First-Up' this time to move to a new front line location called Rendova. The crews were briefed just yesterday.

They move out of Tulagi at 0825-hrs, a rare daytime movement, for the nearly three and a half hour trek cutting across the New Georgia Sound, known as 'The Slot', passing by Savo Island just north of Guadalcanal. They pull into PT base Russells a little past 1200 hours and put 500 gallons of 100 octane fuel in their tanks to be ready to move out early the next day. They moor for the night and get to watch the movie "Lost Horizons", the only movie Liebenow ever saw during his service in the war. Russells was a nice base according to Liebenow and West, however they never got to stay more than a night at any one time.

They stayed until the afternoon of the next day, June 29, by which time the offensive by the Marines and Army against New Georgia and Rendova is well underway.

At 1743-hours RON-9 begins its move from Russell Island base to a new base at Rendova. Unlike the day light crossing from Tulagi to Russells, this move will be under cover of darkness in the less secure area along western New Georgia Island. The 12 PTs of RON-9 are on their way.

Arriving at the Rendova Harbor the PTs choose Lumbari Island, in the harbor area, as the base of operations. Across the water a short distance is the major Japanese airbase at Munda on New Georgia Island.

The Army's artillery group, according to West, had set up positions on high ground on the edge of Rendova Harbor. They started shelling the key Japanese base and airfield at Munda, which was across the narrow straights on New Georgia Island. The firing of the 155 Howitzers continued around the clock shooting every 5 to 10 minutes. The PTs were anchored in proximity to the 155s such that, while on deck West could hear the 157's dishes, in the galley, rattle with every round fired. It also made it hard to get some sleep.

The 155 Howitzers could hurl a shell up to 3 miles, and could also provide coverage for other anticipated US landings on New Georgia Island. Obviously this became a problem for the Japanese and they had to respond. That would happen soon enough.

"GREEN DRAGONS" boats (nicknamed by their crew because of the coloring) approach Rendova through the Reynard Entrance to Rendova Harbor at dawn on June 30, 1943 carrying the Marines' big guns and Marine and Army cargo. Photo by Marine Sgt. Sarno. [NARA 127-GW-1051-56817]

The location for the PTs was Rendova Harbor whose outer limits were defined and protected by sand bars which formed a somewhat curved arc closing in the harbor except for a few inlets. As the island was secured by the Marines and Army that day, there were no facilities, so the PTs drop anchor in the harbor at Lumbari Island and tie together the bows, in groups of two or three, known as 'nests'. Before leaving Tulagi the RON-9 PTs had been directed to provision their boats with two weeks of food knowing it would be a while before they had a real base setup at Rendova. However, as the LCTs came into Rendova Harbor with water, food and supplies for the US Army and Marine forces now on the island, the crewmen of the PTs managed to 'liberate' food and water supplies for themselves.

As for access coming out of the harbor, PTs could go left for a short distance and then head right, and circle around the west and north side of New Georgia Island and into Vella Gulf; which was the location of the bulk of their interdiction missions. They could also come out of the harbor and turn west (left), but that was the Solomon Sea and on the open seas the 80-foot long PTs lost some of their fighting advantages.

Aerial view of Reynard entrance to Rendova Harbor
[NARA 80-G-42070]

Key points to photo above
PT Base Rendova – Lumbari Is. (out of photo range)
Bau Island

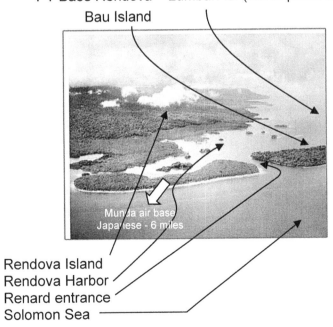

Munda air base
Japanese - 6 miles

Rendova Island
Rendova Harbor
Renard entrance
Solomon Sea

June 30, 1943: Rendova Harbor. The PTs of RON-9 moored in 'nest' configuration (a nest is when PTs are in groups of two or three). Behind the PTs is Lumbari Island; the base for PT Skippers and Command Officers in the first weeks at Rendova.   [NARA 80-G-52582]

RENDOVA PATROLS AND MISSIONS

JUNE 30 – JULY 1, 1943 – RENDOVA ①

The 157 boat's bow was now steady as it moved through protected Renard inlet leading into Rendova lagoon. Just as sunrise was breaking on the horizon, the 157 was moving to the lagoon's entrance. The nearly ten plus hours on station had been rather uneventful at the assigned Renard entrance by Tambatuni Island. The night had been black as there was almost no moon. A new moon the next night would make it the darkest it could be. On nights such as these you could put your hand out in front of you and not see it. You could only search by sound and look for any tell-tale light that had inadvertently escaped from an enemy ship. No US ships were expected to be near the 157's location so any hint of activity would be quickly acted on by Liebenow… although an event where a US ship had apparently been torpedoed by RON-9's Commander Kelley could give one pause, but you could not let that thought linger. That pause would be the difference in being the aggressor or the fleeing defender. You spend hours in the inky darkness ever watching. In an instant that can change.

As was the case on most patrols, half the crew would catch some sleep on the deck while the other half would position themselves to watch. West's personal favorite spot to sleep was right behind the day cabin. Using his life jacket as a pillow, that area is cocooned by the day cabin's rear wall in front and the curved wall panels on either side. On the backside of this area was the hatch down to the engine room. That would reduce the noise around you. The collective eyes of those on watch would cover the three-hundred and sixty-five degrees around the boat. Liebenow would be awake the entire patrol however. An incident which occurred months earlier while they were traveling from New Caledonia gave his Squadron leader, Commander Robert B. Kelly, the cause to have a conversation with Liebenow that 'Skippers never sleep'. And so it was.

That is all that is on your mind as you slowly move about with your PT's flapper valves closed to silence the engines' exhaust noise. It comes down to response time that makes the difference between having options for an attack or having to high-tail out and 'lay smoke' using your smoke generator on the PT stern to generate a smoke cloud which hides you, hopefully, from enemy fire. But tonight is so dark even laying of smoke doesn't make sense unless enemy search lights beamed on you…and your enemy doesn't like that much, as it also gives away their own speed and position.

The Marine invasion of New Georgia and Rendova had begun only the day before, the last day of June, and met with little resistance on Rendova. The Marines and Army had cleared Rendova quickly allowing the 12 PTs of RON-9, with RON-9 Commander Kelley on the 153, and some boats of RON-10 and RON-5 to use Rendova's harbor on the northwest side. There are no facilities on the lagoon so the PTs are on their own. Should a PT fire torpedoes there are no docks from which to reload the tubes so when a PT is empty of torpedoes they'll have to make the nearly 400 mile round trip trek to Tulagi and back. That's a night trip each way and at low speeds to avoid kicking up an effervescent wave which makes an ideal arrow pointing to you as the target. That's nearly twenty-hours…in each direction

On Rendova, the Army's 155 artillery pieces were quickly brought in and set up at the back of Rendova Lagoon and had begun round the clock shelling across the narrow water passage at the Japanese airfield at Munda. Sooner or later the Japanese would have to counter this threat but this night saw nothing for the PT-157 and its patrolling fellow PTs, the 156 and 161.

JULY 1/2 – RENDOVA Ⓒ

No Patrol. *Liebenow said when possible the boats were sent out on alternating night patrols. This would give crews a rest and undoubtedly allow time for the crews to make repairs, clean guns, pump fuel and most importantly rest.*

JULY 2/3 – RENDOVA ② – 'SQUEEZE PLAY'

In the afternoon the Japanese air force stage a bombing raid on the US's new 155 Howitzer artillery positions that are farther down the Rendova Harbor, a closer position from which to fire on the Japanese held Munda airfield. The 155s had been continuously firing on the airfield around the clock and the Japanese were now attempting to stop the shelling. The US 90mm air defense response, however, is heavy and accurate, so that most, if not all of the two engine, light bombers were hit. As West stood on the deck with his binoculars, he watched as several of the bombers began to burn and or simply explode. "Japanese planes tended to explode", West said, "because they lacked the resealable fuel tanks. One tracer in their gas tank and the tank would blow up". As he watched this destruction of the bombers he could see small black specks falling from the airborne carnage. He followed many of the specs and realized some of them were Japanese air crewmen. They have no parachutes! They are hitting the water and Lumbari Island which is right behind them. It is literally raining bodies all around them. In minutes the attack is over, but the dead bodies are everywhere.

———————————— ● ————————————

According to Welford West, before the PT-157, PT-156 and the PT-161 with RON-9 Lt. Commander Kelly on-board, left for patrol, they received intelligence to look for possible Japanese ships in the area.

As usual, the missions of PTs in the Solomons were carried out at night. The advantage of night fighting for PTs was that it made it difficult for enemy airplanes to spot and hit them. The disadvantage was of course spotting the enemy, especially on moonless nights. Only a few PTs were equipped with radar in the summer of 1943.

The PTs 157, 156 and 162 moved out of Rendova Harbor at 1830-hrs with their mission to patrol the area just outside and around Rendova Harbor. Both Liebenow and West clearly recall just how dark it was that night. The astrological calendar for this night shows it was indeed a 'new' moon meaning there was *no moon* light. That leaves only the light of the stars. Seeing other boats on a moonless night is quite difficult, however, not impossible. Welford West, at the 157's wheel, had been in the Merchant Marines before the war so was already accustomed to searching the ocean by night.

The mission for these three PT's, this night, was to move up and down (north/south) in the narrow straights between their harbor at Rendova and the Japanese held island of New Georgia; whose nearest point was the Japanese base and airfield at Munda. After exiting the harbor, the 157 headed in a northerly direction. Although this was a moonless night there was the very last touch of haze on the western horizon, as West explained, and against that haze he could see the distant silhouette of the destroyer coming toward them at high speeds.

By the direction the destroyer was moving, it had come in from the Solomon Sea (which means it was moving in a west to east direction) and therefore likely sent in from the large Japanese port of Rabaul to the north on New Britain Island. The 157 proceeded north moving across the bow of the incoming destroyer far enough out to allow spacing to make a 180-degree turn and line up for a torpedo run on the destroyer's starboard side. It was total darkness now. The desired angle to fire would be to hit them amidships; that is broadside. Firing a torpedo from behind, as some PTs had done, showed that newer Japanese destroyers could out run a Mark VIII torpedo. The broadside attack, however, was the most dangerous! If you're discovered, more of the enemy destroyer's guns could direct their fire at you.

Just as the 157 began to make its port turn to swing around back onto the destroyer, a second Japanese destroyer appeared out of the total darkness about 5-degrees off the starboard side of the PT's bow, and no more than 50-feet away! West, at the wheel, and Liebenow, right beside him, saw this second destroyer at the same instant. Liebenow yelled to West to turn hard; however West was already turning the wheel, with all that he had (using the wheel grip on the boat's wheel that sticks out and allows the wheel to be turned like a crank). The distance of the 157's bow to the destroyer's hull, at its closest, appeared to be no distance at all. Liebenow and West are convinced they hit and no doubt it looked like a collision for sure. At a cruise speed of 25-knots (29-mph) you are moving at 42.5-feet in one second! West said in addition to a hard turn to avoid the collision with the destroyer, the saving grace was the destroyer's own sizeable bow wake acting as a cushion of water that hit the 157 and actually helped push the PT's bow away from hitting the destroyer's hull.

The first destroyer, on which the PT-157 had originally planned to make the torpedo run, had itself altered its course to move closer (to its port side) and parallel to the second destroyer, which had slowed a bit to allow the first destroyer to catch up. To avoid a collision with the first destroyer, the 157 continued its turn and now found itself running parallel to and in the same direction with the destroyers; one on the port side and one on the starboard!

The first destroyer had likely moved closer to the second destroyer knowing that such close quarters would reduce, if not eliminate, any PT that was between them and certainly remove the ability of a PT to fire torpedoes in the very limited space between them. The PT-157 was in this 'squeeze' by itself, cut off from the 156 and 161.

The Japanese destroyers had realized now that there were PTs in and around them. However with the moonless night it was not possible for them to see the PT's locations and movements. Although the Japanese ships had searchlights, and would use them on many other occasions, they chose not to do so this night. The 157 had to hold their fire on the destroyers as it would immediately give away their own position. Now the ships respond with two streams of cross fire, one from their bows and the second from their sterns, angled at each other but slightly away from each other (so as to not hit each other), hoping to hit the still invisible PTs. The only good thing, said West, about being caught directly between the two Japanese ships is that the ships had to limit their crossfire technique to avoid hitting the other. West still muses today that each time a bigger gun from either of the destroyers fired, he ducked just a bit all the while knowing that the thin pieces of the helm's plywood walls would have hardly helped if the shell was accurate.

In the most recent interviews, West said that the first gauntlet (from the stern of both destroyers) of fire began just as the 157's stern was moving ahead, with its slightly faster speed than the parallel destroyers' pace, of the line of fire which limited the damage to the 157. Had they come through a few seconds earlier, the enemy fire would have raked the entire length of the 157 and it would likely have hit the PT's large, high octane fuel tanks with an explosive result. The 157 had no choice but to move out of this squeeze position and through these crossfire gauntlets to make their escape before their position would be discovered. West maintained the course and 1400-rpms as Liebenow had ordered. Liebenow's remark to West was something along the lines of 'we're not blown up yet, so maintain [the current] course and speed' meaning we're not dead yet so keep doing what we're doing. In addition to the forward and aft crossfire gauntlets, the 157 was also receiving fire from an above angle by Japanese .51–cal guns that were positioned in the destroyers' upper 'crows nests' and 20mm guns mounted higher on the ships than those now firing the gauntlets. This downward firing was done in random spray patterns as these gun positions also could not see the PT-157.

If there had been any moonlight of any kind, the PT-157 would have been visible and not survived this encounter. With the moonless night and the PT blending among the waves in the dark ocean, this was their only means of protection.

During these moments, a 20mm from one of the two destroyers went through the 157's deck and tore into the center of the three Packard engines tearing its supercharger and damaging a second engine. To have hit the *center* engine which is only possible only by the attacking destroyers' 20mm guns shooting at a *down angle* and gives an indication just how close the 157 was to both of the hunters. Dan Jamieson, the chief motormac (motor mechanic) as well as Aust, who were in the engine room, were miraculously unhurt, and nursed the damaged engine to keep it running and used it when they needed it for the rest of this patrol. The damage to the center engine, however, included a severed ¾" fuel line (high octane gas), according to West, that was connected to the dead engine, resulting in gas fumes throughout the engine room. West said Liebenow ordered Jamieson, Aust and Shaw up to the deck as any spark, especially from the tracer rounds from the Japanese, into the engine room and the 157 would have possibly exploded. West figured Liebenow thought was the motormac's odds of survival in such a case would be far greater on deck then at the flash point of the engine room. West heard later that the moments after Jamieson had come up onto deck from his engine room, he (Jamieson) looked about at the crossfire, and said 'I come out to see some action, and now I've seen it. I want to go home!'. For someone usually in the engine room during the course of a mission, this was quite a moment to be up on deck and see the fireworks around them.

As they approached the second cross-fire gauntlet of fire (coming off the destroyers' bows) the stream of firing stopped. Today, West said he assumes that both of the Japanese 20mm guns had to change their ammo drum at that very moment the 157 moved through (the momentarily quiet gauntlet line) and was able to get just ahead of the destroyers and be free of the fire. The gauntlet fire did resume right behind them. However, they were now beyond that and a few moments later the two destroyers broke off. Apparently there was a command decision on the part of the destroyers' commander that staying in the area with torpedo equipped PTs was not worth the risk. The two destroyers then began a turn back toward the open Solomon Sea, from which they came. They spilt in different directions, possibly as an evasive action.

The moonless night had been their sole key protection. And now the PT-157 sat out in the water alone. For a few moments the 157 slowed and Liebenow did an assessment of their condition. No one had been hit. Jamieson, now that the threat of enemy tracer fire was gone and the fire and/or explosion that could come from it, scrambled below to work on the engines. He popped back up to say although the second engine was leaking oil he could nurse that engine and use it for limited periods of time.

With the destroyers turning they would be vulnerable in a broadside torpedo launch from the 157. With only a few moments left to consider his options before the destroyers would be lost to them in the black ink night, Liebenow redirected Jamieson again back to his station in the engine room and directed West off the wheel and to his torpedo tube battle stations and make ready to fire. Liebenow took the wheel and turned the 157 about and lined up to make a torpedo run at one of the two departing destroyer. We see the heart and adrenaline of the boxer, educated college thinking and military training in Liebenow appear at this moment. He and the 157 have taken the blows and now it's his turn to hit back.

West said at the proper distance from target Liebenow slowed the PT ever so slightly to allow the 157's two rear torpedoes to be fired. Once fired and both 'fish' were in the water and past the bow Liebenow turned the boat hard to port and headed back to base. Liebenow said he, as well as a few of the crewmen, saw torpedo explosions as they hit the destroyer. West, however, did not see the torpedo hits as his attention was on watching the darkness ahead and avoid getting tangled with yet another destroyer. Once, and almost twice on this night, almost being hit by destroyers was more than enough for West. The 157 itself was shot up with damaged engines. All the crew had come through this mission unhurt. They head back t0 Rendova.

The 157 now proceeded back to its nearby base with only one engine running, the second partially damaged engine disengaged and third engine dead. Liebenow said he radioed to base and noted their 'two fish gone and two cold potatoes'; which was the quick code for two torpedoes were launched and two dead engines. They later were told by Lt. Cmdr. Kelly (who was on-board the PT-161) there had been four Japanese destroyers, and told Liebenow he also saw at least one of the 157's torpedo hit on the destroyer.

If those four destroyers were indeed sent in to silence the US Army's 155 Howitzers, then they were too distracted by the actions of the 156, 157 and 162 to complete their task. They did not inflict any harm to the 155 Howitzers. 'Just doing our job' is what both Liebenow and West said of this night.

In the publication 'History of United States Naval Operations in World War II' author Samuel Eliot Morison notes that the four destroyers were actually part of a nine Japanese destroyer group and these four destroyers were detached from the group with the specific purpose to destroy the PTs in the area. However, that same publication noted that the PTs used smoke. The 157 did not; possibly the 156 and 162 did. As West said, it was so dark smoke would not have helped their situation. It also states that the torpedoes fired did not hit their target. There was a bright flash from the destroyer that Liebenow directed his torpedoes to. Both he and Commander Kelly later reported seeing the flash. Research shows the damage was not sufficient to have inflicted serious damage to the destroyer as Japanese navel history logs did not record damage to their ships. The Japanese Naval records mistakenly report having sunk two PTs that night.

JULY 4/5/6 – RENDOVA ©

By the log and MTB Daily Action Reports, the 157 did not go out on patrol during these days. Neither Liebenow's or West's memory could recall why but it can be assumed that the PT-157's damaged engines needed some repairs. Motormac Dan Jamieson, who Liebenow and West said was a magician with engines, would have been working on them in this period. Jamieson had no spare parts and the closest place to get any would be back at Tulagi. That wasn't in the cards. Possibly Jamieson's years of prior experience had anticipated the need for make-shift repairs and he had stored some raw materials such as tubing and/or flat metals in the engine room from which he could fabricate needed parts. We do know that; as of July 9th the rare photo of a PT underway in daylight shows what appear to be all engines running…at least for now.

Around this time, some 24-hours after watching the Japanese bombers get shot down and the crewmen falling into the water and land, West said many of those crewmen could be seen floating in the water. They didn't have parachutes, but they did have their life-jackets which had kept those that landed on the water afloat. But now the bodies were developing the natural, internal gases caused by decomposing, and their bodies were swelling. West said one of the bodies, which had 'blown up the size of a 55-gallon drum', was floating nearby another PT. It was too close to that boat for one crewman on that PT who put the PT's dingy boat in the water, went to the body and tossed a rope loop around it. He then proceeded to tow it, rowing by hand, out toward the harbor's Renard entrance so that it maybe swept out to the open sea.

All of the PTs stationed at Rendova were ordered to stay in Rendova Harbor on the night of July 4/5 as there was anticipated to be action by Japanese and American destroyers and cruisers. They were not to be disappointed. From Rendova Harbor the crews were standing on their decks watching the Battle of Kula Gulf on the horizon. The accounts of the number of rounds fired in a short period of time by both sides, and especially the American cruisers, was phenomenal.

Unknown until after the war and a review of Japanese naval records, was that during this naval battle, the Japanese losses include the ship Niizuki. It was the Niizuki on July 2 that led 4 ships, of a 9 ship task force, with the specific assignment to intercept any PTs coming out of Rendova Harbor; which they did with the 157, 156 and 161, before they could get near the main part of the Japanese task force. The main body of this enemy fleet was to try and shell the new American 155-howitzers, which they did not, that were continuously shelling the Japanese airbase at Munda. Another ship with Niizuki, the Amigiri, was also among the nine destroyers in the group. She will gain fame later in early August as we'll see.

Commander Kelly would, when possible, send out half of RON-9 to patrol on assigned station points, while the second half were held in reserve as a 'striking force', to use Kelly's Action Report term. When the good intelligence indicated a high probability of more targets, more of the PT's (if not all) would be sent out on patrol.

This break from the routine patrols for the 157 was rare. They wanted to be in action. In their minds that was the only way to win the war. That was their way to stay sharp at the cat and mouse game with the Japanese. They finally move out on patrol on July 7th.

JULY 7/8- RENDOVA ③ and ④
In the afternoon (1115 hours) of the 7th, the 157 is underway in a three hour trip to Segi Point (location point '4') to pick up a Major Frederick and party and bring him to Rendova, arriving shortly before 1800 hours.

A little less than a half hour later the 157 is underway for patrol with RON-9 Commander Kelly on board, and the PTs 156 and 161. As is Kelly's style, many nights he selects a PT with which to go out on patrol.

About an hour later a Japanese float plane drops a bomb 400-yards off the 157's stern. No damage done and the patrol continue without any further events. At 0110 hours a plane drops two bombs 200-yards of the 157's starboard beam. No damage done. The patrol leaves its station at 0600 hours and gets into Rendova at 1715 hours.

In these patrols Japanese planes are frequently shadowing the PTs and dropping flares to spot PT locations. When moving out of Rendova, West says the Japanese could likely see from their positions on New Georgia the PTs on their way to their assigned stations, as it would be dusk,. He recalls how the Japanese planes would be right on them as the PTs left Rendova Harbor and start dropping flares right away and throughout much of the patrol. On one patrol a flare actually landed on the deck of the 157 (which West immediately kicked into the water). The planes seemed more interested in knowing their locations then picking a fight. We might assume their primary job was to track and report PT locations to warn any of their nearby fleet.

The PT-157 takes on 1350 gallons of 100 octane gas. It was a PT Skipper's desire to keep the tanks full at all times. A fuel tank with 100 octane gas and a lot of air is a dangerous mixture should enemy incendiary fire find its way into the tank.

JULY 8/9- RENDOVA ©
No Patrol; on alert at base

JULY 9 (DAY) – RENDOVA ⑤
This will be a special mission day. Commander Kelly is aboard as well as a Marine Correspondent, Samuel Stavisky, and his photographer, Marine Sgt. Jerry Sarno.

It is almost 0900 hours, and in an unusual daylight move, the 157 is underway to take Kelly to PTs 153 and 158 that ran aground the night of July 2/3. Kelly wants to remove the vital documents and disable and/or destroy any equipment such as radar that Liebenow believes one of the boats did have.

Stavisky and Sarno were eager guests of Kelly on this mission (this is a 'mission' as it has a specific purpose whereas a 'patrol' is when you move about in an assigned area and either find the enemy…or not). Their assignment was to move around the active battlefront areas looking for stories of soldiers and sailors for the papers back home. They knew of Kelly and had heard of his exploits certainly, but now they had moved up to Rendova to spend a few days with him. In Stavisky's book, *Marine Combat Correspondent,* he talks of his visit to Rendova. Most importantly also are Sarno's photos of the PT-157's crew, with Kelly on the foredeck in a pose across the deck and a second photo of the 157 underway at high speed to the location of grounded PTs.

Photos of this mission were professional grade. Some were even made with a 4"x5" format camera, taken by Sgt. Jerry Sarno, were recently provided by the National Archives [NARA] research commissioned by the author. These highly detailed photos give us a rare look of a PT on a mission in a combat area in daylight. As PTs routinely patrol at night, such photos are not possible so this is a very unique moment.

'Under way'. This is one of those rare moments with the 157 running fast in daylight on an actual mission. A second, nearly identical version of this photo had become one of the two most popular photos among the 157 crew after the war. The other is the one of the crew on deck seen on page 11. However both of these photos, recently uncovered at NARA, are much clearer, and with no damage, than those previously seen. [NARA # 127-GW-1051-57382]

Liebenow moved the 157 close enough to the location of the 153 and 158 to let Kelly and two crewmen, one of whom was Sam Koury and the other a visitor on-board, Q/M-1/C Robert C. Link, paddle out in the 157's dingy to the abandoned PTs. (see page 48).

There was enemy gunfire from the shore. However, it was not accurate. Kelly went on board and did retrieve the log books, and likely disable the radios (this may be the reason Sam Koury was along). Stavisky reported in his book that while returning to the 157, Kelly was calling out to Liebenow to keep the bow of the 157 pointed to shore so as to not give the Japanese a broad target at which to shoot.

Shoving off: RON-9 CMDR Kelly, (farthest away in the dingy boat) with machine gun, 157's Radioman Sam Koury in the middle, using Dan Jamieson's life vest, and Q/M-1C Robert Link with helmet and life jacket with 'LINK' on stenciled on the back, prepare to paddle out in the 157's dingy to the two abandoned boats. Motormac Dan Jamieson is standing with his back facing us in the photo while torpedo man Welford West (in front of Jamieson) looks down into the boat. [NARA # 127-GW-1051-56385]

The mission was completed without damage to the 157 or crew.

JULY 9/10 – RENDOVA ©

No patrol and no fuel pumped. Must be a lot of sleeping and reading going on. The crew of the 157 wasn't big on card playing.

JULY 10/11 – RENDOVA ⑦

Initially all PTs were held in Harbor. However, at 1:45 in the morning, the 157, with RON-10 Commander Warfield on-board, take off with PTs 156 and 161 out of Rendova Harbor and sit on station patrolling a picket line from Wana Wana Island. The Action Reports says initially all boats were in Rendova Harbor until they received some intelligence which says some unidentified ships are headed their way. Lt. Commander T. G. Warfield scrambles all boats, with himself on the PT-157, out to see what they can find. Although the presence of Warfield is understandable as he is Commander of RON-10 and RON-10 now has some of its PTs at Rendova, it is interesting that he is on the 157, a RON-9 boat. He is technically now in charge at Rendova. Although he and Kelly are the same rank, Warfield outranks Kelly based on graduate year at the Naval Academy. Neither Liebenow or West can recall where Kelly was this night and why Warfield chose to ride out, which he seldom did. Nevertheless, all boats stay out until 0600. Having found nothing, they head back to Rendova.

Warfield was a traditional Navy Officer as discussed earlier in this book, and that comes into play now. West recalls this night, as during patrol when Lt. Cmdr. Warfield comes across the 157's Radioman Sam Koury apparently sleeping against or in the raft on the foredeck while on watch. Rather than nudge Koury or start talking to Koury to roust him, Warfield immediately threatens to court-martial Koury. That did not, however, occur.

JULY 12/13 – RENDOVA ⑧

After Cmdr. Kelly's apparent absence from Rendova the previous night, he is now back. At 2015 the 157, with Commander Kelly on board, and in the company of PTs 103, 104, 105, 117, 154, 155, 156, 160, 161 and 162 heads toward Blackett Straight. There was apparently some anticipation of a large Japanese movement that caused 11 PTs on this patrol. They arrive back in Rendova Harbor at 0645.

DeWilde enters the destination of their mission which was rare in his log entries. So far at Rendova we have seen the 157 in the repeated patrols with the same PTs (most typically the 156 and the 161)

JULY 14/15 – RENDOVA ④

On this patrol the 157 is again back in the local patrol mode with the PTs 156 and 161. They head out at 1905 and are on station in only 45 minutes, so this appears to be a 'home guard' position. They leave the station and head to Rendova at 0030 for the short trip back.

JULY 15/16 – RENDOVA ⑨

During the day a large air battle takes place over the waters just outside of the Rendova Harbor, West recalls. "The Japanese sent in a lot of fighters ahead of the bombers that were sent to bomb Guadalcanal. I watch the fighting with my binoculars and see them clear as day. When one of our planes got hit, the plane would smoke and begin to descend. A few bailed out and parachuted of course. When one of their planes got hit, they always seemed to explode. It was like watching a movie. The [Japanese] bombers saw what was happening and turned back." A few of the PTs were ordered to go and retrieve (what are now dead) Japanese pilots as U.S. Navy intelligence was always looking for documents; none were found.

They patrol Ferguson Passage with the 156 and 161. Nothing occurs although they get shelled from enemy shore batteries as they pass near Munda Point.

JULY 16/17 – RENDOVA Ⓒ

Available as 'strike force'

JULY 17/18 – RENDOVA ⑩

In the company of the 159 and 160, they leave Rendova at 1845 and are on station at Vella Gulf. At 0505 they are back to base Rendova.

This is a much more intriguing patrol than stated in the log recap for this patrol. During the patrol, ships are spotted in the distance. The 159's was the lead boat and its skipper, orders by radio (which using the radio is against the RON-9 standing rule not to break radio silence unless there is an emergency), the 157 and the 160 to prepare to attack with torpedoes. Liebenow sees, however, the distant ship fire the 'friendly' flare sequence. He replies to the 159's skipper that "they are 'friendlies' " (i.e. not Japanese). The 159's skipper repeats his *'prepare to attack'* order again, and again Liebenow says *'but these are friendlies*!'. Again the 159's skipper (Hayes) is barking at Liebenow to *'prepare to attack!'*. With this Liebenow moves the 157 to torpedo firing speed and at the last moment Liebenow turns the 157's bow off the target ship so as to point to an island, and fires the two forward torpedoes (which is all he has left since the firing of the two aft torpedoes on July 2/3 in 'squeeze play').

Having seen the experience of Kelly mistakenly torpedoing the U.S.S McCawley only a few weeks prior, Liebenow's decision is to avoid putting himself in that same position. PT skippers and crews were to follow orders even when on remote islands isolated from the rest of the world. This, Liebenow knew, would be a situation that would bring him front and center to his commanding officer Kelly.

No surprise then that next morning Commander Kelly called Liebenow into his tent and asked him why he did not fire his torpedoes at the targeted ship when he was [repeatedly] instructed to! Liebenow begins to explain that he saw the right flares colors sequence fired by one of the ships that identified them as 'friendlies'. Kelly is about to tear into Liebenow for not following orders when he is interrupted by a radio call. On the call is a Navy commander, who apparently is reviewing his ship's action reports, and demanding to know why a couple of his PTs had launched torpedoes at his ships the previous night. At the conclusion of this call Kelly turns to Liebenow and tells him 'get out of here'. The subject never came up again.

JULY 18 (AFTERNOON)– RENDOVA Ⓒ TO PT BASE RUSSELLS Ⓑ

The 157 has now spent its final two torpedoes. Rendova still has no facilities for the PTs from which to pump fuel or reload torpedoes so they'll have to return to Tulagi to get their torpedoes reloaded. They also need to have the center engine again looked at. Motormac Jamieson has worked some miracles to keep the two engines, damaged in the 'squeeze play' patrol, from nearly two week ago. The center engine had been hardest hit with portions literally shot off the engine, but now running with Jamieson and Aust work.

In the afternoon of the 18th (1320-hrs), the 157, with the escort of the 159 and 160 head toward Russells Island. At 1535-hrs DeWilde writes in the log "sustained casualty on center engine, proceeded independently". Whatever magic MotorMac Jamieson had done to keep that engine running has given out. The 159 and 160 departed company with the 157 and the 157 proceeding to Russells (whether the 159/160 went on to Russells or turned back to Rendova is not known). Fortunately, having the two outer engines running, the handling at the helm of the 157 would not have been affected by yaw effect which would have been the case if it had been one of the outer engines that were dead.

The 157 makes it to Russells without further event and moors for the night.

July 19 – Russells Island Ⓑ

At 0835 the 157 is underway out of Russells and headed across The Slot to Tulagi. Their noon-time arrival at Tulagi is nearly the amount of time it took when they left Tulagi and headed to Russells on June 28th, so the 157's dead center engine issue hasn't slowed them up. They moor at Galley Dock and take a *big* 1200-gallon gulp of fuel. At 1514 the 157 is moored and will await its turn at the repair docks to have its center engine replace.

July 20 – Tulagi Ⓐ

There is nothing for the 157 to do but wait its turn at the engineering dock for engine repairs...so all hands are ashore.

West will grab a jeep and local guide to show him around Tulagi. He did get to see much on their previous time at Tulagi but this time he wants to sightsee! The seas and sky around Tulagi are more secure now than when he last left Tulagi so he is going to take advantage and explore the island.

Of everything Liebenow did on shore, the one and most prominent thing he recalls is having the first hot, fresh water shower he has had in months. He has been wearing the same white tee-shirt and shorts for some time now, and this shower is something he feels to this day.

Macht and Aust go into the nearby jungle to search for shot down Japanese planes after the last big air raid on Tulagi. Macht wrote "After the raid Ted Aust & I took our dingy & rowed over into the jungle looking for souvenirs. We found 2 or 3 planes there & got several good souvenirs. The last wreck we looked into [and] the (deceased) pilot was still in the plane. We went through the clothing & found his wallet with pictures of himself & his wife & 2 kids. When I saw that it hit me real hard as the propaganda material had depicted them as some sort of ogre. What a shock to find out they were family men just like us." Naval Intelligence found out about their 'souvenirs' and recovered them for intelligence purposes.

July 21 – Tulagi Ⓐ

DeWilde writes following account in the log book with what appears to be remarkable details of the timing of these events. DeWilde is either bored or exercising his personal organization ability (he was a college graduate with a mind for numbers) or both. Nevertheless he has captured a great time/motion demonstration of the Tulagi repair efficiency.

0804 - The 157 is moving to the engineering dock

0815 - Docked at the Engineering dock

0845 - Repair engineers begin the process to remove the center engine. This first requires the removal of the rear deck panel that sits over the engines.

1330 - Installed new center engine. [West believes the original Packard 1250 engine was replace with the newer, updated Packard 1500 engine that had more power]

1409 – Repairs completed and the 157 is back on its way to it mooring.

Liebenow was told by the repair crews that the 157 had over 65 bullet holes, only some of which (ones in which water would leak below) were repaired including the larger hole made by the round that penetrated the engine room and damaged the two engines. All these holes could only have come from the 'Squeeze Play' patrol of July 2/3.

West said that they also found that in one of the two torpedo tubes that were fired, a Japanese .51-cal bullet had pierced one of the torpedo tubes and lodged itself inside the tube between the tube and the air flask section of the torpedo. When the torpedo was fired that night, it dragged this bullet inside the length of the tubes leaving a permanent groove inside the tube. West said the groove wasn't large enough to warrant the replacement of the tube so they left it that way. What they couldn't have known at that time was that in a few months the tubes would be replaced with hanging racks to use the more reliable aerial type torpedoes after the defective design of the Mark VIII torpedoes was confirmed.

JULY 22 – TULAGI (A)

The crew continues to take rest & relaxation.

Much like it was in Liebenow's luck to have run into his neighbor from Fredericksburg, VA, Capt. Manley Wright, shortly before leaving Tulagi, he now runs into a college friend, Aubrey Harlow, who is also involved with PTs.

JULY 23 – TULAGI (A)

At 0948 it takes the 157 a little over 10 minutes to get to the torpedo dock. By 1103 it has taken on 4 of the Mark VIII torpedoes. At 1325 it takes over an hour to fill up on 1600 gallons of fuel from the S.O. (Supply Officer).

JULY 24– TULAGI – PT BASE RENDOVA (C)

A little past noon and the 157 is on its way to Rendova. No stop over at Russells this time. It takes nearly 5-1/2 hours to cover the 200+ miles to Rendova getting in at 1740.

Almost immediately after the 157's docking, RON-9's XO (Executive Officer), Lt. Hank Brantingham quickly comes on board to tell Liebenow that Kelly is away and that Commander Warfield is overseeing PT operations at Rendova. This is not music to Liebenow's ears as Warfield is the 'traditional' style of officer discussed earlier in this book.

It is also noted that the 157 is 'moored in assigned berth' so some docks apparently have been constructed while the 157 was away! The crew can now walk off the boat onto land (if they so desire). This is a PT base now! [*from this point forward the author will refer to Rendova location as 'PT Base Rendova*]

JULY 25– PT BASE RENDOVA (C)

1030 in the morning and a single Japanese plane is strafing the PTs at Rendova. The plane is chased off by guns from the PTs.

The 157 takes on 900 gallons from the Rendova S.O. so now there is a *fueling dock* as well. The days of having to hand crank the fuel are gone! More indications that this is no longer the desolate, distant harbor but now truly an Advanced Naval PT Base.

JULY 25/26 – PT BASE RENDOVA (10)

1800-hrs and the 157 with PTs 109 and 159 are on their way out to Vella Gulf. This is the first patrol for the 157 with PT-109. Lt. Kennedy is tent mates with Liebenow from now until the night of August 1/2.

They leave station at 0500 and are back in Rendova 2-hrs and 15 minutes later. Apparently they went slowly back to base, likely trying to avoid having their wakes spotted as they are close to Kolombangara Island – still a major Japanese stronghold.

Noted, almost in passing, is that on the 26th at 2000-hrs while sitting at their berth in Rendova a Japanese plane drops a 200-lb bomb that lands 200-yards off the 157's stern.

JULY 26/27 – PT BASE RENDOVA ⑧

Stay at Rendova. Available strike force

JULY 27/28 – PT BASE RENDOVA ⑫

Patrol area is 2 miles north of Gizo Straight with PTs 159 and 162. Out at 1812-hrs and on station at Vella Gulf at 2100-hrs. Leave station at 0440-hrs and arrive Rendova at 0700-hrs. Refuel with 850 gallons. All pretty routine.

The patrol actions are moving farther north from Rendova. That is requiring a lot of drive time as in the case here. It's almost 3-hrs in each direction. That adds the wear and tear on the boats, engines and crews. To be more effective, save time, wear and additional fuel issues, the PTs will need to move to another, closer location.

JULY 28/29 – PT BASE RENDOVA ©

Stay at Rendova. Available strike force

JULY 29/30 – PT BASE RENDOVA ©

Stay at Rendova. Available strike force

JULY 30/31 – PT BASE RENDOVA ⑬

Back again on patrol to Vella Gulf trolling between Meresu Cove (Kolombangara Is.) and Gizo Island with the 159 and 162. This time it only takes an hour less to get to Vella Gulf each way.

JULY 31/AUGUST 1 – PT BASE RENDOVA ©

Stay at Rendova. Available strike force

AUGUST 1/2 – PT BASE RENDOVA ⑪

Just before dusk, eighteen Japanese planes come across Rendova Harbor, coming in from the Rendova Island side to hide their approach, to make a surprise, one pass raid against the PTs boats anchored in the harbor. West was below deck on the 157 writing a letter when the explosions hit. As he scrambled up the day cabin ladder to the deck, Quartermaster DeWilde was already in the forward turret firing the 20-mm gun at the Japanese planes. The planes had taken surely them by surprise and the one-pass-and-gone approach of the enemy planes pretty much assured that none of the planes were hit by the PT's return fire.

As a result of the raid, bombs did hit the 117 and 164 at the dock, destroying them both and killing two men on the ground. That is a pretty poor hit rate for 18 planes but good news for the RON-9 crews.

Welford recalls looking over at the 117, which was now cracked and spilt across the deck separating the bow from the rest of the boat, and being able to look directly into the radio room of the 117.

Like the night of July 2/3 when the 157 was caught in 'Squeeze Play', this is a moonless night and again the Japanese are preparing a 'Tokyo Express', meaning many ships with supplies and personnel moving south; however, the US is already anticipating. The RON-10 commander and now the temporary acting RON-9

Commander W. T. Warfield, the PT skippers and the crews know this and in response *all* PTs in Rendova Harbor are ordered out on assigned patrols tonight.

Direct Hit: The PT-117 has received a direct hit. One man on board at the time of air attack but uninjured. [Acme Photo]

Tokyo Rose reports a few days later that <u>all</u> the PTs at Rendova were sunk. Her music may still be good, however, what has sunk was her credibility with RON-9 and nearby Rendova personnel.

The 157 was in the following foursome on patrol this night:

AREA B (BLACKETT STRAIT)
DIVISION B - OFF VANGA VANGA
Lt. H. J. Brantingham PT 159 OAK 27
Lt. (jg) W. F. Liebenow PT 157 OAK 21
Lt. (jg) J. R. Lowrey PT 162 OAK 36
Lt. (jg) J. F. Kennedy PT 109 OAK 14

The 157 had of course been on several recent patrols with the 159 and 162. The 109, having recently arrived at Rendova, had not yet been on close patrol with the 157.

Liebenow said the boats were patrolling in this order shown above. Each boat skipper was to watch the boat ahead of them and its wake so they could stay in close quarters with each other (again, no running lights or radio contact is allowed). So the 157 was to keep an eye on the 159; the 162 an eye on the 157, and the 109 to keep an eye on the 162. At some point on patrol, the 162 lost visual contact with the 157. The 159 and 157 were still in close proximity to each other. Once you lose visual contact, you are on your own.

Brantingham's boat (159), had radar and it confirmed that Japanese ships were approaching. Brantingham pulled his boat alongside the 157 and told Liebenow about the ships, and to prepare to attack (with torpedoes). Brantingham fired all 4 torpedoes and the 157 got off two torpedoes. West said the two torpedoes were right on target, however, there were no explosions from their torpedoes (so again the issue of the torpedoes' defects arises). The 157 had launch failure on the remaining two torpedoes.

The 159's torpedoes, when fired, had ignited the oil in the torpedoes tubes (the other torpedo problem) and of course that alerted the Japanese to their presence and they immediately began firing at the 159, which of course was also the direction of the 157. The 159 and 157 then laid smoke to cover and make good each other's escape. Aust recalls "My battle station in a torpedo attack was rear starboard torpedo. Well, we were idling up the coast - we generally patrolled at idling speed with mufflers closed so that there was just a low rumbling sound, blub-blub-blub. Suddenly, "Target ahead - attack! Attack!, and all hell broke loose! Huge search lights came on and flares and shells started dropping around us. We made our torpedo run; our targets were clearly outlined against the shore ...right up to it. The Japs sure knew these waters. Just as we fired the aft torpedoes, I hit the firing pin with my hammer, and a shell hit the water very close by, splashing water all over me. As the boat was turning away, I felt a burning in my right knee. I thought, S---!! I'm hit ... but it was the heat from the torpedo tube. My leg had moved against it as turned. Whew!! Then it was ... run like hell! Our target erupted at water level, and all hell was going on behind us. We followed the lead boat away and then cut our speed and lay to waiting to see what would happen next. It was so dark you couldn't see a thing."

Once out of danger the 159 and 157 came along side each other and Brantingham said that without any torpedoes left he was returning to base (Rendova) , and instructed Liebenow to look for the ships again (and get the torpedoes fired if possible), stay on station and finish the patrol. They did so but, not having radar, had lost the Japanese ships. They then moved a bit in a direction where they assumed the 162 and 109 might be looking to reconnect with them. On a moonless night searching for fellow PTs was a risky business. As the 'Squeeze Play' patrol on July 2/3, also a moonless night, demonstrated, a ship could come right on you and it would be nearly impossible to see, as Lt. Kennedy and the 109 crew would find out shortly.

About 2 hours after the 159 left, both West and Liebenow said they did see a flash in the distance but it was far off, well beyond their designated patrol area. There was no way to tell the source of that flash and it could be any number of reasons. The 157 stayed at its station area location for the rest of their patrol time...which was shortly before dawn. They headed back to base before airplanes could spot their wake in the first hint of daylight.

Liebenow's 157 was the farthest out and so was the last of all the PTs to return to Rendova Harbor that morning. Liebenow said that when the 157 returned, Lowrey, skipper of the 162, reported in the post patrol debriefing that the 109 had been hit by a Japanese ship resulting in a large ball of flame. He said they searched but found no survivors. That was a tough break, Liebenow thought, for Kennedy. He had met Kennedy at PT training in Melville, Rhode Island, and Kennedy had only just arrived at Rendova a week or so before and was bunking in the same tent with Liebenow and William (Bill) Battle.

Looking at the number of empty, freshly fired torpedo tubes of the PTs on the morning of August 2, it would be apparent to all that this was the busiest night RON-9 had had since arriving in Rendova.

In Robert Bulkley's book, *At Close Quarters: PT Boats in the US Navy,* he says this night was a major event for PTs. Eight PTs fired a total of 30-torpedoes and yet, although many hits were observed, no Japanese ships were sunk, and of course the PT-109 was lost. It is noted by Bulkley that coast watchers found several torpedoes on island beaches and considering that many of these torpedoes were fired on target at very close quarters, would again indicate the fault lies with the torpedoes, not the crews. Two of those torpedoes were possibly from the 157 or the 159 as they were pointed in the direction of Kolombangara when they fired.

Bulkley also comments that the PTs should have passed the word down the line to other PTs as the enemy ships moved from north to south. That would have required the use of radio which was not permitted (only in case of extreme emergency) as the Japanese ship-board RDF's (Radio Direction Finder) equipment would be able to find the PTs.

The 157 crew has returned by 0800 in the morning but then the 157 leaves just past noon for Russells Islands. The reason for this move, with the 157 still having two torpedoes, is not noted in the log nor does Liebenow or West recall why. It does take the 157 a little over 5 hours to reach Russells. Russells was, however, like a haven Liebenow does recall. He always felt safe and could relax a bit here.

AUGUST 3– RUSSELLS ISLANDS Ⓑ

At 1400-hrs the two new torpedoes are loaded onboard. In an effort to shorten the reload distance from Rendova PTs apparently equipment has been brought to Russells to make more of a 'full service station'. Next the 157 gets a very large fuel gulp of 2100 gallons from YOG-49. A YOG was a refueling tanker; however, even with fuel pumps it took an hour and forty minutes to fill up. These tankers could sit in the harbor, allow boats to refuel alongside without having to take up limited docking spaces that could be used for more critical operations (such as loading torpedoes). Following this refueling, the 157 returns to its Russells berth for the night

AUGUST 4 – RUSSELLS ISLANDS ② - TO RENDOVA ⑥

Just after 0900 the 157 makes the 5-hour trek back to Rendova

AUGUST 5/6 – PT BASE RENDOVA ⑩

Back on patrol now with the 159 and 162 in Vella Gulf. DeWilde puts in a log entry "Reference COM MTBs Rendova Action Report to COMINCH < "Commander-in-Chief", U.S. Navy > dated Aug 6 1943". Whenever Q/M Waldo DeWilde puts this in a log entry it means that something more significant was reported however he didn't want it in the log in the event that the 157 and the crew were captured. Unfortunately, the document to which DeWilde refers could not be located at NARA.

How DeWilde makes reference to a report that is yet to be written into a log book was explained by Liebenow. DeWilde, as possibly all the log book keepers, would wait until they saw the MTB Daily Action Reports which were taken from the debriefs of the skippers. This would typically happen the following day, be reviewed by the log keepers, for each of the PTs, and referenced if and when needed in each PTs own log book.

AUGUST 7/8 – PT BASE RENDOVA ⑮

Although on this day the 157 will be on a mission as opposed to a patrol, and as straightforward as the mission's objective is, it will forever mark the lives of those on the 157.

The events around the rescue of the crew of the PT-109 have been told in great detail mostly by those who were not present (see candidate John F. Kennedy's quote to Liebenow on page 77). The recounting of that night, therefore, are from the perspective of Liebenow and West who were there and integral to the 'pick-up', as Kennedy, late in 1960, referred to this night to Liebenow.

Update 2014: In discussing the rescue of the crew of the PT-109, one aspect was not included previous printings of the book and so is now added. That is the arrival of the 'Kennedy coconut'. Welford West recalls the event....

It was getting to be late afternoon as the afternoon shadows, Welford recalls, were beginning to get long. That would be somewhere between 4:00 to 5:00. He was in the cockpit area of the bridge. It would be about the time the crews are stirring from the daylight doldrums preparing themselves and their boats for the possible missions. Although most of the crew of the 157 is on-board, Liebenow was on shore (which would be Lumbari Island; the small island in Rendova Harbor that served of the officers' tent quarters along with the larger tent for daily briefings/debriefings before and after the night's missions).

Welford looked up to see a native canoe approaching with about five to six of the local island natives. It is likely that as canoe entered Rendova Harbor they approached, or were approached, by US military. Hearing that the destination of the canoe was the group of PTs, they would have directed them in the direction of the PTs, which could be seen anchored in the harbor. Looking at the map of the area, great credit must be given to the natives who rowed about 18-miles along the coast, then about 20 more miles over the open Solomon Sea to reach Rendova. The night crossing also avoided detection by Japanese patrols.

The canoe approached the PTs and came along side the port side of the 157. Two or three natives and the climbed aboard the 157 and handed a coconut, wrapped in paper, to one of the 157's crewmen. The coconut had the now famous message inscribed:

"NAURO ISL...COMMANDER...NATIVE KNOWS POS'IT...HE CAN PILOT...11 ALIVE...NEED SMALL BOAT...KENNEDY".

The coconut was passed around by the 157's crew. This was indeed an usual and exciting revelation to the crew! [It should not have been, however, as the Coast Watcher network had already informed its commanders of this situation however the word had not yet been communicated to US naval command.] The natives, were directed to row over to nearby Lumbari Island to PT operations so as to deliver their information (i.e the coconut and paper that it was wrapped in) to the PT commander; Commander Warfield. It is now only a few hours before the evening briefings at which the area missions to the PTs' and their appointed location so Warfield has to make some quick decisions on what to do and who will do it.

That set off the chain of events that became the rescue of the crew of the PT-109.What Liebenow does say is this rescue mission of the 109 survivors was treated as a possible enemy trap. The 'Kennedy coconut' may be a trick, or Kennedy may have been forced to write it. The 157 was assigned by Cmdr. Warfield to be the lone pickup boat while the PT-171, which had radar, went ahead of the 157 to use its radar to sweep the area for enemy activity prior to 157 moving in to the shore for the 'pick up'.

157 Log entry....

> "1553 underway for Onaiavisi Inlet. 1630 laying to in Onaiavisi. 1730 three native guides came aboard, underway for assigned berth and moored at 1755. 2030 underway for Furgeson passage with Exec Officer MTB RON 9, Com MTB RON 2 and party aboard. 2330 laying to the west of Pailerongoso Island. 2345 Boat Captain PT 109 came aboard, underway for northwest side of Cross Island. Underway in Ferguson Passage. 0030 laying to 0.4 Miles east of Banini Island. Sent Small boats ashore to pick up survivors of PT 109. 0215 two officers and 8 men came aboard and underway for PT base Rendova. 0515 moored in assigned berth, survivors left ship. 0800 mustered crew at quarters, no absentees. 1315 commenced fueling and completed fueling at 1415. Received 750 gallons of 100 octane fuel from SO Advance Naval Base Rendova. 1830 underway for patrol in company of PTs 159, 162. 2130 On station in Gizo Straight. Made daily inspection of magazines and all other daily inspections required by current security orders. Conditions normal."

As they headed out of Rendova, Liebenow and West recall the following were on-board: the PT-157's crew (see page 10 for a listing of the crew), RON-9 Executive Officer Hank Brantingham, RON-2 (Kennedy's Squadron) Lt. Alvin Cluster, Chief Pharmacist's Mate Fred Ratchford and Pharmacist Mate Lawrence (to provide any triage level medical care to the rescued crewman), the two natives, who had brought the coconut, to guide them to Kennedy's location, Press correspondents Leif Erickson (AP) and Frank Hewlett (UP).

After locating Kennedy, who by now was with a 'coast watcher' Sub-Lieutenant Arthur Reginald Evans (Australian Coast Watcher), Kennedy came out from shore with the 2 natives in a canoe. They all came aboard and Kennedy, and two natives with him, came straight up the 157's bridge where Liebenow, Warfield, Cluster and two original natives were waiting. Kennedy, Liebenow said, appeared to be very happy to be back on a PT. The immediate conversation between Liebenow and Kennedy was very brief with Liebenow asking Kennedy the obvious 'how did you get hit by a Jap destroyer?' to which Kennedy said simply 'I don't know Lieb'.

Aust said of this moment one of the party on board said, "We wanna see Jack" ... one jerk flashed a light at the tiny dock on which the survivors waited, and West, our torpedo man, said, "put out the f------light!" ... and the jerk said, "What's the matter'? 'Fraid some one will see us?!" <Aust notes with a bit of sarcasm> "Of course not! ...we were only 10-15 miles inside Jap-held islands and surrounded by reefs. Oh, well, there are all kinds of people in this world. We don't need them, but we sure got them!"

Liebenow in telling of this moment to the author today, reflects, and said that of all the PT Skippers who really would know how it could happen it would be him. It was just one month before on the night of July 2/3, also a moonless night, when Liebenow and West didn't see the Jap destroyer right in front of them until they were less than 100-feet away and nearly got themselves cut in two during the patrol. Such is testimony as to just how dark the nights where with only light from the stars.

Liebenow, in telling of the events of this night, also gives great credit to the work of the coast watchers, many of whom worked and lived behind enemy lines. 'That was a most dangerous job!' Liebenow would say.

Kennedy then turned to the guides that came on board with him and asked them to direct Liebenow to the island on which the rest of the 109 crew were waiting.

At this point, Liebenow stood at the 157's wheel as they began the move toward the shore to pick up the rest of the 109's crew. The bridge cockpit was full with Liebenow, Kennedy, Brantingham, Cluster, and four local natives.

As Liebenow began to move through the shallows and coral reefs, Welford West, who had the most experience at sea before the war, at Liebenow's request, stood on the bow and, using a lead-line, gave depth readings and directed Liebenow as he slowly guided the 157 through the shallows as close to the shore as possible. The combined work of Liebenow and West managed to move the 157 to within two boat lengths of the shore. *Both Liebenow and West note this distance and are today rankled by some armchair historians who have incorrectly said they were a quarter-mile off shore. (author's comment: this may have been due to QM DeWilde's log entry stating "0030 laying to 0.4 Miles east of Banini Island. Sent Small boats ashore to pick up survivors of PT 109" DeWilde's frist comment regarding Banini Island was apparently meant as a navigation reference point; not the 157's destination point from which they affected the pick-up).*

Most of the 109 crew walked out from the shore and waded the short distance to the 157, West and 157's rear turret gunner, Ray Mach, put the 157's dingy boat into the water, rowed to the shore at least two times, West recalls, and retrieved the wounded 109 crewmen that could not swim.

The 109 crew were taken below where the wounded were treated by the Pharmacist's Mates, Ratchford and Lawrence; the crew was fed, and some 'medicinal' alcohol distributed.

At the time, this rescue, to the crew of the 157, was just another mission among many they had done. After all the 157 and other PTs, had done clandestine drop-off and pick-ups of coast watchers and soldiers at many islands before and after this incident. These were not noted in the daily MTB reports nor in PT log books (in the event of capture you didn't want the enemy reading your dairy!). As a 'rescue mission', however, it did it did receive a special note in the MTB report (see page 134). Prior to the 109 sinking Lt. had been in Rendova less than a week. He was a tent mate of Liebenow and Liebenow thinks that is one of thinks that is one of the reasons why he was chosen to do the pickup. Although Ron-9 Cndr. Kelly was not at Rendova during this period (he was at Lever Harbor), Cmdr. Warfield likely chose the 157 as he knew of Kelly's confidence in 157's ability. Whereas a scheduled drop-off/pick-up of a 'coast watcher' or soldiers would be at a designated time and a location with sometimes easier access, the location of the 109 survivors was likely not going to be easy to get to. The combination of Liebenow's seamanship along with West's ability to run a lead line did indeed make them an ideal combination for threading the needle through the anticipated maze of shallows and reefs on a near moonless night. The 157's Motormac, Ted Aust, commented "...our boat, 157, was chosen as it always seemed to be handy for special missions".

It is true there was a large contingent of non-157 on board but those that were there, other than the 157's crewmen, were either the Officers of RON-9 and RON-2, who were responsible for Kennedy, or medical personnel to handle the wounded 109 crewmen. It was not until later, when Lt. Kennedy becomes President, that the details of this particular mission that included the 157 were well publicized.

Many versions of who was on-board and what happened that night abound. As Aust notes (and which also gives us an interesting engine room perspective)...

> "Later, as stories came out of this experience, I laugh about one report that said one of our boats directed us through the reefs by radar. No Way! ... I sat in the engine room, 135°-140° heat for 2-3 hours shifting engines as we advanced slowly, then backing up and going around the hidden reefs. No radar can "see" under water. Sonar, yes ... but we had no such thing"

Another coincidence: *Much like Liebenow running into his childhood friend at Tulagi (Capt. Manley Wright on page 37), Chief Pharmacist's Mate Ratchford is another coincidence. Before the war Fred Ratchford served under Dr. George Boyd Tyler (US Navy MC) who was in charge of the dispensary in Bancroft Hall at Annapolis Naval Academy. Dr. Tyler was a Commander in the U. S Naval Medical Corp and the father of Liebenow's wife, Lucy Tyler Liebenow.*

CPO Fred T. Ratchford

AUGUST 8/9 – PT BASE RENDOVA ⑮

It's the evening after the night the 157 picked up the 109 surviving crew and the 157 is out again on patrol with the 159 and 162. After fueling up with 750 gallons, they leave Rendova at 1830 and are on station exactly three hours later at Gizo straight. 6 hours later they leave station and arrive at Rendova around 0700.

AUGUST 10 – PT BASE RENDOVA ⑥

No Patrol or mission. They're on 'ready alert' status.

AUGUST 11/12 – PT BASE RENDOVA ⑮ TO RUSSELLS ISLANDS Ⓑ

Out at 1810-hrs with PTs 159 and 161 to Gizo Straight. Two hours into their trip to Gizo an enemy plane drops two bombs without hitting any of the PTs. The PTs fired on the aircraft. Three minutes later another plane (a Nakjima 95 with floats) passes 500 feet overhead. No report in the log regarding being fired on or fire at this second plane. At 0420-hrs headed back on the three hour trip to Rendova.

The 157 refuels at Rendova and heads on out to what will be a nearly 6-hour trip to Russells Islands; again.

This is the last time they will see Rendova. The 157 gets orders to locate to PT Base Lever Harbor where Kelly and half of RON-9 PTs have been for almost three weeks. Although they travel by themselves to PT Base Russells they are joined by the remaining PTs of RON-9, namely the 152, 154, 161 and 162. Once at Russells they will all head up the east side of the New Georgia Island, through the body of water nicknamed 'The Slot', to Lever Harbor. The Slot used to be the highway for the Japanese to move south unobstructed. No, it is the road by which the Allies are moving north. The pursuit continues.

Rendova posed significant challenges to the PT-157 and the other boats of RON-9. The crews having had to stay on-board day and night, and getting their 'feet wet' in the first direct combat experience, is now over. There is certainly more fighting, much more, to be done but as they approach 'Lever' they are now veterans of First-Up action.

LEVER HARBOR PATROLS AND MISSIONS

The Life: Lever Harbor was a very, very different atmosphere from Rendova. Whereas Rendova had no existing facilities, PT Base Lever Harbor had buildings built well before the war by the Lever Brothers, a soap company, for their staff and production facility.

In Rendova the crews, except the Skippers, stayed on board their PTs 24-hours a day. The PTs anchored out in the harbor and were exposed all day to the sun and occasional rains. At Lever the PTs would move under the overhanging trees and come to within a few feet of the shore. The crew built ramps with coconut logs allowing them now to step off the boat and onto land! This was personal freedom to move about. And now the PTs themselves, now under the overhang, were not exposed to the sun.

At Rendova the meals were cooked in the PT galleys. Food was sparse and limited mostly to K-rations, Spam and whatever they could scrounge from the Army and Marine supply LSTs coming into the harbor. At Lever Harbor they were served at least one meal a day in the Lever Brothers production facility which was now a chow hall.

The crew also could get their clothes washed now by the native population in exchange for Navy fish rations. They washed the clothes by beating them on the rocks so this wasn't a modern method by any means but still, after having lived in the same clothes for weeks on end this was a welcome change of life!

Welford recalls how the palm trees were all in rows; everywhere. That was due to the palm trees being production trees for the Lever Brothers' soap business.

The Fight: The nature of the fight against Japanese by the First-up PTs changes a great deal from Lever Harbor onward. To the Japanese the loss of their large naval ships is unsustainable and they must change their tactics...and do! What is not apparent immediately, but is noticed quickly, is that the Japanese are relying on barges more then capital ships to move men and material.

As of August 1943 the Japanese are slowly retreating and using the barges to do so. Barges are very low in the water and have a shallow draft. They can hug the shoreline making them nearly invisible to the PTs (and yet on nights with moonlight the PTs are fairly visible to them). And you can't torpedo a shallow draft barge which thereby nullifies one of the more effective weapons the PTs have (although the Japanese don't seem to realize the shortcomings of the Mark VIII torpedoes, they still had to respect them). By hugging the coast line these barges also get a tremendous advantage of having protection from their shore batteries covering their every movement. Each day there are new defensive shore batteries being set up and it will get more and more difficult for the PTs to move within effective firing range as the shore batteries and special heavily armed barges make it more precarious for the PTs.

Internal memos from Commander Kelly up the chain of command describe these issues in Action Reports and separate memos (one from Kelly is included in this book in Appendix E on page 163). Unlike Kelly's rather routine Daily Action Reports while in Rendova, the nature of the barge style war requires his quick analysis and almost daily adjustments as to how to attack the barges while not putting a heavy risk on the PTs.

The patrols of Rendova were the opening rounds in this fight with long distance jabs from their torpedoes. With the Lever Harbor patrols the fight now changes to counter-punch the new enemy tactics. Once the PTs get into their assigned patrol areas they will move away from their low speed, no wake mode and make high speed runs, with all deck guns blazing, at the barges. This becomes a period of even more daring aggressiveness by the PTs. And a wrong turn or speed setting here will cost a PT and its crew dearly.

In response, the PTs are adding more and larger caliber guns, and even light cannons, to their decks in a period of experimentation to see what they need to do in the way of armament and attack tactics to counter this new Japanese strategy. Although they appeared to have had them just a few days before, the Action Reports of August 23 '43 specifically notes the 157 and 159 have 'jury rigged' 37MM light cannons on the foredecks. Liebenow recalls these cannons were provided courtesy of the local U.S. Marines. The difficulty in using the cannon is that the PT had to point their boats at the target in order to aim the cannon. The effectiveness of the combination of cannon to the PTs' existing two 20MM guns and two twin 50-cals is being measured.

The results of these patrols, including comments on individual runs at the enemy, by the PTs are being monitored closely by Kelly. He also has added the amount of ammo used into the Daily Action Reports to apparently support his point that a lot of ammo is being expended without the desired results. The PTs are causing a 'harassing effect', to use Kelly's words to the Commander, South Pacific in his memo of September 8th recapping the events of the August patrols. The PTs continue to quickly adopt and adjust; that initiative is a true strength of the US Military.

AUGUST 13 – PT BASE RUSSELLS ISLANDS Ⓑ

No tasks noted for the day. The 157 takes on 1200-gallons of 100 octane fuel needed for the trip tomorrow from Russells to *Lever Harbor*.

AUGUST 14/15 – PT BASE LEVER HARBOR ⬚17

Early morning and the 157 is underway from Russells Islands with PTs 154, 159, 161 and 162. Six hours later they arrive at PT Base Lever Harbor. This reunites the 157 and the other PTs with the rest of RON-9; many of whom had moved previously (late July) to Lever Harbor while the 157 was at Tulagi getting it center engine replaced.

No rest this night, however, as the 157 moves out with the 154, 159, 160, 161 & 162 as well as the 126, 115 & 116 to their stations in Vella Gulf. They will set up a picket line from Boko Point, Vella Lavella to stretch out 5 miles to the east.

Japanese aircraft are active throughout the night. This includes the dropping of flares by the planes at unknown targets. One of the planes even fires tracers at the water but they were no closer than one mile from the nearest PT.

They leave the Gulf at 0530 and are back in Lever Harbor in a little over two hours.

On patrols the PTs watch for Japanese planes dropping flares as they try and spot PTs. When the flares are spotted it does cause the PTs to stop in the water to eliminate their tell-tale wakes. Without the wakes, spotting a PT at night is not very easy as they tend to blend in with the water and waves. At one point, this night, a Japanese plane flies 300-500 feet right over the PT-160, with Commander Kelly aboard, but never spotted the 160 even though there was bright moonlight.

AUGUST 15/16 – PT BASE LEVER HARBOR ⬚16

The Action Report of 16 August 1943 by Commander Kelly lays out the actions of both the PT-157 and PT-154 this night. The following combines that report plus the 157 log book plus the eyewitness details by both Liebenow and West.

At 2100-hrs the two PTs head out of Base Lever Harbor and 5 minutes later pick up the Marine APc-25 and two LCTs (see page for 38 for an example of a loaded LCT as it enters Rendova Harbor) which the PTs will escort (headed to resupply Marines on New Georgia, pushing from the north towards Munda airfield, and were running low on supplies). West recalls this to be a very bright moonlit night (records show it was indeed a full moon). Fifty-five minutes later a lone plane flies over the formation. A little over an hour later (2310-hours), near Visuvisu Point (see Oak Map 3 on page 31), a single Japanese float airplane appears, and drops one bomb 300 yards off the

APc Boat: Over 115 of the APc-1 class boats were built between 1942-1943. The photo above of the PCs-38 is identical to the APc-25. Photo: U.S. Naval History and Heritage Command, Photo No. NH 96395

APc-25; according to the MTB log. West knows the bomb landed closer than that as, he was later told, the APc-25 had water on the deck from the explosion. Nat Smith's research of the APc25's log show that one crewman of the LCT 325 was wounded in both legs and another received superficial wounds. Both PTs now begin a series of zigzag maneuvers and laying smoke puffs to create visible wakes and prop wash to draw the attention of the plane. That diversion succeeds as the plane drops two more bombs and strafes the PTs and then departs.

With the bright moonlight there was no mistaking it was a Japanese plane. Even so the gunners on RON-9 PTs are under orders not to shoot unless instructed to do so by the skipper. This was due to previous experiences by PTs whose gunners had fired on planes at night not realizing that in some instances they were 'friendlies'. The reverse has also been true when friendly planes have shot at PTs. Both planes and boats are now learning to hold fire and only fire when their skippers or pilots tell them it is OK to do so.

Nearly three hours later, three enemy planes appear approaching the US formation from behind. They apparently found the formation by tracking the boats' wakes. The planes began a series of runs at which each time they would drop a bomb and strafe the PTs. The counter measure for this was that as a plane lined up for its bombing run, and moments before the plane would drop a bomb, West, manning the smoke generator, would release a puff of smoke and at the same moment, Liebenow would turn the 157 in either a hard port or hard starboard direction. A very carefully timed pattern here, much like a quarterback's timing throw to a receiver, only in this case you didn't want to catch the ball. The planes did bite on the smoke as the bait and the bomb would go through the smoke puff into the water and explode harmlessly away from the PT which was already safely off in its new direction.

This sequence of the planes bombing/strafing runs and the PTs smoke puff/change course maneuver went on for about five to six bombs West recalls. Each time the plane was getting a little more accurate and beginning to figure out the smoke puff maneuver. One of the planes drops its bomb only 50-yards away from the 157; now it's getting too close. At this point a change in diversion maneuver by the PTs is needed.

The 154 and 157 now began to circle each other. The 157 was now riding in the 154's prop wash while the 154 was following the 157's prop wash. Like two dogs chasing the other's tail as it were. The idea of this maneuver is that with the PTs moving circular movement instead of a line the planes could no longer 'line-up' on a bombing/strafing run. It would also give the PTs a concentration of fire power with the PTs now able to shoot at the same plane/s if and when they are allowed to do so by their skippers.

The usual way for PTs to hide from aircraft is to cut engines which stop the tell-tale prop wash and bow wakes. However, in this case the 157 and 154 *did* want to keep the planes interest so that it does not go back after the Marine's boats. The 157 and 154 are now running in circles. They are riding in each other's prop wash. Although it is a full moon, this makes it very difficult for the enemy pilot to know where the PTs are exactly, as the prop washes and bow wakes churn up the water which helps hide the PTs' true location. Despite the full moon, the pilots are still hindered by limited light and certainly there is no color distinction at this low light (everything lit by moonlight light is more or less black and white) to tell what is prop wash, bow wake or boat.

Likely having dropped most, if not all, of their bombs at this point, the planes circled. One of the planes is paying particular attention and its gunner is firing down on the 157. The 157's forward gunner, James 'Smitty' Smith fires a few rounds from his 20mm at one of the planes. This is against standing orders, however, this seems to be enough to convince the planes to leave...and they do. As for Smitty's shots; with success comes forgiveness for his breaking of orders, and nothing is recorded about his actions except in the minds of those who were there.

The Marine convoy, meanwhile, has arrived at destination point: Enogai. The 157 and 154 go to check on the Marine boats. As they come up along side the boats, Liebenow recalls hearing cheers from the crews on the boats. The Marines and ship's crewmen watch this dance know full well that these PT crews have deliberately put themselves in the line of fire to protect them.

Both the 157 and 154 return to their originally assigned patrol area and complete the night's patrol duty until 0500 when they return to base Lever Harbor.

Aside from the first bomb the Japanese planes have totally ignored the Marine convoy and the PT's diversionary actions have been a total success. No PT or Marine personnel were wounded nor any real damage to either of the PTs.

In the Daily Action report Commander Kelly recommends that the Marine supply convoys change to daylight schedules as "the LCTs make excellent targets on bright moonlight nights and it is not felt that the PTs can provide them adequate A.A.[anti-aircraft] protection". The 154 and 157 did their job but this is not a long term solution. Had the Japanese not gone after the PTs' diversions and instead stayed focused on the Marine boats the results would have been disastrous.

AUGUST 16/17 – PT BASE LEVER HARBOR Ⓓ

The 157 does not go out this night.

In Kelly's Daily Action Report he is noting, ever more strongly, that PT's actions against the barges are with significant disadvantages and are 'both ineffective and costly'.

AUGUST 17/18 – PT BASE LEVER HARBOR ⟦19⟧

This night the 157 goes out with the 116, 126 and 159 to Kula Gulf. The 157 and 159 are paired as 'Section A'. The 126 and 116 are 'Section B'. The patrol area is a triangle of Bairoko – Arundel – Vila in the Kula Gulf which includes the coastline of the southern tip of the large Japanese held island of Kolombangara Island and the northwest coast of New Georgia Island. Although it doesn't appear to be very far from Lever Harbor, it is noted in the log that it took nearly 2-1/2 hours to get to station.

What follows is the history from those that were there and is not in any of the U.S. Navy documentation....but this is what happened that night.

On this patrol the 157 is paired with the 159 and they are sent out to look for some possible large ships in the area in their assigned sector which includes part of Kolombangara Island. Kolombangara is a large volcano cone (see aerial map on page TBD) and contains 10,000 Japanese military personnel.

Aboard the radar equipped 159 is RON-9's Executive Officer Brantingham. His presence indicates some expectation of action by these two PTs that night

As the two PTs were hugging close to the shore of the big island of Kolombangara the 159 is scanning with its radar for ships. Kolombangara was a well fortified Japanese held island.

The 159's radar picks up a ship coming toward them and motions to 157 for them to back along the shore of Kolombangara to cloak them against the backdrop of the island. They back in, stern first, with their exhaust flappers engaged so that the PT's exhaust noise is run through the underwater muffler system and silenced. The 159 is to the 157's port (left) side and about 200-yards in front of and off to the side of the 157. West said they were so close they could smell the Japanese defenders cooking their fish meals.

As the two PTs sit, bow pointed out, the ship can be as it approaches on this moonlit night. It is a cruiser. The ship also appears to be now cutting slightly closer to the shore now. As the ship get to about 45-degrees off the PTs' bows the 159 suddenly, without notifying the 157, fires two torpedoes. West is at the helm and this firing comes as a total surprise. Worse, the 159 torpedo firing has resulted in the always problematical 'flash' as the oil in the top tubes has ignited! The on-coming ship that has seen the flash and their response is to immediately firing flares just above the are area of the PTs lighting them up plain as day and the commencement of firing on their position. With the 157 is on the closest side of the on-coming ship it is now the most exposed. West said the volume of fire was very heavy…and large caliber stuff. Some of it included 5 inch shells. The 157's Motormac, Jamieson, who came up to the deck briefly, told West later he saw the trail of a large shell whistle just above and to the side of his head. The mystery to this day is that all this firing seemed to be flying *just above the boat*. Had the firing been lower by five to ten feet the 157 would have been cut to ribbons. Nevertheless, Liebenow orders two of its torpedoes to be fired. The 159, although ahead of the 157, is off to the side far enough not to be in the path of the 'fish' just fired. With the two torpedoes away he then orders West, who is still at the helm, to full throttle up and get the hell out of there which the 159 is already in the process of doing.

Both the 159 and 157 are now under fire by the targeted ship which has moved closer and is now just a few degrees off the starboard bow. As they accelerate they are heading nearly directly toward the ship and then turn hard to port. That puts them in the same direction as the ship, however, the PT's speed and evasive maneuvers allow them both to make a great haste getaway.

West is noticing though that the 157 is just not accelerating as it should when he suddenly remembers that in the surprise moment of the 159's firing its torpedoes, and the immediate return firing on them by the ship, that he has forgotten to reposition the silencing flappers from 'on' to 'off' position. He now corrects this and the 157 is back on its usual high speed.

There is no damage to the 157 from enemy fire and no crew on either boat has been wounded. Why the return fire on the PT was a touch high, and therefore ineffective, was an odd but obviously welcomed occurrence.

West, however, later finds one casualty or, rather, six. All of the six mufflers of the 157's exhaust silencing system, which were meant to be used only at 7-knots or less, and are made of copper to resist corrosion with the salt water, have been distorted and ballooned out due to the pressure of the exhaust gases during high speed acceleration. It is a small price to pay for another remarkable patrol.

The PT's torpedoes did not hit the destroyer (or failed to detonate or ran too low) and the destroyer's guns did no damage to the PTs ...*which in this case may have been good for all involved.*

What follows is speculation here by the author, but also has third party support...

The details of this patrol are not in the 157's deck log (As was routine, torpedo firings were not entered in the 157's log) nor included in the MTB Daily Action Report...but they did happen as written. The author's sources indicate the destroyer that was fired at with torpedoes was a U.S. Navy ship.

That this was a U.S ship would also explain why trained gunners on the destroyer firing at the PTs were slightly overshooting the PTs (no damage was reported). Sitting as they were at the start, the gunners on the destroyer would have easily been able to knock the PTs to pieces. The destroyer, having fired flares above the PTs, apparently recognized they were 'friendlies' and we might assume wanted to keep the PTs too occupied to try and fire more torpedoes, all the while doing so without hurting them. Once the PTs were no longer pointing the torpedo tubes at the destroyer a 'cease-fire' may have been issued from the destroyer's Captain. This also would explain why the destroyer quickly stopped firing at the PTs even though the PTs were still well within range of the destroyer's guns. How so many guns from the destroyer could miss two PTs is hard to explain otherwise.

Incidents of friendly fire are one of the PT's constant concerns. Such occurrences did happen, and as we saw, it happened on a patrol the 157 had in July, and of course Kelley's mishap with the U.S.S. McCawley. The technology of IFF (Indentify Friend or Foe) is very basic still and the coordination of the two groups, PT operations and Task Force operations, operating in the same water with two different assignments is constantly giving US Pacific Command real problems. Fortunately here, there are no casualties!

AUGUST 19 – PT BASE LEVER HARBOR Ⓓ

'On alert as striking force'

AUGUST 20/21 – PT BASE LEVER HARBOR ⒙

1750-hrs and underway for Kula Gulf with the PT 159 to intercept enemy barges moving from Bairoko to Vila. It's overcast and occasional rain until midnight at which time the sky clears revealing a bright moonlight. The 159 and 157 make a few courageous runs at the barges. The damage to the barges is 'indeterminate since all barge appeared to reach Vila".

The 157 is noted in the RON-9 Action Report as firing from its 37MM cannon! Liebenow said these were courtesy of local U.S. Marines....who now had a good appreciation for the escort work the PTs were providing on a regular basis as the Marines move between Lever Harbor and Enogai.

The 157's crew mounted the cannon's rear leg onto coconut logs and bolted them to the deck. Although there was some play in the movement of the cannon it was pretty much aimed by moving the boat into position to a line of fire. [Author's note - Imagine having to aim the boat to get a line to target and also the pitching of the boat. Hitting anything under that condition would have to involve a great amount of luck!]

This night also results in another 'secret letter designated MTBLH/A16-3 Serial 10 dated 22 August 1943' entry in the 157's log book. That is referring to the MTB Daily Action Report which can be found in Appendix C on page 145.

AUGUST 22/23 – PT BASE LEVER HARBOR ⬚18

It's an overcast and rainy night. The 157 and patrol is back at barges again! They're still trying to disrupt barge traffic in the Bairoko-Arundel-Vila area…1744-hrs and underway for Kula Gulf with PTs 154, 159 & 161. It is specifically noted on the RON-9 Action Report that the 157 and the 159 now has a 'jury-rig' 37MM on the bow although the 157's cannon fire is in the Action Report from the patrol the previous night. With this note Kelly appears to be notifying the upper chain of command that this 37MM is an experimental adaptation as the PTs try to find solutions for the difficulties of inflicting damage on the barges.

The 157 is using its forward turret 20MM and new 37MM close to within 500-yards of Japanese barges as is the 159. The enemy's return fire was intense so the PTs went at higher speeds on 5 more runs. Then both the 157 and 159 make a final pass as the enemy fire is now becoming more accurate so they then break off the firefight.

Not noted in the 157's deck log nor the MTD daily report was an incident while the 157 and 161 ('Section B' on this patrol) were returning to PT Base Lever Harbor from Kula Gulf. It was just at first light when two planes, just above the water, were seen coming fast straight at the pair of PTs. It looks to be a strafing run by the planes. With all guns of both PTs trained on the planes, both PTs held fire even as the planes were quickly closing in. Had any one gun fired from the planes or the PTs, the barrage that both of the PTs (that is 4-20mm, 2-twin 50-cal) could fire on the two planes would have certainly heavily damaged or more likely downed both planes. The planes continued to close in quickly. It was now past the moment when the PT would have to open with defensive fire. The planes suddenly wig-wagged their wings and then pulled up. These were a pair of Corsairs. The salty language from the collective crewmen of both PTs could be heard above the noises of the PT's Packard engines. How close those two pilots came to being a 'friendly fire' casualty they would never know.

The 157's log book again notes a 'secret letter' which is the MTB Daily Action Report in Appendix C (starting on Page 101), This one is designated MTBLH/A16-3 Serial 12 dated 23 August 1943'. These reports by Kelly are very different in the depth of detail than what he wrote about the patrols while in Rendova. He is obviously trying to send a message…a message of growing frustration that the use of PTs is not appropriate for barge busting. On the risk/reward calculation in his head, the risks are far outweighing the reward. They're not really sinking anything.

AUGUST 24 – PT BASE LEVER HARBOR Ⓓ

On alert. All PTs remain at base by orders of the Commander of Task Force 31. That means the regular Navy doesn't want any issue with friend or foe identification between them and the PTs.

AUGUST 25/26 – PT BASE LEVER HARBOR ⬚16

Tonight is an escort mission. With the 154 and 161 the 157 will escort the U.S.S. APc-25 (coastal transport ship) From Lever Harbor to Enogai. RON-9's XO, Lt. Hank Brantingham, is aboard the 157. This is an almost 9-1/2 hour roundtrip with a 1-1/2 hours layover while a Enogai.

AUGUST 26/27 – PT BASE LEVER HARBOR Ⓓ

'On alert as striking force'

AUGUST 27/28 – PT BASE LEVER HARBOR [18]

It's a no-moon night. The darkest it can be. Back to Kula Gulf. Underway at 1835-hrs with the 115 and 154. Lt. Brantingham is again on the 157. They leave station early at midnight under orders from Task Force Commander 31 and they get back to Lever Harbor at 0215-hrs.

At 0645-hrs it's now daylight and the 157 is back out going to Enogai. They anchor at Enogai at 0800. Two hours later the 157 is on its way back to Lever Harbor and arrives shortly before noon. Over the past 18 hours the 157 has been on night patrol and daylight mission. At 1310 the 157 gulps 900 gallons of fuel. Neither Liebenow nor West can recall the unusual nature of this daytime mission to Enogai.

West says there were some back-to-back patrols/missions where you were so tired you would start walking to another part of the boat and forget why you were walking in the direction and what you were doing. We might assume this could be one of those times.

AUGUST 28/29 – PT BASE LEVER HARBOR Ⓓ

No patrols or missions by any PTs as they are again ordered to stay on base by Task Force Commander 31.

At Lever Harbor: Liebenow (center) sitting with RON-9's Supplies Officer (sitting to Liebenow's right), Cato, and Signal Officer, Sells. Sells would always ride with Commander Kelly whenever Kelly would go out on a PT except when Kelly rode on the 157. The 157's Radioman, Sam Koury, had exceptional signals skills so, as Liebenow noted, Sells could remain at base on those nights that Kelly was on the 157.

AUGUST 30/31 – PT BASE LEVER HARBOR [20]

Although the 157's Deck Log entry reads as a rather routine event, '1814 underway for patrol in company of PT's 115, 154 & 159'. 2043-hrs and on station at Kula Gulf. This will be Liebenow's last patrol as Skipper of the 157.

The second purpose of this patrol was not actually a patrol but a mission. Although the PT-157 went out with the 115, 154 & 159, the 157 has a specific assignment to insert two Marines at a beach location behind enemy lines. Lt. Brantingham is also onboard the 157.

The 157 was again being called on for a special mission Liebenow recalls. They are going to insert two Marines beyond enemy lines on the heavily fortified, Japanese held island of Kolombangara. He noses the bow up to the beach. Liebenow stood on the foredeck and watches as the two Marines jump into the shallow water and into the jungle. He could back out the 157 immediately but he intends to wait a few minutes to make sure that all stays quiet on shore. If the Marines sense any problem he wants to be able to pull them right back on the 157 and high tail it out. Feeling all is clear he signals the helmsman to back out and get under way to their patrol location. He then sits on the deck with his back against the front of the day cabin (right beneath the 'aces 'n' eight logo of a deck of cards) with his feet flat on the deck still watching the shore line. After waiting a few minutes he tries to get up when he realizes his right knee is locked in its bent position. He is certainly in pain and he calls out to West who instantly comes up to Liebenow as does Smitty who saw what happened from his perch in the forward turret. He might have been concerned that Liebenow may have been hit by some unheard gun fire from the shore. Seeing it is a locked knee was good news. The bad news is that the leg won't go straight. With Smitty holding Liebenow, West works to straighten Liebenow's leg all the while saying to himself 'God, help me fix this. I don't won't to lose this skipper from our boat'. This is very painful for Liebenow and the results to straightening the knee is very limited. The 157 proceeds to their assigned patrol station until their usual departure time (meaning giving them enough time to get back to base before daylight when they can easily be seen). Liebenow's leg is a bit better but now very sore and he's walking with a limp.

After return from patrol, Kelly is forced to remove Liebenow as Skipper of the PT-157. He instructs Liebenow to hitch a ride on any boat headed back to Guadalcanal's blue beach medical facility where there are facilities to examine his knee.

It is the last day of August and last 'First-Up' mission for the 157 with Liebenow as Skipper. The loss of Liebenow will alter the crew chemistry of the 157. The earlier writings in this book of 'traditional' officers will now come into play as Lt. Ruff is moved from XO to Skipper of the 157. A time of adjustment is about to begin.

SHORTLY THERE AFTER

Liebenow goes to Field Hospital BLUE BEACH on Guadalcanal. By now the knee is moving more but still not with full motion. The doctor tells Liebenow that he has two choices. He can wrap the knee and Liebenow can head back to Base Lever Harbor and hope for the best, or get shipped to Australia for surgery. The doctor warns Liebenow that surgery usually assures some permanent loss of mobility. Unlike arthroscopic tools today that allow cartilage trimming, stitching and other procedures, in 1943 it usually involved a very lengthy incision, frequently total removal of damaged cartridge and long recovery times. Liebenow chooses to take the chance and wrap it and head back to Lever Harbor.

On arrival back to Lever Harbor Liebenow is assigned to Base patrol, meaning no time on the boats. After some time demonstrating further improvement in the use of his knee, Kelly will assign Liebenow to Section Leader. He will now go out most nights on different boats and observe the enemy activity and performance of the crews, but his days as a PT Skipper *in the Pacific* are over.

In late November Liebenow gets priority orders from Bulkeley to head to Melville Rhode Island where he believes he will get a training assignment. However, shortly after arrival he learns he is going to be in a group of seasoned PT officers to serve on British and US PT boats. Shortly before D-Day, Liebenow is given command of the PT-199 and he and the crew rescues over sixty sailors from the U.S.S. Corry.

The crew of the 157 will have a hard time in September. The loss of Liebenow moves Ensign John Ruff to Skipper of the 157. Ruff's style is so very different from Liebenow's and the adjustments are difficult for some of the crew.

SAM KOURY KILLED SEPT 11 1943
LEVER HARBOR PT 157 NEW GEORGIA

Even more difficult, however, is the death of the crewman, Radioman Sam Koury, on September 11, 1943. While the 157 was making runs at enemy barges, Sam was bringing ammo to West who was manning the newly added 38-cal on the 157's foredeck. Streams of enemy tracers were flying across the deck (tracers are bullets that light-up when fired allowing the gunner to see the path of the bullets being fired). Considering that for each tracer there are three other non-tracer rounds, this means the number of bullets is very, very intense. West and the deck crew have yelled to Sam to 'get down!'. Koury, however continues to carry the ammo up. An instant later Sam is hit by an enemy .51-cal through the hips. He slumps over the 157's life raft. He is given morphine to endure the ride back. The 157 reaches the wooden hulled service

ship, U.S.S. APc-23, in Lever Harbor at 2200-hrs on September 10. They provide Sam medical attention however dies at 0200 hours on September 11. At 0655-hrs Sam Koury's remains are put aboard the PT-161, transported south to Russells Islands and buried. In 1948 the U.S Navy moved his remains back to his home town of Leesville, Louisiana. His casket arrives by train and he is buried on March 19th 1948. Sam is home again.

SAM RAYMOND KOURY
LOUISIANA
RM1c USNR
WORLD WAR II
FEB 25 1918   SEPT 11 1943

EPILOGUE

The PT-157, Liebenow, West and the 157…

Liebenow: In late 1943 Commander Bulkeley was forming another PT group for the waters off of Europe. When Bulkeley asked Kelly who he would want to transfer, he responded with Liebenow. Kelly sends urgent communiqués regarding the early, poor results of 'barge busting' activities to the upper echelons of naval command and stating flat out that PTs were not suited to barge busting operations. The Command responds with a 'try harder' message. There is a sense of frustration in Kelly's tone. His PTs are throwing themselves into a nightly gauntlet against well defended barges, a near suicide run each time for the PTs, with little results to show for their daring. The author and another knowledgeable source independently have arrived to the same conclusion and that is Kelly transferred Liebenow to Bulkeley's new European operation as the best option for Liebenow. Liebenow is one of Kelly's most valued skippers and to have him face the continue nightly barge busting runs in the plywood boats apparently was something Kelly didn't think made the best use of Liebenow; and this transfer, maybe, will save Liebenow from his 'last patrol' on Kelly's watch.

Liebenow was transferred, with priority orders, to the European theater at the end of 1943 and performed OSS drop offs and pickups of agents along the German held French coast. He was given command of the PT-199 the day before D-Day and was at the front on D-Day. The 199 rescued over 60 sailors of the USS Corry, which was hit by German shore fire and sunk. Near the end of his service Liebenow was on a larger US ship but that wasn't suited to his personality. It was 'traditional' Navy.

For his actions on the PT-157 while in the Solomons he was awarded the Silver Star. For his action in the Atlantic he received a Bronze Star.

Liebenow mentioned that at one of the PT veterans' reunions, some 30+ years later, he was asked why the 157 seemed to get a number of special assignments. His answer, with tongue in cheek, was that 'the 157 was more 'special', to which one of the 157's own crewmen yelled out 'it was because the 157 was more expendable!' ….which brought a good round of laughter.

Welford West: after having spent more than 18 months on the 157, was showing the physical toll of riding on a PT boat for that long. CPO Pharmacist Mate Ratchford, who was on the 157 the night they picked up the survivors of the PT-109 (page 58), put Welford on a cot and gave him medication which knocked him out for almost 24-hours. After 18-months of the rough rides from the mahogany V-hull of the PT on ocean waves his body was just worn out. It was the first patrol that West ever missed. He was reassigned, by Ratchford, back to the States in April 1944 where after some R&R (rest & relaxation), he became an instructor in torpedoes at the PT training school at Melville, Rhode Island.

The PT-157: At the end of World War II the PTs in the Pacific were considered not worth returning back to the states. According to the Department of the Navy – Naval Historical Center:

"PT-157's squadron [RON-9] subsequently took part in the operations up the Solomons chain and, after May 1944, in the New Guinea area. Later in the Pacific War, it served in the Philippines. No longer needed after the fighting had ended, in late November, 1945 PT-157 was taken out of service and destroyed"

Opposite page: While still in the Pacific…After decommissioning of the PTs, their weapons and equipment were removed and the PTs were burned in local harbors

THE SECRETARY OF THE NAVY
WASHINGTON

The President of the United States takes pleasure in presenting the SILVER STAR MEDAL to

LIEUTENANT WILLIAM FREDERICK LIEBENOW, JR.
UNITED STATES NAVAL RESERVE

for service as set forth in the following

CITATION:

"For conspicuous gallantry and intrepidity in action as Commanding Officer of a Motor Torpedo Boat operating in the Solomon Islands Area on the nights of July 2-3 and August 15-16, 1943. Although one engine of his boat was demolished during a vigorous attack on four enemy destroyers, Lieutenant (then Lieutenant, Junior Grade) Liebenow expertly maneuvered his crippled vessel into firing position and scored an accurate torpedo hit on one destroyer, withdrawing his craft without further damage to his boat and personnel. Subsequently attacked by enemy planes while escorting a slow speed convoy, he promptly and skillfully executed diversion tactics, laying smoke puffs, flashing lights and creating a conspicuous wake which successfully drew the burden of the attack to his boat and saved the convoy ships from damage. Lieutenant Liebenow's excellent seamanship, decisive action and courageous devotion to duty were in keeping with the highest traditions of the United States Naval Service."

For the President,

James Forrestal.

Secretary of the Navy

Citation and Medals

of

William F. Liebenow and Welford H. West

Lt. (jg.) William F. 'Bud' Liebenow

Skipper of the PT-157, December 1942 – September 1, 1943

- Awarded the **Silver Star** Medal during his tour in the Pacific for the actions noted on the Citation on the opposite page.
- Awarded the **Bronze Star** Medal for his actions of June 1944 while in command of PT-199 in Europe.
- **Additional Medals listed on separation papers**:
  Asiatic-Pacific Area Campaign, 3 Stars
  European – Africa Middle Eastern Area Campaign, 1 Star (D-Day)
  American Area Campaign

Torpedoman 1/C Welford H. West

Torpedoman P.O. 1/C of the PT-157, USN, November 1942 – April 1944

- **With reference to the actions mentioned in the Citation on page**:
  Welford West's assigned deck positions on the two actions cited:
  - July 2-3: At the helm when the PT-157 scored the torpedo hit on the enemy destroyer.
  - August 15-16: Was manning the smoke generator creating the noted smoke puffs during the cited convoy escort action.
- **Medals listed on Welford West's separation papers**:
  Pacific – Asiatic Area Campaign, 1 Star
  American Area Campaign
  Victory World War II
  Good Conduct

LIEBENOW AND KENNEDY – 1960

1960 – A couple of former PT Skippers

[Above] John F. Kennedy and William F. Liebenow during some whistle stops in Grand Rapid Michigan, the area in which Liebenow and his family lived at the time, during Kennedy's campaign for United States Presidency,

J.F.K [said] to me on the whistle stop train "Lieb, if I get the votes of everybody that claims to have been on your boat the night of the pickup I'll win this election in a land slide"

  - *William F. 'Bud' Liebenow* – September 2011

FIRST-UP
Chronicles of the PT-157

A P P E N D I X   A

T I M E L I N E O F PT-157

(June 29 – September 1, 1943)

PT-157 Time Line: June 28 – September 1, 1943

June 28 - day	RON-9 moves from PT base Tulagi to naval Base Russells Island.
June 29/30 - night	RON -9 Moves from Naval Base Russells (Island) to Rendova Harbor. 157 goes on patrol with 156, 161.
June 30/July 1 – night	On patrol.
July 1/2 – night	No patrol; ready reserve
July 2/3 – night	On patrol with 156, 161. On this moonless night the 157 gets caught between two Japanese destroyers. The 157 is damaged but functional and, after escaping the 'squeeze play' manages to fire two torpedoes before returning to base.
July 3/4 – night	No patrol; ready reserve. [Not sure if the engines allow the 157 to go on patrol.]
July 4/5 – night	No patrol; ready reserve. [Not sure if the engines allow the 157 to go on patrol.]
July 5/6 – night	All PTs ordered to stay in harbor as a precaution of anticipated enemy movements with ships that the US Navy destroyers will intercept. The distant Naval Battle of Kula Gulf can be seen by the crews from the deck of their PTs.
July 6/7 – night	No patrol; 'Ready Reserve' in Rendova Harbor. [state of 157s engines unknown]
July 7 – day	The 157 heads out near mid-day to Segi Point to pick up a Major Frederick and party and bring them to Rendova Harbor at near 6:00 in the evening.
July 7/8 night	30-minutes after dropping off Major Frederick and his party the 157 with Commander Kelly on-board and with PTs 156, 161 head out to patrol. On their way an unidentified float plane drops a 400-lb bomb to the stern of the 157. A little after 1:00am Japanese planes drop 2 two-hundred pound bombs off the starboard beam.
July 9 –day	The 157 with Commander Kelly on board plus Marine combat correspondent Samuel Stavisky and photographer Marine Sgt. Jerry Sloan the head out just before 9:00am to the reef off Kundu Kundu. Kelly is going to destroy sensitive equipment and retrieve the log books of the PTs 153, 156 that ran around a few nights before.
July 9/10 – night	No patrol; 'Ready Reserve' in Rendova Harbor
July 11 – night	Leaves Rendova at almost 2:00am with Commander Kelly on board and with the 156 & 161.
July 12/13 – night	All boats (12) of RON-9 leave Rendova Harbor. The Commander of RON-10, T. G. Warfield, is on-board the 157. This scramble of all boats was due to intelligence reports to Warfield that enemy ships might be moving into the area.
July 13/14 – night	No patrol; 'Ready Reserve' in Rendova Harbor.
July 14/15 – night	On patrol west of Rendova with PTs 156, 161.
July 15/16 - night	On patrol Vella Gulf with PTs 156, 161.
July 17/18 - night	On patrol Vella Gulf with PTs 150, 160. Lead boat orders, by radio, the 157 to fire torpedoes however Liebenow has seen the distant ship fire a friendly signal. After

the 3rd order to fire, Liebenow fires two torpedoes off target to comply with orders but avoid hit 'friendly' ships.

July 18 – day	Liebenow gets called before Kelly to answer why he hesitated to fire when ordered. During this conversation Kelly received word by radio the ships were indeed US Naval Warships (i.e. 'friendlies' and Kelly dismisses Liebenow). The 157, now empty of torpedoes, proceed to Base Tulagi via Base Russells in the company of PTs 150 and 160. Along the way the 157s previously damaged engine fails and they continue on their own 'independently'.
July 19 – day	The 157 heads from Base Russells to Base Tulagi.
July 20 – day	Moored at Base Tulagi. R&R (Rest & Relaxation) for the crew.
July 21 – day	Base Tulagi - The 157's center engine is replaced at the engineering dock.
July 22	Moored at Base Tulagi. R&R (Rest & Relaxation) for the crew.
July 23 – day	Base Tulagi – Four torpedoes are loaded.
July 24 – day	The 157 on its way back from Tulagi to Rendova
July 25/26 – day/night	At 1030-hrs a Japanese planes strafes the PTs in Rendova Harbor. The 157 mans all guns and returns fire. At receiving 900-gallons of fuel, the 157 heads out at 1800-hrs with PTs-109 and 159 to Vella Gulf.
July 26 – day	After returning to base and refueling a Japanese plane drops a bomb 200-yds from the 157's stern.
July 27/28 – night	On patrol in Vella Gulf with the PTs 159 and 162.
July 28/29 - night	On 'Alert' status in Rendova Harbor (i.e. no patrol; held in reserve).
July 29/30 - night	On 'Alert' status in Rendova Harbor (i.e. no patrol; held in reserve).
July 30/31 - night	On patrol in Vella Gulf with the PTs 159 and 162.
July 31/August 1	On 'Alert' status in Rendova Harbor (i.e. no patrol; held in reserve).
Aug 1/ 2	August 1st morning starts with a raid on the PTs moored in Rendova Harbor by 18 Japanese planes. This attack is a pre-emptive raid to reduce the PTs presence during the Japanese 'Tokyo Express' run coming that night; of which the US is already aware is coming. That night on patrol the 157 is out with the 159 (lead), with the 162 and 109 following the 157. The 159/157 lose contact with the 162 & 109. The 159 and 157 fires torpedoes During morning de-brief, the Skipper of the 162 reports that the PT- 109 was lost with all hands. At noon the 157 heads for Base Russells
August 3 – Day	The 157's gets two 2 torpedoes (fired the night before) replaced.
August 4- day	The 157 makes the return trip to Rendova.
August 5/6 - night	On patrol in Vella Gulf with the PTs 159 and 162. There is some action of note indicated by DeWilde's reference to the MTB Daily Action Report however this report was never submitted up to Pacific command.

August 6/7 – night	On 'Alert' status in Rendova Harbor (i.e. no patrol; held in reserve).
August 7/8 – night	Responding to a message from PT-109 Skipper Lt. J. F Kennedy inscribed on a coconut brought to them by two local natives, the 157 successfully navigates through shoals and coral and reaches the crewman who are taken on-board; and all return to base.
August 15/16 – night	The 157 and 154 are escorting Marine supply ship convoy when they come under two separate attacks by Japanese aircraft. Both of the PTs run a series of distracting, evasive maneuvers to draw enemy fire away from the convoy. The convoy and the 157 and 154 make it safely to its destination.
August 16/17 – night	On 'Alert' status in Rendova Harbor (i.e. no patrol; held in reserve).
August 17/18 – night	On patrol in Kula Gulf with PTs 116, 126 & 159. Likely friendly fire incident.
August 18/19 - night	On 'Alert' status in Rendova Harbor (i.e. no patrol; held in reserve).
August 19/20 - night	On 'Alert' status in Rendova Harbor (i.e. no patrol; held in reserve).
August 20/21 – night	On patrol in Kula Gulf with PT-159. The 157 now has a 37MM bolted to its bow as an experiment in seeing how effective it might be again the enemy barges.
August 21/22 – night	On 'Alert' status in Rendova Harbor (i.e. no patrol; held in reserve).
August 22/23 – night	On patrol in Kula Gulf with PTs 154, 159 & 161. The 157 has a 'jury rigged' 37MM on its bow as noted in the MTB Daily Report. However the MTB Daily Report notes shots fired by the 157's 37MM on the night of August 20/21.
August 23/24 – night	On 'Alert' status in Rendova Harbor (i.e. no patrol; held in reserve).
August 24/25 – night	On 'Alert' status in Rendova Harbor (i.e. no patrol; held in reserve).
August 25/26 – night	Escort Marine APC 25 with 154 & 161
August 26/27 – night	On 'Alert' status in Rendova Harbor (i.e. no patrol; held in reserve).
August 27/28 – night	On patrol in Kula Gulf with PTs 154 & 115.
August 28 – day	At 0545 the 157 goes to Enogai, stays for two hours and then return to Lever Harbor.
August 28/29 – night	On 'Alert' status in Rendova Harbor (i.e. no patrol; held in reserve).
August 29/30 – night	On 'Alert' status in Rendova Harbor (i.e. no patrol; held in reserve).
August 30/31 – night	On patrol in Kula Gulf with PTs 154, 115 & 159. However the 157 is dropping off 2 US Marines at Rei Cove behind the enemy lines on Kolombangara Island. Liebenow's knee locks up and he is relieved of his command of the PT-157 by Cmdr. Kelly and ordered to Guadalcanal to see a doctor about his knee.

APPENDIX B

DECK LOG OF THE PT-157
Log book entries by Quartermaster Waldo DeWilde

Appendix

The documents in this section, those past July 12 1943, were requested by the author from the National Archives and Records Administration [NARA]. Some pages were of poor quality due to deterioration of the original documents. The pages provided from NARA, which were in digital format, and the author has made some adjustments to enhance their readability.

ALL documents in this section are declassified

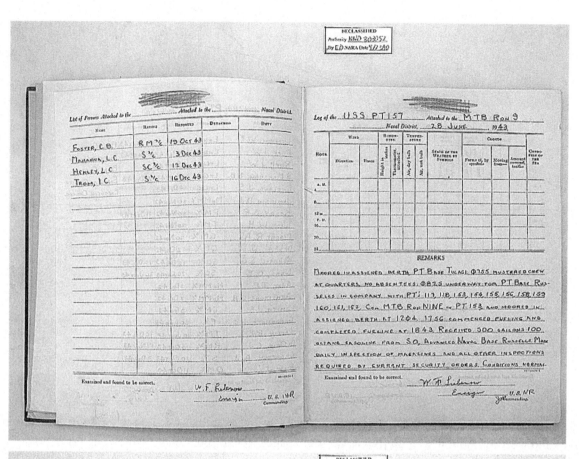

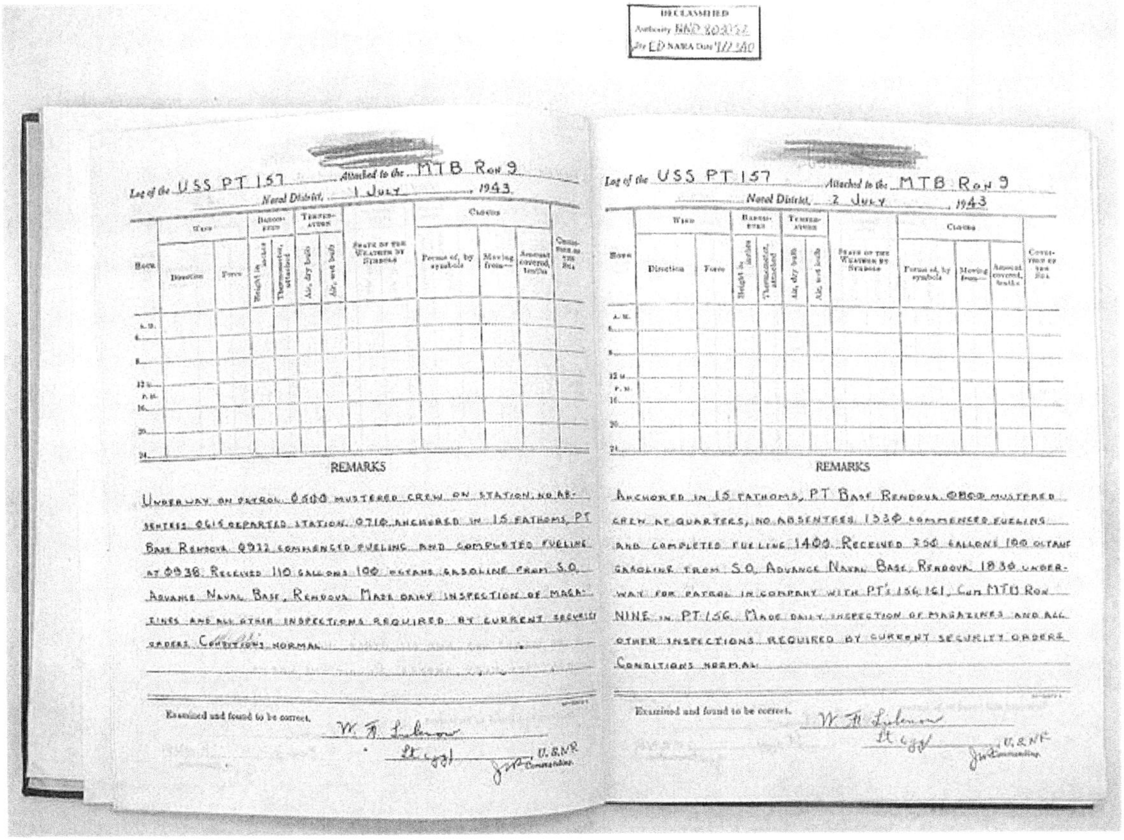

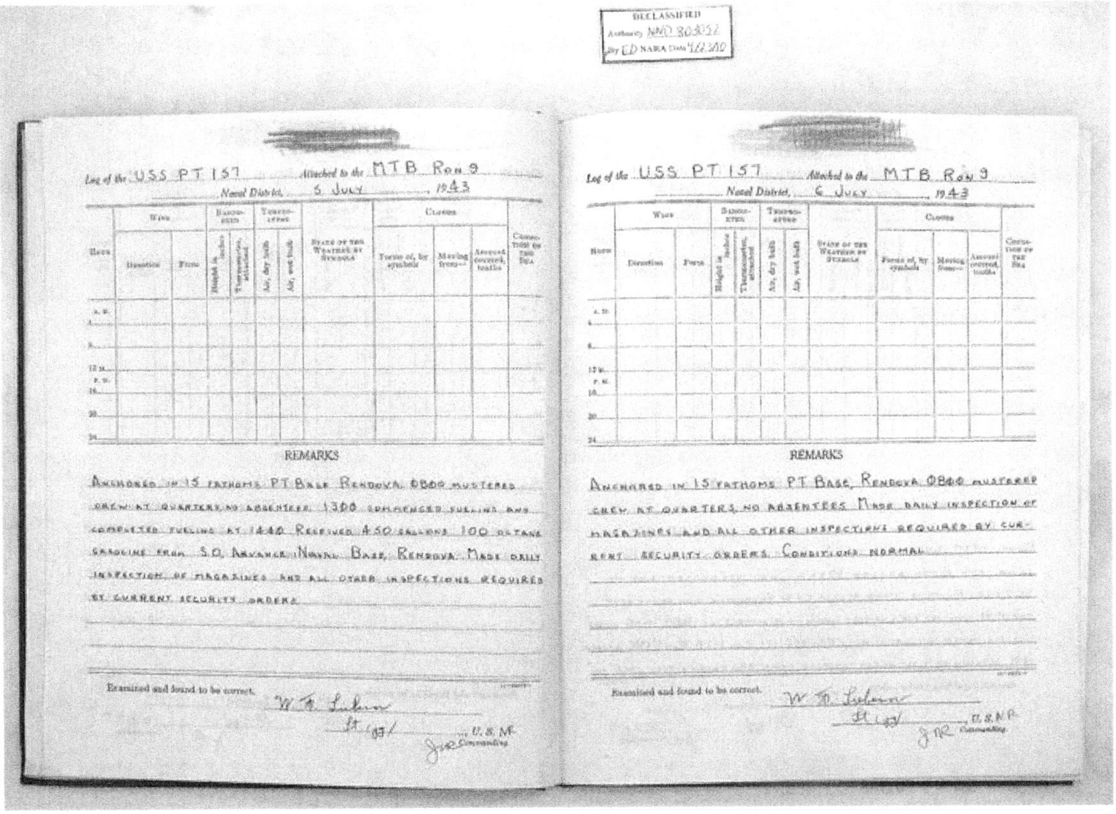

Log of the U.S.S. PT 157 — Attached to the MTB Ron 9 — Naval District — 7 July 1943

DECLASSIFIED
Authority NND 803052
By ED NARA Date 4/23/10

REMARKS

Anchored in 15 fathoms, PT Base Rendova. 0700 mustered crew at quarters, no absentees. 1116 underway for Seci Point, New Georgia. 1415 moored starboard side to LCT 182, Seci Point. 1527 underway for Rendova with Major W.R. Frederick and party aboard. 1737 moored starboard side to LCT 134 Rendova. 1750 Major W.R. Frederick and party left ship. 1751 underway for assigned berth and moored at 1807. 1830 underway for patrol in company with PT's 156, 161, Com MTB Ron NINE aboard. 1857 unidentified float plane dropped bomb 400 yards astern. 1915 an

Examined and found to be correct.
W. F. Liebner Lt USNR Commanding

Station west of Rendova. Made daily inspection of magazines and all other inspections required by current security orders. Conditions normal.

Examined and found to be correct.
W. F. Liebner Lt USNR Commanding

Log of the U.S.S. PT 157 — Attached to the MTB Ron 9 — Naval District — 8 July 1943

DECLASSIFIED
Authority NND 803052
By ED NARA Date 4/23/10

REMARKS

Underway on patrol. 0110 Jap planes dropped two bombs, 300 yards off our starboard beam. 0600 departed station and anchored in 15 fathoms, PT Base Rendova at 0715. 0800 mustered crew at quarters, no absentees. 1518 commenced fueling and completed fueling at 1742. Received 1350 gallons 100 octane gasoline from SO, Advance Naval Base, Rendova. Made daily inspection of magazines and all other inspections required by current security orders. Conditions normal.

Examined and found to be correct.
W. F. Liebner Lt USNR Commanding

Log of the U.S.S. PT 157 — Attached to the MTB Ron 9 — Naval District — 9 July 1943

REMARKS

Anchored in 15 fathoms PT Base Rendova. 0800 mustered crew at quarters, no absentees. 0852 underway for reef off Kundurumb, Com MTB Ron NINE aboard. 0926 lying to off PT's 153, 158 aground on reef, Com MTB Ron NINE. Went to beached boats. 0956 Com MTB Ron NINE came aboard with shots from enemy shore battery landing 200 yards short. 0952 underway for PT Base Rendova and anchored in 15 fathoms at 1015. Laflin, R.E. TM's reported aboard for duty. Made daily inspection of magazines and all other inspections required by current security orders. Conditions normal.

Examined and found to be correct.
W. F. Liebner Lt USNR Commanding

Log of the USS PT 157 — Attached to the MTB Ron. 9 — Naval District — 10 July 1943

REMARKS

Anchored in 15 fathoms, P.T. Base Rendova 0800 mustered crew at quarters no absentees. Made daily inspection of magazines and all other inspections required by current security orders. Conditions normal.

Examined and found to be correct.
W. F. Liebenow
Lt. USNR
Commanding

Log of the USS PT 157 — Attached to the MTB Ron. 9 — Naval District — 11 July 1943

REMARKS

Anchored in 15 fathoms, P.T. Base Rendova. 0145 underway on patrol in company with PTs 159, 161, Com MTB Ron TEN aboard. 0230 on station west of Rendova. 0600 departed station and anchored in 15 fathoms P.T. Base Rendova at 0645. 0700 Com MTB Ron TEN left ship. 0800 mustered crew at quarters no absentees. Made daily inspection of magazines and all other inspections required by current security orders. Conditions normal.

Examined and found to be correct.
W. F. Liebenow
Lt. USNR
Commanding

Log of the USS PT 157 — Attached to the MTB Ron 9 — Naval District — 12 July 1943

REMARKS

Anchored in 15 fathoms P.T. Base Rendova 0800 mustered crew at quarters no absentees. 0932 commenced fueling and completed fueling at 1105. Received 550 gallons 100 octane gasoline from S.O. Advance Naval Base Rendova. 2015 underway for patrol in Blackett Strait in company with PTs 103, 104, 105, 117, 164, 155, 156, 159, 160, 161, 162. Com MTB Ron TEN aboard. 2245 on station. Made daily inspection of magazines and all other inspections required by current security orders. Conditions normal.

Examined and found to be correct.
W. F. Liebenow
Lt. USNR
Commanding

Log of the USS PT 157 — Attached to the MTB Ron 9 — Naval District — 13 July 1943

REMARKS

Underway on patrol in Blackett Strait. 0415 departed station and anchored in 17 fathoms. P.T. Base Rendova at 0847. 0800 mustered crew at quarters no absentees. 1218 commenced fueling and completed fueling at 1255. Received 550 gallons 100 octane gasoline from S.O. Advance Naval Base Rendova. Made daily inspection of magazines and all other inspections required by current security orders. Conditions normal.

Examined and found to be correct.
W. F. Liebenow
Lt. USNR
Commanding

Log of the U.S.S. PT 157 ___ Attached to the MTB Ron 9
Naval District, 14 JULY , 1943

Hour	Wind		Barometer	Temperature			State of the Weather by Symbols	Clouds			Condition of the Sea
	Direction	Force	Height in inches	Thermometer, attached	Atta, dry bulb	Atta, wet bulb		Forms of, by symbols	Moving from—	Amount covered, tenths	
a. m.											
8											
12 m.											
p. m.											
16											
20											
24											

REMARKS

Anchored in 17 fathoms PT Base Rendova. 0800 mustered crew at quarters no absentees 1845 underway for patrol in company with PT's 156 161 1950 on station west of Rendova. Made daily inspection of magazines and all other inspections required by current security orders Conditions normal.

Examined and found to be correct.

W. F. Liebenow
Lt (jg)
U.S.N.R.
Commanding.

Log of the U.S.S. PT 157 ___ Attached to the MTB Ron 9
Naval District, 15 JULY , 1943

Hour	Wind		Barometer	Temperature			State of the Weather by Symbols	Clouds			Condition of the Sea
	Direction	Force	Height in inches	Thermometer, attached	Atta, dry bulb	Atta, wet bulb		Forms of, by symbols	Moving from—	Amount covered, tenths	
a. m.											
8											
12 m.											
p. m.											
16											
20											
24											

REMARKS

Underway on patrol west of Rendova. 0030 departed station and anchored in 17 fathoms PT Base Rendova at 0117 0800 mustered crew at quarters no absentees 0940 commenced fueling and completed fueling at 1010. Received 200 gallons 100 octane gasoline from S.O. Advance Naval Base Rendova 2140 underway for patrol in company with PT's 156 161 Made daily inspection of magazines and all other inspections required by current security orders. Conditions normal.

Examined and found to be correct.

W. F. Liebenow
Lt (jg)
U.S.
Commanding.

Log of the U.S.S. PT 157 ___ Attached to the MTB Ron 9
Naval District, 16 JULY , 1943

Hour	Wind		Barometer	Temperature			State of the Weather by Symbols	Clouds			Condition of the Sea
	Direction	Force	Height in inches	Thermometer, attached	Atta, dry bulb	Atta, wet bulb		Forms of, by symbols	Moving from—	Amount covered, tenths	
a. m.											
8											
12 m.											
p. m.											
16											
20											
24											

REMARKS

0000 on station in Vella Gulf 0140 departed station and anchored in 15 fathoms PT Base Rendova at 0500 0800 mustered crew at quarters no absentees 1200 commenced fueling and completed fueling at 1225. Received 600 gallons 100 octane gasoline from S.O. Advance Naval Base Rendova. Made daily inspection of magazines and all other inspections required by current security orders. Conditions normal.

Examined and found to be correct.

W. F. Liebenow
Lt (jg)
U.S.N.R.
Commanding.

Log of the U.S.S. PT 157 ___ Attached to the MTB Ron 9
Naval District, 17 JULY , 1943

Hour	Wind		Barometer	Temperature			State of the Weather by Symbols	Clouds			Condition of the Sea
	Direction	Force	Height in inches	Thermometer, attached	Atta, dry bulb	Atta, wet bulb		Forms of, by symbols	Moving from—	Amount covered, tenths	
a. m.											
8											
12 m.											
p. m.											
16											
20											
24											

REMARKS

Anchored in 15 fathoms PT Base Rendova 0800 mustered crew at quarters no absentees 1845 underway for patrol in company with PT's 159, 160 in Vella Gulf. Made daily inspection of magazines and all other inspections required by current security orders. Conditions normal.

Examined and found to be correct.

W. F. Liebenow
Lt (jg)
U.S.N.R.
Commanding.

Log of the USS PT 157 — Attached to the MTB Ron 9 — Naval District, 18 July, 1943

REMARKS

Underway on patrol in Vella Gulf. Reference: Com MTB's Rendova memorandum to Com Nav Base New Georgia (action report) dated 18 July 1943. 0505 anchored in 15 fathoms PT Base Rendova. 0800 mustered crew at quarters, no absentees. 1320 underway for PT Base Russells in company with PT's 159. 160. 1635 sustained casualty on center engine, proceeded independently. 1710 moored at assigned berth PT Base Russells. Made daily inspection of magazines and all other inspections required by current security orders. Conditions normal.

Examined and found to be correct.
W. F. Liebenow
Lt (jg) U.S.N.R.
Commanding.

Log of the USS PT 157 — Attached to the MTB Ron 9 — Naval District, 19 July, 1943

REMARKS

Moored in assigned berth PT Base Russells. 0700 mustered crew at quarters, no absentees. 0835 underway for PT Base Tulagi, and moored at Gauly Dock at 1158. 1325 commenced fueling and completed fueling at 1450. Received 1200 gallons 100 octane gasoline from S.O. Advance Naval Base Tulagi. 1500 underway for assigned berth and moored at 1514. Made daily inspection of magazines and all other inspections required by current security orders. Conditions normal.

Examined and found to be correct.
W. F. Liebenow
Lt (jg) U.S.N.R.
Commanding.

Log of the USS PT 157 — Attached to the MTB Ron 9 — Naval District, 20 July, 1943

REMARKS

Moored in assigned berth PT Base Tulagi. 0745 mustered crew at quarters, no absentees. Made daily inspection of magazines and all other inspections required by current security orders, conditions normal.

Examined and found to be correct.
W. F. Liebenow
Lt (jg) U.S.N.R.
Commanding.

Log of the USS PT 157 — Attached to the MTB Ron 9 — Naval District, 21 July, 1943

REMARKS

Moored in assigned berth PT Base Tulagi. 0800 mustered crew at quarters, no absentees. 0804 underway for engineering dock and moored at 0815. 0845 removed center engine. 1330 installed new center engine. 1352 underway for assigned berth and moored at 1400. Made daily inspection of magazines and all other inspections required by current security orders. Conditions normal.

Examined and found to be correct.
W. F. Liebenow
Lt (jg) U.S.N.R.
Commanding.

Log of the U.S.S. PT 157   Attached to the MTB Ron 9
Naval District, 22 July , 1943

Hours	Wind		Barometer	Temperature		Clouds				Condition of the Sea
	Direction	Force	Height in inches	Thermometer, attached	Air, dry bulb	Air, wet bulb	State of the Weather by Symbols	Forms of, by symbols	Moving from—	Amount covered, tenths	
A. M.											
4											
8											
12 M.											
P. M.											
16											
20											
24											

REMARKS

Moored at assigned berth PT Base Tulagi. 0750 mustered crew at quarters, no absentees. Made daily inspection of magazines and all other inspections required by current security orders. Conditions normal.

Examined and found to be correct.   W. F. Liebenow
Lt (jg)
, U.S.N.R.
Commanding

Log of the U.S.S. PT 157   Attached to the MTB Ron 9
Naval District, 23 July , 1943

Hours	Wind		Barometer	Temperature		Clouds				Condition of the Sea
	Direction	Force	Height in inches	Thermometer, attached	Air, dry bulb	Air, wet bulb	State of the Weather by Symbols	Forms of, by symbols	Moving from—	Amount covered, tenths	
A. M.											
4											
8											
12 M.											
P. M.											
16											
20											
24											

REMARKS

Moored in assigned berth PT Base Tulagi. 0800 mustered crew at quarters, no absentees. 0935 underway for torpedo dock and moored at 0948. 1130 took on 4 Mark VIII torpedoes. 1325 commenced fueling and completed fueling at 1440. Received 1600 gallons 100 octane gasoline from SO, Advance Naval Base Tulagi. 1345 underway for assigned berth and moored at 1550. Made daily inspection of magazines and all other inspections required by current security orders. Conditions normal.

Examined and found to be correct.   W. F. Liebenow
Lt (jg)
, U.S.N.R.
Commanding

Log of the U.S.S. PT 157   Attached to the MTB Ron 9
Naval District, 24 July , 1943

Hours	Wind		Barometer	Temperature		Clouds				Condition of the Sea
	Direction	Force	Height in inches	Thermometer, attached	Air, dry bulb	Air, wet bulb	State of the Weather by Symbols	Forms of, by symbols	Moving from—	Amount covered, tenths	
A. M.											
4											
8											
12 M.											
P. M.											
16											
20											
24											

REMARKS

Moored in assigned berth PT Base Tulagi. 0800 mustered crew at quarters, no absentees. 1218 underway for PT Base Rendova. 1740 moored in assigned berth PT Base Rendova. Made daily inspection of magazines and all other inspections required by current security orders. Conditions normal.

Examined and found to be correct.   W. F. Liebenow
Lt (jg)
, U.S.N.R.
Commanding

Log of the U.S.S. PT 157   Attached to the MTB Ron 9
Naval District, 25 July , 1943

Hours	Wind		Barometer	Temperature		Clouds				Condition of the Sea
	Direction	Force	Height in inches	Thermometer, attached	Air, dry bulb	Air, wet bulb	State of the Weather by Symbols	Forms of, by symbols	Moving from—	Amount covered, tenths	
A. M.											
4											
8											
12 M.											
P. M.											
16											
20											
24											

REMARKS

Moored in assigned berth PT Base Rendova. 0800 mustered crew at quarters, no absentees. 1030 manned all guns and turned back Jap fighter who was strafing berth. 1330 commenced fueling and completed fueling at 1410. Received 900 gallons 100 octane gasoline from SO, Advance Naval Base Rendova. 1800 underway for patrol in company with PTs 103, 159. 2020 on station in Vella Gulf. Made daily inspection of magazines and all other inspections required by current security orders. Conditions normal.

Examined and found to be correct.   W. F. Liebenow
Lt (jg)
, U.S.N.R.
Commanding

FIRST-UP
Chronicles of the PT-157

Log of the USS PT 157   Attached to the MTB Ron 9
Naval District, 26 JULY 1943

	Wind		Barom-eter	Temper-ature				Clouds			Condi-tion of the Sea
Hour	Direction	Force	Height in inches	Thermometer attached	Air, dry bulb	Air, wet bulb	State of the Weather by Symbols	Forms of, by symbols	Moving from—	Amount covered, tenths	
A. M.											
4											
8											
12 M.											
P. M.											
16											
20											
24											

REMARKS

Underway on patrol in Vella Gulf 0500 departed station 0715 moored in assigned berth PT Base Rendova. 0800 mustered crew at quarters, no absentees. 0907 commenced fueling and completed fueling at 0938. Received 850 gallons 100 octane gasoline from S.O. Advance Naval Base Rendova. 2000 Jap plane dropped bomb 100 yards off our stern. Made daily inspection of magazines and all other inspections required by current security orders. Conditions normal.

Examined and found to be correct.
W. F. Liebenow
Lt (jg) , U.S.N.R.
Commanding.

Log of the USS PT 157   Attached to the MTB Ron 9
Naval District, 27 JULY 1943

	Wind		Barom-eter	Temper-ature				Clouds			Condi-tion of the Sea
Hour	Direction	Force	Height in inches	Thermometer attached	Air, dry bulb	Air, wet bulb	State of the Weather by Symbols	Forms of, by symbols	Moving from—	Amount covered, tenths	
A. M.											
4											
8											
12 M.											
P. M.											
16											
20											
24											

REMARKS

Moored in assigned berth PT Base Rendova. 0800 mustered crew at quarters no absentees. 1812 underway for patrol in company with PTs 159, 162. 2100 on station in Vella Gulf. Made daily inspection of magazines and all other inspections required by current security orders. Conditions normal.

Examined and found to be correct.
W. F. Liebenow
Lt (jg) , U.S.N.R.
Commanding.

Log of the USS PT 157   Attached to the MTB Ron 9
Naval District, 28 JULY 1943

	Wind		Barom-eter	Temper-ature				Clouds			Condi-tion of the Sea
Hour	Direction	Force	Height in inches	Thermometer attached	Air, dry bulb	Air, wet bulb	State of the Weather by Symbols	Forms of, by symbols	Moving from—	Amount covered, tenths	
A. M.											
4											
8											
12 M.											
P. M.											
16											
20											
24											

REMARKS

Underway on patrol in Vella Gulf 0440 departed station and moored in assigned berth PT Base Rendova at 0700. 0730 commenced fueling and completed fueling at 0800. Received 850 gallons 100 octane gasoline from S.O. Advance Naval Base Rendova. 0800 mustered crew at quarters, no absentees. Made daily inspection of magazines and all other inspections required by current security orders. Conditions normal.

Examined and found to be correct.
W. F. Liebenow
Lt (jg) , U.S.N.R.
Commanding.

Log of the USS PT 157   Attached to the MTB Ron 9
Naval District, 29 JULY 1943

	Wind		Barom-eter	Temper-ature				Clouds			Condi-tion of the Sea
Hour	Direction	Force	Height in inches	Thermometer attached	Air, dry bulb	Air, wet bulb	State of the Weather by Symbols	Forms of, by symbols	Moving from—	Amount covered, tenths	
A. M.											
4											
8											
12 M.											
P. M.											
16											
20											
24											

REMARKS

Moored in assigned berth PT Base Rendova. 0800 mustered crew at quarters, no absentees. Made daily inspection of magazines and all other inspections required by current security orders. Conditions normal.

Examined and found to be correct.
W. F. Liebenow
Lt (jg) , U.S.N.R.
Commanding.

91

Log of the USS PT 157   Attached to the MTB Ron 9
Naval District,   30 JULY   , 1943

Hour	Wind		Barometer	Temperature				State of the Weather by Symbols	Clouds				Condition of the Sea
	Direction	Force	Height in inches	Thermometer, attached	Air, dry bulb	Air, wet bulb			Form of, by symbols	Moving from—	Amount covered, tenths		
A. M.													
8													
12 M.													
P. M.													
16													
20													
24													

REMARKS

MOORED IN ASSIGNED BERTH PT BASE RENDOVA. 0800 MUSTERED CREW AT QUARTERS, NO ABSENTEES. 1808 UNDERWAY FOR PATROL IN COMPANY WITH PT's 159, 162. 2005 ON STATION IN VELLA GULF. MADE DAILY INSPECTION OF MAGAZINES AND ALL OTHER INSPECTIONS REQUIRED BY CURRENT SECURITY ORDERS. CONDITIONS NORMAL.

Examined and found to be correct.   W. F. Liebenow
Lt (jg)   , U. S. N R
JWR Commanding.

Log of the USS PT 157   Attached to the MTB Ron 9
Naval District,   31 JULY   , 1943

Hour	Wind		Barometer	Temperature				State of the Weather by Symbols	Clouds				Condition of the Sea
	Direction	Force	Height in inches	Thermometer, attached	Air, dry bulb	Air, wet bulb			Form of, by symbols	Moving from—	Amount covered, tenths		
A. M.													
8													
12 M.													
P. M.													
16													
20													
24													

REMARKS

UNDERWAY ON PATROL IN VELLA GULF. 0430 DEPARTED STATION AND MOORED IN ASSIGNED BERTH PT BASE RENDOVA AT 0612. 0800 MUSTERED CREW AT QUARTERS, NO ABSENTEES. 0836 COMMENCED FUELING AND COMPLETED FUELING AT 1005. RECEIVED 800 GALLONS 100 OCTANE GASOLINE FROM S.O. ADVANCE NAVAL BASE RENDOVA. MADE DAILY INSPECTION OF MAGAZINES AND ALL OTHER INSPECTIONS REQUIRED BY CURRENT SECURITY ORDERS. CONDITIONS NORMAL

Examined and found to be correct.   W. F. Liebenow
Lt (jg)   , U. S. N R
JWR Commanding.

Log of the USS PT 157   Attached to the MTB Ron 9
Naval District,   1 AUGUST   , 1943

Hour	Wind		Barometer	Temperature				State of the Weather by Symbols	Clouds				Condition of the Sea
	Direction	Force	Height in inches	Thermometer, attached	Air, dry bulb	Air, wet bulb			Form of, by symbols	Moving from—	Amount covered, tenths		
A. M.													
8													
12 M.													
P. M.													
16													
20													
24													

REMARKS

MOORED IN ASSIGNED BERTH PT BASE RENDOVA. 0200 ENEMY PLANE DROPPED BOMB 800 YARDS EAST OF BERTH. 0800 MUSTERED CREW AT QUARTERS, NO ABSENTEES. 1545 ATTACKED BY ENEMY DIVE BOMBERS, DIVERTED FROM BERTH BY HEAVY RETURN FIRE. 1825 UNDERWAY FOR PATROL IN COMPANY WITH PT's 159, 162. MADE DAILY INSPECTION OF MAGAZINES AND ALL OTHER INSPECTIONS REQUIRED BY CURRENT SECURITY ORDERS. CONDITIONS NORMAL.

Examined and found to be correct.   W. F. Liebenow
Lt (jg)   , U. S. N R
JWR Commanding.

Log of the USS PT 157   Attached to the MTB Ron 9
Naval District,   2 AUGUST   , 1943

Hour	Wind		Barometer	Temperature				State of the Weather by Symbols	Clouds				Condition of the Sea
	Direction	Force	Height in inches	Thermometer, attached	Air, dry bulb	Air, wet bulb			Form of, by symbols	Moving from—	Amount covered, tenths		
A. M.													
8													
12 M.													
P. M.													
16													
20													
24													

REMARKS

UNDERWAY ON PATROL IN VELLA GULF. REFERENCE: COM MTB's RENDOVA ACTION REPORT TO COMINCH DATED 1 AUGUST, 1943. 0615 MOORED IN ASSIGNED BERTH PT BASE RENDOVA. 0800 MUSTERED CREW AT QUARTERS, NO ABSENTEES. 1210 UNDERWAY FOR PT BASE RUSSELLS AND MOORED IN ASSIGNED BERTH AT 1735. MADE DAILY INSPECTION OF MAGAZINES AND ALL OTHER INSPECTIONS REQUIRED BY CURRENT SECURITY ORDERS. CONDITIONS NORMAL.

Examined and found to be correct.   W. F. Liebenow
Lt (jg)   , U. S. N R
JWR Commanding.

FIRST-UP

Chronicles of the PT-157

Log of the USS PT 157   **Attached to the** MTB Ron 9
   Naval District, 3 AUGUST 1943

Hour	Wind		Barometer	Temperature		State of the Weather by Symbols	Clouds			Condition of the Sea
	Direction	Force	Height in inches	Thermometer, attached	Air, dry bulb / Air, wet bulb		Forms of, by symbols	Moving from—	Amount covered, tenths	
A. M.										
4										
8										
12 M.										
P. M.										
16										
20										
24										

REMARKS

MOORED AT ASSIGNED BERTH PT BASE RUSSELLS. 0800 MUSTERED CREW AT QUARTERS, NO ABSENTEES. 1009 UNDERWAY FOR TORPEDO DOCK AND MOORED AT 1017. 1400 COMPLETED LOADING TORPEDOES. 1405 UNDERWAY FOR YOG 49 AND MOORED ALONGSIDE AT 1415 - 1440 COMMENCED FUELING AND COMPLETED FUELING AT 1624. RECEIVED 2100 GALLONS 100 OCTANE GASOLINE FROM YOG49. 1731 UNDERWAY FOR ASSIGNED BERTH AND MOORED AT 1740. MADE DAILY INSPECTION OF MAGAZINES AND ALL OTHER INSPECTIONS REQUIRED BY CURRENT SECURITY ORDERS. CONDITIONS NORMAL

Examined and found to be correct.

W. F. Liebenow
Lt (jg) , U. S. NR
Commanding.

Log of the USS PT 157   **Attached to the** MTB Ron 9
   Naval District, 4 AUGUST 1943

Hour	Wind		Barometer	Temperature		State of the Weather by Symbols	Clouds			Condition of the Sea
	Direction	Force	Height in inches	Thermometer, attached	Air, dry bulb / Air, wet bulb		Forms of, by symbols	Moving from—	Amount covered, tenths	
A. M.										
4										
8										
12 M.										
P. M.										
16										
20										
24										

REMARKS

MOORED IN ASSIGNED BERTH PT BASE RUSSELLS. 0800 MUSTERED CREW AT QUARTERS, NO ABSENTEES. 0910 UNDERWAY FOR PT BASE RENDOVA AND MOORED IN ASSIGNED BERTH AT 1418. MADE DAILY INSPECTION OF MAGAZINES AND ALL OTHER INSPECTIONS REQUIRED BY CURRENT SECURITY ORDERS. CONDITIONS NORMAL

Examined and found to be correct.

W. F. Liebenow
Lt (jg) , U. S. NR
Commanding.

Log of the USS PT 157   **Attached to the** MTB Ron 9
   Naval District, 5 AUGUST 1943

Hour	Wind		Barometer	Temperature		State of the Weather by Symbols	Clouds			Condition of the Sea
	Direction	Force	Height in inches	Thermometer, attached	Air, dry bulb / Air, wet bulb		Forms of, by symbols	Moving from—	Amount covered, tenths	
A. M.										
4										
8										
12 M.										
P. M.										
16										
20										
24										

REMARKS

MOORED IN ASSIGNED BERTH PT BASE RENDOVA. 0615 MUSTERED CREW AT QUARTERS, NO ABSENTEES. 0655 COMMENCED FUELING AND COMPLETED FUELING AT 0712. RECEIVED 450 GALLONS 100 OCTANE GASOLINE FROM S.O. ADVANCE NAVAL BASE RENDOVA. UNDERWAY FOR PATROL IN COMPANY WITH PT's 159, 162. 2100 ON STATION IN VELLA GULF. MADE DAILY INSPECTION OF MAGAZINES AND ALL OTHER INSPECTIONS REQUIRED BY CURRENT SECURITY ORDERS. CONDITIONS NORMAL

Examined and found to be correct.

W. F. Liebenow
Lt (jg) , U. S. NR
Commanding.

Log of the USS PT 157   **Attached to the** MTB Ron 9
   Naval District, 6 AUGUST 1943

Hour	Wind		Barometer	Temperature		State of the Weather by Symbols	Clouds			Condition of the Sea
	Direction	Force	Height in inches	Thermometer, attached	Air, dry bulb / Air, wet bulb		Forms of, by symbols	Moving from—	Amount covered, tenths	
A. M.										
4										
8										
12 M.										
P. M.										
16										
20										
24										

REMARKS

UNDERWAY ON PATROL IN VELLA GULF. REFERENCE: COM MTBs RENDOVA ACTION REPORT TO COMINCH, DATED 6 AUGUST 1943. 0700 MOORED IN ASSIGNED BERTH PT BASE RENDOVA. 0715 MUSTERED CREW AT QUARTERS, NO ABSENTEES. 0748 COMMENCED FUELING AND COMPLETED FUELING AT 0839. RECEIVED 800 GALLONS 100 OCTANE GASOLINE FROM S.O. ADVANCE NAVAL BASE RENDOVA. MADE DAILY INSPECTION OF MAGAZINES AND ALL OTHER INSPECTIONS REQUIRED BY CURRENT SECURITY ORDERS. CONDITIONS NORMAL.

Examined and found to be correct.

W. F. Liebenow
Lt (jg) , U. S. NR
Commanding.

Log of the USS PT 157 ____ Attached to the MTB Ron 9
Naval District, 7 August, 1943

Hour	Wind		Barometer	Temperature		State of the Weather by Symbols	Clouds			Condition of the Sea
	Direction	Force	Height in inches. Thermometer attached	Air, dry bulb	Air, wet bulb		Forms of, by symbols	Moving from—	Amount covered, tenths	
A.M.										
4										
8										
12 M.										
P.M.										
16										
20										
24										

REMARKS

Moored in assigned berth PT Base Rendova. 0800 mustered crew at quarters, no absentees 1553 underway for Onaiavisi Inlet. 1630 lying to in Onaiavisi Inlet. 1730 3 native guides came aboard, underway for assigned berth and moored at 1755. 2030 underway for Ferguson Passage with Exec Officer MTB Ron 9, ComMTB Ron 2, and party aboard 2330 lying to west of Pai-Bronsoso Island. 2345 Boat Captain PT 109 came aboard, underway for north west side of Cross Island Made daily inspection of magazines and all other inspections

Examined and found to be correct.
W. F. Liebenow
Lt (jg)
JnR Commanding.

Log of the ____ Attached to the ____
Naval District, ____, 19__

Hour	Wind		Barometer	Temperature		State of the Weather by Symbols	Clouds			Condition of the Sea
	Direction	Force	Height in inches. Thermometer attached	Air, dry bulb	Air, wet bulb		Forms of, by symbols	Moving from—	Amount covered, tenths	
A.M.										
4										
8										
12 M.										
P.M.										
16										
20										
24										

REMARKS

Required by current security orders. Conditions normal

Examined and found to be correct.
W. F. Liebenow
Lt (jg)
JnR Commanding.

Log of the USS PT 157 ____ Attached to the MTB Ron 9
Naval District, 8 August, 1943

Hour	Wind		Barometer	Temperature		State of the Weather by Symbols	Clouds			Condition of the Sea
	Direction	Force	Height in inches. Thermometer attached	Air, dry bulb	Air, wet bulb		Forms of, by symbols	Moving from—	Amount covered, tenths	
A.M.										
4										
8										
12 M.										
P.M.										
16										
20										
24										

REMARKS

Underway in Ferguson Passage 0030 lying to 0.4 miles east of Banini Island. Sent small boats ashore to pick up survivors of PT 109. 0215 two officers and 8 men aboard and underway for PT Base Rendova. 0515 moored in assigned berth, survivors left ship. 0800 mustered crew at quarters, no absentees. 1320 commenced fueling and completed fueling at 1415. Received 750 gallons 100 octane gasoline from S.O. Advance Naval Base Rendova. 1830 underway for patrol in company with PT's 159, 162. 2130 on station

Examined and found to be correct.
W. F. Liebenow
Lt (jg)
JnR Commanding.

Log of the ____ Attached to the ____
Naval District, ____, 19__

Hour	Wind		Barometer	Temperature		State of the Weather by Symbols	Clouds			Condition of the Sea
	Direction	Force	Height in inches. Thermometer attached	Air, dry bulb	Air, wet bulb		Forms of, by symbols	Moving from—	Amount covered, tenths	
A.M.										
4										
8										
12 M.										
P.M.										
16										
20										
24										

REMARKS

In Gizo Strait Made daily inspection of magazines and all other inspections required by current security orders. Conditions normal.

Examined and found to be correct.
W. F. Liebenow
Lt (jg)
JnR Commanding.

Log of the USS PT 157 — Attached to the **MTB Ron 9**
Naval District, **9 August**, 1943

Hours	Wind Direction	Force	Barometer Height in inches	Thermometer attached	Temperature Air, dry bulb	Air, wet bulb	State of the Weather by Symbols	Clouds Forms of, by symbols	Moving from—	Amount covered, tenths	Condition of the Sea
A.M.											
4											
8											
12 M.											
P.M. 16											
20											
24											

REMARKS

Underway on patrol in Gizo Strait 0330 departed station, underway for PT Base Rendova 0710 moored in assigned berth 0800 mustered crew at quarters no absentees. 1105 commenced fueling and completed fueling at 1140. Received 750 gallons 100 octane gasoline from S.O. Advance Naval Base Rendova. Made daily inspection of magazines and all other inspections required by current security orders. Conditions normal.

Examined and found to be correct.
W. F. Liebenow
Lt (jg)
JM Commanding. , U.S.N.R

Log of the USS PT 157 — Attached to the **MTB Ron 9**
Naval District, **10 August**, 1943

Hours	Wind Direction	Force	Barometer Height in inches	Thermometer attached	Temperature Air, dry bulb	Air, wet bulb	State of the Weather by Symbols	Clouds Forms of, by symbols	Moving from—	Amount covered, tenths	Condition of the Sea
A.M.											
4											
8											
12 M.											
P.M. 16											
20											
24											

REMARKS

Moored in assigned berth PT Base Rendova 0800 mustered crew at quarters, no absentees. Made daily inspection of magazines and all other inspections required by current security orders. Conditions normal.

Examined and found to be correct.
W. F. Liebenow
Lt (jg)
JM Commanding. , U.S.N.R

Log of the USS PT 157 — Attached to the **MTB Ron 9**
Naval District, **11 August**, 1943

Hours	Wind Direction	Force	Barometer Height in inches	Thermometer attached	Temperature Air, dry bulb	Air, wet bulb	State of the Weather by Symbols	Clouds Forms of, by symbols	Moving from—	Amount covered, tenths	Condition of the Sea
A.M.											
4											
8											
12 M.											
P.M. 16											
20											
24											

REMARKS

Moored in assigned berth PT Base Rendova 0800 mustered crew at quarters, no absentees. 1815 underway for patrol in company with PT's 159, 161. 2015 enemy plane dropped two bombs on last section south of Ferguson Passage, both misses. Boats fired on plane, results undetermined. 2017 Nakajima 95 with floats passed overhead at 500 feet. 2130 on station in south Gizo Strait. Made daily inspection of magazines and all other inspections required by current security orders. Conditions normal.

Examined and found to be correct.
W. F. Liebenow
Lt (jg)
JM Commanding. , U.S.N.R

Log of the USS PT 157 — Attached to the **MTB Ron 9**
Naval District, **12 August**, 1943

Hours	Wind Direction	Force	Barometer Height in inches	Thermometer attached	Temperature Air, dry bulb	Air, wet bulb	State of the Weather by Symbols	Clouds Forms of, by symbols	Moving from—	Amount covered, tenths	Condition of the Sea
A.M.											
4											
8											
12 M.											
P.M. 16											
20											
24											

REMARKS

Underway on patrol in Gizo Strait. 0420 departed station and underway for PT Base Rendova 0710 moored in assigned berth. 0715 mustered crew at quarters, no absentees. 0712 commenced fueling and completed fueling at 0756. Received 950 gallons 100 octane gasoline from S.O. Advance Naval Base Rendova. 1350 underway for PT Base Russells and moored in assigned berth at 1312. Made daily inspection of magazines and all other inspections required by current security orders. Conditions normal.

Examined and found to be correct.
W. F. Liebenow
Lt (jg)
JM Commanding. , U.S.N.R

Log of the USS PT 157   Attached to the MTB Ron 9
Naval District, 13 August, 1943

Hour	Wind		Barometer	Temperature		State of the Weather by Symbols	Clouds			Condition of the Sea
	Direction	Force	Height in inches	Thermometer, attached	Air, dry bulb	Air, wet bulb		Forms of, by symbols	Moving from—	Amount covered, tenths	
A.M. 4											
8											
12 M. P.M. 16											
20											
24											

REMARKS

Moored in assigned berth PT Base Russells. 0800 mustered crew at quarters no absentees. 1015 commenced fueling and completed fueling at 1050. Received 1200 gallons 100 octane gasoline from SO, Advance Naval Base Russells. Made daily inspection of magazines and all other inspections required by current security orders. Conditions normal.

Examined and found to be correct.

W. F. Liebenow
Lt (jg)
JMR Commanding. U.S.NR

Log of the USS PT 157   Attached to the MTB Ron 9
Naval District, 14 August, 1943

Hour	Wind		Barometer	Temperature		State of the Weather by Symbols	Clouds			Condition of the Sea
	Direction	Force	Height in inches	Thermometer, attached	Air, dry bulb	Air, wet bulb		Forms of, by symbols	Moving from—	Amount covered, tenths	
A.M. 4											
8											
12 M. P.M. 16											
20											
24											

REMARKS

Moored in assigned berth PT Base Russells. 0515 mustered crew at quarters, no absentees. 0525 underway for PT Base Lever Harbor in company with PT's 154, 159, 161, 162. 1125 moored in assigned berth. 1445 commenced fueling and completed fueling at 1520. Received 350 gallons 100 octane gasoline. 1816 underway for patrol in company with PT's 154, 155, 156, 159, 160, 161, 162. 2040 on station in Vella Gulf. Made daily inspection of magazines and all other inspections required by current security orders. Conditions normal.

Examined and found to be correct.

W. F. Liebenow
Lt (jg)
JMR Commanding. U.S.NR

Log of the USS PT 157   Attached to the MTB Ron 9
Naval District, 15 August, 1943

Hour	Wind		Barometer	Temperature		State of the Weather by Symbols	Clouds			Condition of the Sea
	Direction	Force	Height in inches	Thermometer, attached	Air, dry bulb	Air, wet bulb		Forms of, by symbols	Moving from—	Amount covered, tenths	
A.M. 4											
8											
12 M. P.M. 16											
20											
24											

REMARKS

Underway on patrol in Vella Gulf. 0530 departed station and underway for PT Base Lever Harbor. 0745 moored in assigned berth. 0800 mustered crew at quarters no absentees. 1230 commenced fueling and completed fueling at 1325. Received 750 gallons 100 octane gasoline. 2100 underway for Kula Gulf in company with PT 154. 2110 AP's and LCT's joined us. Made daily inspection of magazines and all other inspections required by current security orders. Conditions normal.

Examined and found to be correct.

W. F. Liebenow
Lt (jg)
Commanding. U.S.NR

Log of the USS PT 157   Attached to the MTB Ron 9
Naval District, 16 August, 1943

Hour	Wind		Barometer	Temperature		State of the Weather by Symbols	Clouds			Condition of the Sea
	Direction	Force	Height in inches	Thermometer, attached	Air, dry bulb	Air, wet bulb		Forms of, by symbols	Moving from—	Amount covered, tenths	
A.M. 4											
8											
12 M. P.M. 16											
20											
24											

REMARKS

Underway in Kula Gulf. Reference: Com MTB, Lever Harbor, secret letter MTBLH/A16-3, serial 003, dated 16 August 1943. 0513 moored in assigned berth PT Base Lever Harbor. 0730 mustered crew at quarters, no absentees. 0745 commenced fueling and completed fueling at 0835. Received 550 gallons 100 octane gasoline. Made daily inspection of magazines and all inspections required by current security orders. Conditions normal.

Examined and found to be correct.

W. F. Liebenow
Lt (jg)
JMR Commanding. U.S.NR

Log of the USS PT 157   Attached to the MTB Ron 9
Naval District, 17 August 1943

	Wind		Barom-eter	Temper-ature		State of the Weather by Symbols	Clouds			Condi-tion of the Sea
Hour	Direction	Force	Height in inches Thermometer attached	Air, dry bulb	Air, wet bulb		Forms of, by symbols	Moving from	Amount covered, tenths	
A. M.										
4										
8										
12 M.										
P. M.										
16										
20										
24										

REMARKS

Moored in assigned berth PT Base Lever Harbor. 0800 mustered crew at quarters no absentees 1820 underway for patrol in company with PT's 116, 126, 159. 2100 on station in Kula Gulf. Made daily inspection of magazines and all other inspections required by current security orders. Conditions normal.

Examined and found to be correct.
W. F. Liebenow
Lt (jg)   U.S.N.R.
Commanding.

Log of the USS PT 157   Attached to the MTB Ron 9
Naval District, 18 August 1943

	Wind		Barom-eter	Temper-ature		State of the Weather by Symbols	Clouds			Condi-tion of the Sea
Hour	Direction	Force	Height in inches Thermometer attached	Air, dry bulb	Air, wet bulb		Forms of, by symbols	Moving from	Amount covered, tenths	
A. M.										
4										
8										
12 M.										
P. M.										
16										
20										
24										

REMARKS

Underway on patrol in Kula Gulf. Reference: Com MTB Lever Harbor, secret letter, MTBLH/A16-3, Serial 005, dated 18 August 1943. 0653 moored in assigned berth PT Base Lever Harbor. 0800 mustered crew at quarters, no absentees 1000 commenced fueling and completed fueling at 1100. Received 750 gallons 100 octane gasoline. Made daily inspection of magazines and all other inspections required by current security orders. Conditions normal.

Examined and found to be correct.
W. F. Liebenow
Lt (jg)   U.S.N.R.
Commanding.

Log of the USS PT 157   Attached to the MTB Ron 9
Naval District, 19 August 1943

	Wind		Barom-eter	Temper-ature		State of the Weather by Symbols	Clouds			Condi-tion of the Sea
Hour	Direction	Force	Height in inches Thermometer attached	Air, dry bulb	Air, wet bulb		Forms of, by symbols	Moving from	Amount covered, tenths	
A. M.										
4										
8										
12 M.										
P. M.										
16										
20										
24										

REMARKS

Moored in assigned berth PT Base Lever Harbor. 0800 mustered crew at quarters, no absentees. Made daily inspection of magazines and all other inspections required by current security orders. Conditions normal.

Examined and found to be correct.
W. F. Liebenow
Lt (jg)   U.S.N.R.
Commanding.

Log of the USS PT 157   Attached to the MTB Ron 9
Naval District, 20 August 1943

	Wind		Barom-eter	Temper-ature		State of the Weather by Symbols	Clouds			Condi-tion of the Sea
Hour	Direction	Force	Height in inches Thermometer attached	Air, dry bulb	Air, wet bulb		Forms of, by symbols	Moving from	Amount covered, tenths	
A. M.										
4										
8										
12 M.										
P. M.										
16										
20										
24										

REMARKS

Moored in assigned berth PT Base Lever Harbor. 0800 mustered crew at quarters no absentees 1750 underway for patrol in company with PT 159. 2030 on station in Kula Gulf. Made daily inspection of magazines and all other inspections required by current security orders. Conditions normal.

Examined and found to be correct.
W. F. Liebenow
Lt (jg)   U.S.N.R.
Commanding.

Log of the USS PT 157 — Attached to the MTB Ron 9
Naval District, 21 AUGUST, 1943

Hour	Wind		Barometer Height in inches	Temperature			State of the Weather by Symbols	Clouds			Condition of the Sea
	Direction	Force		Thermometer attached	Air, dry bulb	Air, wet bulb		Forms of, by symbols	Moving from—	Amount covered, tenths	
A. M.											
4											
8											
12 M.											
P. M.											
16											
20											
24											

REMARKS

Underway on patrol in Kula Gulf. Reference: Com MTB Lever Harbor, secret letter, MTBLH/A16-3 Serial 0010 dated 22 August 1943. 0740 moored in assigned berth PT Base Lever Harbor. 0800 mustered crew at quarters, no absentees. 1000 commenced fueling and completed fueling at 1105. Received 750 gallons 100 octane gasoline. Made daily inspection of magazines and all other inspections required by current security orders. Conditions normal.

Examined and found to be correct.
W. F. Liebenow
Lt (jg)
U.S. NR
Commanding.

Log of the USS PT 157 — Attached to the MTB Ron 9
Naval District, 22 AUGUST, 1943

Hour	Wind		Barometer Height in inches	Temperature			State of the Weather by Symbols	Clouds			Condition of the Sea
	Direction	Force		Thermometer attached	Air, dry bulb	Air, wet bulb		Forms of, by symbols	Moving from—	Amount covered, tenths	
A. M.											
4											
8											
12 M.											
P. M.											
16											
20											
24											

REMARKS

Moored in assigned berth PT Base Lever Harbor. 0800 mustered crew at quarters, no absentees. 1744 underway for patrol with PT's 154, 159, 161. 2030 on station in Kula Gulf. Made daily inspection of magazines and all other inspections required by current security orders. Conditions normal.

Examined and found to be correct.
W. F. Liebenow
Lt (jg)
U.S. NR
Commanding.

Log of the USS PT 157 — Attached to the MTB Ron 9
Naval District, 23 AUGUST, 1943

Hour	Wind		Barometer Height in inches	Temperature			State of the Weather by Symbols	Clouds			Condition of the Sea
	Direction	Force		Thermometer attached	Air, dry bulb	Air, wet bulb		Forms of, by symbols	Moving from—	Amount covered, tenths	
A. M.											
4											
8											
12 M.											
P. M.											
16											
20											
24											

REMARKS

Underway on patrol in Kula Gulf. Reference: Com MTB Lever Harbor, secret letter MTBLH/A16-3, Serial 0012, dated 23 August 1943. 0700 moored in assigned berth PT Base Lever Harbor. 0800 mustered crew at quarters, no absentees. 1000 commenced fueling and completed fueling at 1045. Received 300 gallons 100 octane gasoline. Made daily inspection of magazines and all other inspections required by current security orders. Conditions normal.

Examined and found to be correct.
W. F. Liebenow
Lt (jg)
U.S. NR
Commanding.

Log of the USS PT 157 — Attached to the MTB Ron 9
Naval District, 24 AUGUST, 1943

Hour	Wind		Barometer Height in inches	Temperature			State of the Weather by Symbols	Clouds			Condition of the Sea
	Direction	Force		Thermometer attached	Air, dry bulb	Air, wet bulb		Forms of, by symbols	Moving from—	Amount covered, tenths	
A. M.											
4											
8											
12 M.											
P. M.											
16											
20											
24											

REMARKS

Moored in assigned berth PT Base Lever Harbor. 0800 mustered crew at quarters, no absentees. Made daily inspection of magazines and all other inspections required by current security orders. Conditions normal.

Examined and found to be correct.
W. F. Liebenow
Lt (jg)
U.S. NR
Commanding.

Log of the USS PT 157 — Attached to the MTB RON 9
Naval District, 25 AUGUST, 1943

Hours	Wind		Barometer	Temperatures			State of the Weather by Symbols	Clouds			Condition of the Sea
	Direction	Force	Height in inches	Thermometer attached	Air, dry bulb	Air, wet bulb		Forms of, by symbols	Moving from	Amount covered, tenths	
A.M.											
4											
8											
12 M.											
P.M. 16											
20											
24											

REMARKS

MOORED IN ASSIGNED BERTH PT BASE LEVER HARBOR 0840 MUSTERED CREW AT QUARTERS, NO ABSENTEES 1745 UNDERWAY FOR PATROL IN COMPANY WITH PTs 154, 161 ESCORTING APc 25 TO KULA GULF. MADE DAILY INSPECTION OF MAGAZINES AND ALL OTHER INSPECTIONS REQUIRED BY CURRENT SECURITY ORDERS. CONDITIONS NORMAL

Examined and found to be correct.

W. F. Liebenow
Lt (jg)   U.S.N.R.
for Commanding.

Log of the USS PT 157 — Attached to the MTB RON 9
Naval District, 26 AUGUST, 1943

Hours	Wind		Barometer	Temperatures			State of the Weather by Symbols	Clouds			Condition of the Sea
	Direction	Force	Height in inches	Thermometer attached	Air, dry bulb	Air, wet bulb		Forms of, by symbols	Moving from	Amount covered, tenths	
A.M.											
4											
8											
12 M.											
P.M. 16											
20											
24											

REMARKS

UNDERWAY IN KULA GULF 0350 MOORED IN ASSIGNED BERTH PT BASE LEVER HARBOR 0800 MUSTERED CREW AT QUARTERS, NO ABSENTEES 0900 COMMENCED FUELING AND COMPLETED FUELING AT 0945 RECEIVED 450 GALLONS 100 OCTANE GASOLINE. MADE DAILY INSPECTION OF MAGAZINES AND ALL OTHER INSPECTIONS REQUIRED BY CURRENT SECURITY ORDERS. CONDITIONS NORMAL

Examined and found to be correct.

W. F. Liebenow
Lt (jg)   U.S.N.R.
for Commanding

Log of the USS PT 157 — Attached to the MTB RON 9
Naval District, 27 AUGUST, 1943

Hours	Wind		Barometer	Temperatures			State of the Weather by Symbols	Clouds			Condition of the Sea
	Direction	Force	Height in inches	Thermometer attached	Air, dry bulb	Air, wet bulb		Forms of, by symbols	Moving from	Amount covered, tenths	
A.M.											
4											
8											
12 M.											
P.M. 16											
20											
24											

REMARKS

MOORED IN ASSIGNED BERTH PT BASE LEVER HARBOR 0800 MUSTERED CREW AT QUARTERS, NO ABSENTEES 1833 UNDERWAY FOR PATROL IN COMPANY WITH PTs 118, 154. 2033 ON STATION IN KULA GULF. MADE DAILY INSPECTION OF MAGAZINES AND ALL OTHER INSPECTIONS REQUIRED BY CURRENT SECURITY ORDERS. CONDITIONS NORMAL

Examined and found to be correct.

W. F. Liebenow
Lt (jg)   U.S.N.R.
for Commanding

Log of the USS PT 157 — Attached to the MTB RON 9
Naval District, 28 AUGUST, 1943

Hours	Wind		Barometer	Temperatures			State of the Weather by Symbols	Clouds			Condition of the Sea
	Direction	Force	Height in inches	Thermometer attached	Air, dry bulb	Air, wet bulb		Forms of, by symbols	Moving from	Amount covered, tenths	
A.M.											
4											
8											
12 M.											
P.M. 16											
20											
24											

REMARKS

UNDERWAY ON PATROL IN KULA GULF 0001 LEFT STATION, UNDERWAY FOR PT BASE LEVER HARBOR AND MOORED IN ASSIGNED BERTH AT 0215. 0645 UNDERWAY FOR ENOGAI INLET AND ANCHORED IN 15 FATHOMS AT 0800. 0805 MUSTERED CREW AT QUARTERS, NO ABSENTEES 1037 UNDERWAY FOR PT BASE LEVER HARBOR AND MOORED IN ASSIGNED BERTH AT 1150. 1310 COMMENCED FUELING AND COMPLETED FUELING AT 1400 RECEIVED 900 GALLONS 100 OCTANE GASOLINE. MADE DAILY INSPECTION OF MAGAZINES AND ALL OTHER INSPECTIONS REQUIRED BY CURRENT SECURITY ORDERS. CONDITIONS NORMAL

Examined and found to be correct.

W. F. Liebenow
Lt (jg)   U.S.N.R.
Commanding.

Log of the USS PT 157   Attached to the MTB Ron 9
Naval District, 29 AUGUST, 1943

Hour	Wind		Barometer	Temperature		State of the Weather by Symbols	Clouds			Condition of the Sea
	Direction	Force	Height in Inches / Thermometer attached	Air, dry bulb	Air, wet bulb		Form of, by symbols	Moving from	Amount covered, tenths	
A.M.										
4										
8										
12 M.										
P.M.										
16										
20										
24										

REMARKS

Moored in assigned berth PT Base Lever Harbor. 0800 mustered crew at quarters. No absentees. Made daily inspection of magazines and all other inspections required by current security orders. Conditions normal.

Examined and found to be correct.   W. F. Liebenow
Lt (jg)
J M Commanding.   U.S.N.R

Log of the USS PT 157   Attached to the MTB Ron 9
Naval District, 30 AUGUST, 1943

Hour	Wind		Barometer	Temperature		State of the Weather by Symbols	Clouds			Condition of the Sea
	Direction	Force	Height in Inches / Thermometer attached	Air, dry bulb	Air, wet bulb		Form of, by symbols	Moving from	Amount covered, tenths	
A.M.										
4										
8										
12 M.										
P.M.										
16										
20										
24										

REMARKS

Moored in assigned berth PT Base Lever Harbor. 0800 mustered crew at quarters, no absentees. 1814 underway for patrol, in company with PT's 115, 154, 159, 2043 on station in Kula Gulf. Made daily inspection of magazines and all other inspections required by current security orders. Conditions normal.

Examined and found to be correct.   W. F. Liebenow
Lt (jg)
J M   U.S.N.R
Commanding.

Log of the USS PT 157   Attached to the MTB Ron 9
Naval District, 31 AUGUST, 1943

Hour	Wind		Barometer	Temperature		State of the Weather by Symbols	Clouds			Condition of the Sea
	Direction	Force	Height in Inches / Thermometer attached	Air, dry bulb	Air, wet bulb		Form of, by symbols	Moving from	Amount covered, tenths	
A.M.										
4										
8										
12 M.										
P.M.										
16										
20										
24										

REMARKS

Underway on patrol in Kula Gulf. 0430 departed station, underway for PT Base Lever Harbor and moored in assigned berth at 0705. 0800 mustered crew at quarters no absentees. 0855 commenced fueling and completed fueling at 1000. Received 750 gallons 100 octane gasoline. Made daily inspection of magazines and all other inspections required by current security orders. Conditions normal.

Examined and found to be correct.   W. F. Liebenow
Lt (jg)
J M Commanding.   U.S.N.R

Log of the USS PT 157   Attached to the MTB Ron 9
Naval District, 1 SEPTEMBER, 1943

Hour	Wind		Barometer	Temperature		State of the Weather by Symbols	Clouds			Condition of the Sea
	Direction	Force	Height in Inches / Thermometer attached	Air, dry bulb	Air, wet bulb		Form of, by symbols	Moving from	Amount covered, tenths	
A.M.										
4										
8										
12 M.										
P.M.										
16										
20										
24										

REMARKS

Moored in assigned berth PT Base Lever Harbor. 0800 mustered crew at quarters, no absentees. 1750 underway for patrol in company with PT's 115, 154, 159. 2000 on station in Kula Gulf. Made daily inspection of magazines and all other inspections required by current security orders. Conditions normal. Lt(jg) W. F. Liebenow, USNR transferred to base. Lt(jg) S. B. Marshall, USNR reported on board for duty as Executive Officer.

Examined and found to be correct.   J Roff
Lt(jg)   U.S.N.R
Commanding.

A P P E N D I X   C

DAILY ACTION REPORTS FOR MTB RENDOVA AND LEVER HARBOR GENERATED BY THE SQUADRON COMMANDER

Most of the documents in this section these reports, requested by the author from the National Archives and Records Administration [NARA] were of poor quality due to deterioration of the original documents and/or that the documents themselves are the second or third carbon copy versions; meaning they were light and blurry from the outset. The copies provided from NARA were in digital format so on the more poor quality versions the author has made some adjustments to help in their readability.

The MTB Daily Action Reports for the following dates were never generated or not located by NARA or not applicable to the PT-157:

> July 1-2 through July 5-6
> July 11-12, 13-14, 14-15, 16-17
> July 18-19 through July 25-26
> July 28-29
> August 2-3 through 4-6 (Omitted as the PT-157 was at PT Base Tulagi)
> August 5-6 through August 10-11 (never existed; see page 124)
> August 12-13, 13-14, 18-19 (missing)

ALL documents in this section are declassified

COPY   COPY

Serial 001 (I)   July 1, 1943.
SECRET

Subject: PT Operations night of 30 June and 1 July 1943.
- -

The PT 159 and 162 then retired to the Northwest about three miles where they came upon PT 118, which was dead in the water because of a broken V-drive and reverse gear. They stood by her for over an hour until temporary repairs were effected. During this period PT 158 joined them. When they finally got underway, they resumed their assigned patrol South of Mbalumbalu Island. At 0135 while on the western end of their patrol a plane, presumably enemy dropped a bomb which landed in the water 10 feet off the port quarter of the PT 162. Four of her crew, namely, Kenneth TODD, GM2c, George BROWN, GM1c, Henry COVINGTON, MoMM1c, Robert YATES, RM2c, received injuries from the bomb. The bomb crippled three of PT 162's engines, one of which was later temporarily repaired. All boats departed for base at 0315 arriving at 0530.

In the meantime, PT 153 and PT 160 joined section B until the completion of its patrol.

(B) RENARD ENTRANCE TO HURDY POINT
Lt. H. J. Brantingham   PT 155   OAK 15
Lt. (jg) R. Hunt   PT 117   OAK 3
Ens. H. D. Smith   PT 154   OAK 12

On station at 1900. Report negative except for aircraft flares dropped over PT's at 0200. Returned to base at 0600.

(C) RENARD ENTRANCE TO TAMBATUNI ISLAND
Lt. (jg) R. E. Schneider   PT 156   OAK 18
Ens. J. E. McElroy   PT 161   OAK 33
Ens. W. F. Liebenow   PT 157   OAK 21

Arrived on station at 1915. Report same as Renard Entrance to Onaiavisi Entrance Patrol. Returned to base at 0600.

5. COMMUNICATIONS: Interboat radio communications satisfactory with exception of PT 159 and PT 118, both of whose radios were inoperative. No communications between the forces ashore and the boats. It is considered imperative that satisfactory communications be established immediately.

6. COMMENTS: Due to the strange behaviour of the vessels attacked as reported by the various boat captains the next day, this command has reason to believe that the attack must have been delivered against our own forces. However, Commander General Aperient, Commander, Naval Base, Dowser, and Commander Attack Group, Amphibious Forces assured this command that it had to have been the enemy. All friendly forces had departed the afternoon before and were well clear of the area by the time of the attack. At no time during the torpedo attack were the PT's fired on or challenged. To date confirmation has not been obtained as to what ships were sunk, although it is rumored that they were friendly.

                                          R. B. KELLY
                                          Lt. Comdr., U.S.N.
                                          Commanding Officer

Copy to:
ComSoPac
ComMTBRons, SoPac
ComGen. Dowser

C
O
P
Y

THIRD

MOTOR TORPEDO BOAT SQUADRON NINE
FLEET POST OFFICE, SAN FRANCISCO, CALIFORNIA.

July 7, 1943.

MEMORANDUM FOR COMMANDER, NAVAL BASE, DOWSER

Subject: PT Operations night 6-7 July 1943.

1.   FORCE: Six boats on patrol   Six boats on alert
                at base as striking force.
2.   ENEMY CONTACTS: None
3.   WEATHER: Intermittent rain showers with good visibility
                to East.
4.   PATROLS:

(A) WEST OF KUNDU KUNDU ISLAND TO VICINITY OF KENELO PLANTATION.

FIRST SECTION

Lt. George Cookman	PT 103	OAK 1
Lt. (jg) R. D. Schearer	PT 104	OAK 4
Lt. (jg) George Wright	PT 125	OAK 38

SECOND SECTION

Lt. H.J. Brantingham	PT 155	OAK 15
Lt. (jg) Reed Hunt	PT 117	OAK 3
Ens. H. D. Smith	PT 154	OAK 12

First section arrived on station at 1900 and commenced patrol. At 1935, PT Base received a dispatch that photo coverage on Kahili on 5 July showed 3 CLs, 2 DD leaders, 9 DDs, 1 escort vessel, 5 AKs and one 450' unidentified warship. At 2046, Commander, Motor Torpedo Boat Squadron NINE, ordered first section to shift their patrol 3 miles to the West, informing them that the second section of 3 PTs were proceeding to take over the first section's original patrol station, and that six PTs would be retained at base for striking force. Reports as to enemy shipping were all negative. At 0600 a plane carrying one small white running light and presumably enemy passed over the patrolling PTs and headed in direction Rendova Harbor. All boats returned to base at 0630.

5.   COMMUNICATIONS: Radio communications between boats satisfactory.

R. B. KELLY
Lt. Comdr., U.S.N.
Commanding Officer

Copy to:
  ComSoPac
  ComMTBRons, SoPac
  ComGen, Dowser
  CoMAG, AmpFor, New Georgia
  Com, MTBFlotOne, CTF 31

COPY   FIRST   COPY

MOTOR TORPEDO BOAT SQUADRON NINE
Fleet Post Office, San Francisco, California

Serial 008 (I)   July 8, 1943.
SECRET

MEMORANDUM FOR COMMANDER, NAVAL BASE, DOWSER

Subject: PT Operations night 7-8 July 1943.

    1.   FORCE: Six boats on patrol. Six boats on alert at base as striking
                 force.

    2.   ENEMY CONTACTS: None.

    3.   WEATHER: Infrequent rain showers with good visibility between showers.

    4.   PATROL:
      (a)   SOUTH OF WANA WANA ISLAND TO SOUTH OF FERGUSON PASSAGE.

Lt. O. W. Hayes	PT 159	OAK 27
Ens. O.H.P. Cabot	PT 160	OAK 30
Ens. J. R. Lowrey	PT 162	OAK 36

            Boats left base at 1830. On way to station at 1905, one bomb was
dropped about 100 feet off the starboard quarter of PT 160. No damage or casualties
resulted. Boats were forced to lay to until 1955, when planes apparently left
area, having abandoned search for boats. At 0036 a message was received from
Commander, Naval Base, Dowser, to patrol Ferguson Passage to Vanga Vanga, Kolo-
bangara. At 0045 enemy planes were observed to drop flares to Eastward. At about
0230, message was received from ComMTBRonNINE, directing the first section not to
attempt to enter Ferguson Passage. This patrol was maintained in area 10 miles
South of Ferguson Passage from 0245 to 0410, when boats of this section departed
for base. No visual or radar contact of any shipping in this area was noted.

      (b)   WEST OF KUNDU KUNDU ISLAND TO VICINITY OF KENELO PLANTATION.

Lt. Comdr. R. B. Kelly	PT 157	OAK 0
Ens. J. E. McElroy	PT 161	OAK 33
Lt. (jg) R. E. Schneider	PT 156	OAK 18

            On way to patrol station, observed the bombing of the first section.
Enemy planes flew overhead, and appeared to be four to six in number at altitude
of three to four thousand feet, possibly twin engine bombers, judging by exhaust.
At 1925 several bombs and A/A flashes were observed in vicinity of Rendova
Harbor. At 1945 a bomb hit in vicinity of Kundu Kundu Island. At about 2015
planes appeared to have left the area and section two proceeded to station, arriving at 2040. At about 0040, two or more enemy planes were first observed
overhead, dropping flares at 0105, one of which was yellow and one green. PT
161 and PT 156 were forced to get underway to get out of area of illumination
At 0108 two 100 pound bombs straddled fore and aft of PT 161, which was still
maneuvering to avoid flares. These were very near misses. The helmet and ear-
phones of aft 20MM gunner were blown off by concussion. The cockpit was filled
with water, and the hull was riddled with shrapnel. At 0113 another flare was
dropped very close to the boats illuminating them. At this time no boats moved,

Serial 0008 (I)
SECRET   July 8, 1943.

Subject: PT Operations night 7-8 July 1943.
- -

and no bombs were dropped. Location of bombings and flares was 340 deg. T,
distance six miles from Banieta Point. Shortly thereafter, boats shifted position
to within 3 miles off Banieta Point, where they lay to the remainder of the night.

     5.   COMMUNICATIONS: Excellent between boats, PT Base and Naval Base,
except for jamming by spark transmitter between 0220 and 0245 during transmission
of all messages between boats and base.

     6.   COMMENTS: It appears obvious that the enemy is well cognizant of the
hampering effect of low level glide bombing on PTs at night while on patrol.
This squadron has experienced such bombings four out of the past seven nights.
For the past three nights it has been increasingly persistent. One boat received major damage and four casualties, while two other boats have been hit
by shrapnel. Several additional boats have received near misses never more distant than 150 feet.

     Until effective counter measures can be instituted it is recommended
that routine nightly patrols be discontinued while operating in phosphorescent
waters or on moonlight nights. It is relatively simple for low flying planes to
spot the movements of the PTs and bomb them at leisure.

     It is further recommended that routine searches of desired areas
by conducted by radar-equipped "Blackcats". PTs would be held in readiness
at a strategic nearby location. On making contact the "Blackcats" would radio
PTs the course, speed and location of the approaching forces. PTs would then
intercept and strike.

     In the Rendova Area such a location would be Banieta Point, where there
is suitable anchorage.

                    R. B. KELLY
                    Lt. Comdr., U.S.N.
                    Commanding Officer

Copy to:
  ComSoPac
  ComMTBRons, SoPac
  ComGen, Dowser
  ComAG, AmpFor, New Georgia
  Com, MTBFlotOne
  CTF 31

AK-26(?)   MIDDLE

MOTOR TORPEDO BOAT SQUADRON NINE
FLEET POST OFFICE, SAN FRANCISCO, CALIFORNIA.

Serial 009 (I)
SECRET   July 9, 1943.

MEMORANDUM FOR COMMANDER, NAVAL BASE DUMBEA.

Subject: PT Operations night 8-9 July 1943.

1. FORCE: Six boats on patrol. Six boats on alert at
       base as striking force.

2. ENEMY CONTACT: None.

3. WEATHER: Intermittent heavy rain squalls with good
       visibility between.

4. PATROL:
  (A) BANIETA POINT AREA

Lt. E.J. Brantingham	PT 155	OAK 15
Lt. (jg) Reed Hunt	PT 117	OAK 3
Ens. H. D. Smith	PT 153	OAK 12
Lt. George Cookman	PT 103	OAK 1
Lt. (jg) R. Scheurer	PT 104	OAK 4
Lt. (jg) George Wright	PT 125	OAK 38

All boats departed for patrol station at 1700. They
rendezvoued at 1930 off Banieta Point. Departure was made during
daylight in order to avoid detection by enemy float planes which,
during the past week, have been searching for and bombing PTs at
dusk as they leave base. Enemy plane was observed from base
apparently searching for PTs at 1900 off Western Entrance, Rendova
Harbor. At 2015, patrol boats heard plane overhead apparently
searching for them. It circled for fifteen minutes but did not
detect PTs which were anchored close off shore. One bomb was
dropped apparently from this plane, a few minutes later which hit
3-5 miles Northeast of the position of the PTs. Another plane was
heard at 0313, but it did not detect the boats. At 0545 the final
plane of the night was seen to drop a flare about seven miles North
of the PTs. This plane later dropped bombs on a friendly destroyer
task force, which was bombarding the Munda area. A/A from destroyers
apparently drove it off.

5. COMMUNICATIONS: Satisfactory.

              R. B. KELLY
              Lt. Comdr., U.S.N.
              Commanding Officer.

Copy to:
ComSoPac
ComMTBRons, SoPac
ComGen, Dowser
ComAd, AmpFor, New Georgia.
ComMTBFlotOne
CTF 31

23

THIRD

MOTOR TORPEDO BOAT SQUADRON NINE
FLEET POST OFFICE, SAN FRANCISCO, CALIFORNIA.

FILE NO.

Serial 0010 (I)

SECRET

July 10, 1943.

FROM: COMMANDER, NAVAL BASE, DOWSER.

Subject.   PT Operations night 9-10 July 1943.

1.   FORCE: Six boats on patrol. Seven boats at base
              on alert as striking force.

2.   ENEMY CONTACTS: None.

3.   WEATHER: Clear to midnight with intermittent rain
                  squalls thereafter, visibility fair to good
                  between showers.

4.   PATROL:

(A)   BANIETA POINT AREA

Lt. Comdr. R. B. Kelly	PT 154	OAK 0
Ens. L. I. McKirey	PT 161	OAK 33
Lt.(jg) R. H. Schneider	PT 156	OAK 18
Lt. G. E. Payne	PT 150	OAK 27
Ens. C.P.I. Cabot	PT 160	OAK 30
Ens. J. R. Lowrey	PT 162	OAK 36

All boats arrived and anchored off Baneta Point at
1745. At 1909, the first enemy plane of the **night** was heard to pass
over the PTs. Apparently this same plane returned passing in a
southerly direction over the PTs. Planes were heard at frequent
intervals thereafter, apparently circling the area of the anchored
PTs. They were heard at 1921, 1926 and 1936. All were flying at
very low altitudes. At 1936, plane appeared to drop two bombs 5-6
miles North of the PTs. At 1955, tracer fire and searchlights were
observed over Munda Harbor. At 2107 received following from
ComNavBase, Dowser, "Send 2 MTB's to Ferguson Passage Radar shows
no planes in area X Moonlight will hide wake". At this time a plane
was overhead and had been for two hours. ComTBRon Nine sent the
following reply "Enemy planes overhead continuously 1900- 110
Advise". At 2053 while this message was being transmitted the plane
circled the boats again gliding in and dropping one bomb which missed
boats by about 150 feet. Plane could be heard but not seen except
occasionally through glasses. No more planes were heard until 0410,
when one circled the PTs but did not drop anything. More planes were
heard flying overhead at 0545 and at 0622.

Radar and visual watch of the area between Baneta
Point and Wana Wana Island was negative.

5.   COMMUNICATIONS: Generally satisfactory but own boating
      reception poor between boats and base due to local interference and
      jamming. No contact between boats or NavBase and "Blackcat" covering area.
      It is believed the enemy planes may be using DF to
      locate boats as they frequently circle overhead while boats were
      transmitting.

R. B. KELLY.

24

MOTOR TORPEDO BOAT SQUADRON NINE
FLEET POST OFFICE, SAN FRANCISCO, CALIFORNIA.

Serial 0011 (I)
SECRET   July 11, 1943.

LETTER FROM THE COMMANDER, NAVAL BASE, DOWSER.

Subject: PT Operations night 10-11 July 1943.

1.   FORCE: Twelve Boats on patrol.
2.   ENEMY CONTACTS: None.
3.   WEATHER: Clear with fair visibility.
4.   PATROLS: WANA WANA ISLAND TO BANIETA POINT
         (A) Lt. Comdr. Thomas Warfield   PT 157   OAK 0
             Ens. J. L. McElroy   PT 161   OAK 33
             Lt.(jg) R. L. Schneider   PT 156   OAK 18
         (B) KUNDU KUNDU ISLAND TO BANIETA POINT
             Lt. H.J. Brantingham   PT 155   OAK 15
             Ens. U. D. Smith   PT 154   OAK 12
             Lt.(jg) H. R. Hunt   PT 117   OAK 36
         (C) KENELO PLANTATION, RENDOVA TO BANIETA POINT
             Lt. George Cookman   PT 103   OAK 1
             Lt.(jg) R. D. Shearer   PT 104   OAK 4
             Lt.(jg) T. G. Keresey   PT 105   OAK 7
         (D) MATENI PLANTATION, RENDOVA HARBOR
             Lt. W. F. Hayes   PT 159   OAK 27
             Ens. W.H.P. Cabot   PT 160   OAK 30
             Ens. J. T. Lowrey   PT 162   OAK 36

All boats were retained at base as a striking force
until 1206, when a message was received that 4 unidentified ships
had been spotted to the south, latitude 156° 10' East, sailing on course
120° T at a speed of 9 knots. All twelve boats were ordered to stations
of the above patrol plan at 1225. Patrol was maintained until daybreak,
with negative results, both as to radar and visual watch. At 1336 aircraft was heard to approach and circle PTs. At 0545, an aircraft flare
was dropped midway between Banieta Point and Kundu Kundu Island. This
flare burned out within a few seconds, and it is believed that no PTs
were detected. All PTs returned to base by 0800.

5.   COMMUNICATIONS: Satisfactory. No contact made with
"Blackcat".

Copy to: T. G. WARFIELD
ComSoPac   Lt. Comdr., U.S.N.
ComMTBRons, SoPac   Acting Commanding Officer.
ConGen, Dowser
ComAG, AmpFor, New Georgia
CTF 31
ComMTBFlotOne

MIDDLE

MOTOR TORPEDO BOAT SQUADRON NINE
FLEET POST OFFICE, SAN FRANCISCO, CALIFORNIA.

FILE No.

Serial 0013 (I)
SECRET   13 July 1943.

MEMORANDUM FOR COMMANDER, NAVAL BASE, DOWSER.

Subject: PT Operations night 12-13 July 1943.

1.   FORCE: Twelve boats on patrol.

2.   ENEMY CONTACTS: None.

3.   WEATHER: Clear with good visibility to seaward. Fair
                visibility inshore looking forward Kolumbangara.

4.   PATROLS:

(A) SOUTH PATROL - GIZO TO KOLUMBANGARA
     Lt. Comdr. T. G. Warfield   PT 157   OAK O
     Ens. J. E. McElroy   PT 161   OAK 33
     Lt.(jg) R. E. Schneider   PT 156   OAK 18

(B) NORTH PATROL - GIZO TO KOLUMBANGARA
     Lt. H.J. Brantingham   PT 155   OAK 15
     Ens. H. D. Smith   PT 154   OAK 12
     Lt.(jg) Reed Hunt   PT 117   OAK 3

(C) MIDDLE PATROL - GIZO TO KOLUMBANGARA
     Lt. George Cookman   PT 103   OAK 1
     Lt.(jg) R. D. Shearer   PT 104   OAK 4
     Lt.(jg) R. E. Keresey   PT 105   OAK 7

(D) PAILERONGOSA ISLAND TO MAKUTI ISLAND
     Lt. O. W. Hayes   PT 159   OAK 27
     Ens. O. H. P. Cabot   PT 160   OAK 30
     Ens. J. R. Lowrey   PT 162   OAK 36

        Message was received for PTs to guard Western approaches
to Blackett Strait against enemy shipping. Nine PTs were assigned
patrol stations between Gizo Island and the vicinity of Vanga Vanga,
Kolumbangara. The remaing three PTs were stationed between Pailerongosa
Island and Makuti Island just North of Ferguson Passage. All boats
arrived on station prior to midnight. Landing barges were believed
observed tied up to shore in the vicinity of Vanga Vanga. At 0050 an
aircraft flare was observed to the North and West of the patrolling
PTs. At 0115 a plane flew over PTs 159 and 160 at altitude of 500 feet
as if on a bombing run. Fire was opened upon it, but ceased when it
was identified as a "Blackcat" with no apparent damage done.

        At 0200, Lt. H.J. Brantingham's section sighted four
destroyers sailing in a Southeasterly direction and hugging the shore
line of Kolumbangara. When first observed, these destroyers were in the
vicinity of Vanga Vanga and were seen to pass through our minefield with
impunity. Their speed was estimated at 30 knots. The distance between
the PTs and the destroyers plus the speed of the destroyers and the 27
knot slow speed of the PTs torpedoes prevented any attack being made.

Serial 0013 (I)
SECRET   13 July 1943.

MEMORANDUM FOR COMMANDER, NAVAL BASE, DOWSER.

Subject: PT Operations night 12-13 July 1943.

- -

Information of the sighting was immediately radioed, but no other boats
made visual contact. PT 159, however, picked up 4 contacts on its radar
in the vicinity of Hunda, Kolumbangara. Attempts to close the target
were unsuccessful because of its speed.

            Thereafter, everything was quiet until the order to
return to base by Lt. Comdr. Warfield at 0400. While leaving Ferguson
Passage at 0405, PT 159 again made radar contact of four targets, this
time travelling in a reverse direction to the 0200 sighting. Notice of
contact was radioed to PTs and order for departure to base was cancelled.
PTs were, however, again unsuccessful in closing the targets because
of their speed and distance. Moreover, the torpedoes carried by the
PTs are slower than the targets speed. Radar contact was followed toward Vella Gulf where it was lost. All PTs returned safely to base at
0745, notwithstanding the fact that PTs 159, 160 and 162 were shelled
by shore batteries on Munda Point. All shells fell ½ to 1 mile short.

        5.   COMMUNICATIONS: Satisfactory.

        6.   COMMENTS: There seem to be two possible conclusions
which can be arrived at from PT operations of the night of 12-13 July.
The first is that the enemy has apparently rendered inoperative the
minefield stretching from West of Makuti Island to Vanga Vanga,
Kolumbangara. The second possibility is that the "Bougainville Express"
is once more in operation, this time running to Vila via Vella Gulf
and Blackett Strait, and sailing close inshore to Kolumbangara arriving
in Blackett Strait in the dark of the moon.

                                        T. G. WARFIELD
                                        Lt. Comdr., U.S.N.
                                        Commanding Officer.

Copy to:
  ComSoPac
  ComMTBRons,SoPac
  ComGen, Dowser
  ComAG,AmpFor,New Georgia
  CTF 31
  ComMTBFlotOne

MOTOR TORPEDO BOATS, RENDOVA

Serial 0016 (I)
SECRET   16 July 1943.

MEMORANDUM FOR COMMANDER, NAVAL BASE, DOWSER.

Subject: PT Operations night 15-16 July 1943.

   1.   FORCE: Six boats on patrol. Six boats on alert at
               base as striking force.

   2.   ENEMY CONTACTS: None.

   3.   WEATHER: Clear with excellent visibility.

   4.   PATROL:

   (A) GIZO TO KOLUMBANGARA ISLAND
       Lt. George Cookman9   PT 107   OAK 13
       Lt.(jg) J. K. Roberts   PT 103   OAK 1
       Lt.(jg) R. E. Keresey   PT 105   OAK 7

       Arrived on station at 2315. Left for base at 0340.
Report as to enemy shipping was negative. Aircraft flare sighted
at 0030, 6-8 miles distant in Vella Gulf.

   (B) FERGUSON PASSAGE
       Lt. (jg) R. E. Schneider   PT 156   OAK 18
       Ens. J. E. McElroy   PT 161   OAK 33
       Ens. W. F. Liebenow   PT 157   OAK 21

       Arrived on station at 2250. Departed for base at
0345. Negative report of enemy shipping. During return to base
South of Kundu Kundu Island at 0445 this patrol was shelled by shore
batteries located on Munda Point or on islands due South of Munda
Point. Two guns were engaged in this shelling, firing eight shells
which all fell astern and short 500 yards distance from trailing boat.

   5.   COMMUNICATIONS: Interboat radio communications good.
Naval Base Station, Dowser, Z6Y could not be contacted, nor received
from patrol station.

                                    T. G. WARFIELD
                                    Lt. Comdr., U.S.N.
                                    Commanding Officer.

Copy to:
   ComSoPac
   ComMTBRons,SoPac
   ComGen,Dowser
   ComAG,AmpFor,New Georgia Area
   ComMTBFlotOne
   CTF 31

to be carded 6-11-57
-JJW   *card*

MOTOR TORPEDO BOAT BASE, RENDOVA

File No.
Serial 0018 (I)   18 July 1943.
SECRET

MEMORANDUM FOR COMMANDER, NAVAL BASE DOWSER. [RENDOVA]

Subject: PT Operations night 17-18 July 1943.

1.   FORCE: Twelve boats on patrol. Three boats at
          base on alert as striking force in defense
          of Rendova Harbor.

2.   ENEMY CONTACTS: Six destroyers.

3.   WEATHER: Scattered rain squalls between which there
          was good visibility in bright moonlight.

4.   PATROLS:

(A) FERGUSON PASSAGE TO KOLUMBANGARA ISLAND
    Lt. G. E. Cookman   PT 107   OAK 13
    Lt. (jg) J. K. Roberts   PT 103   OAK 1
    Lt. (jg) R. W. Schearer   PT 104   OAK 4
    Lt. (jg) D. M. Payne   PT 106   OAK 10
    Lt. (jg) R. E. Keresey   PT 105   OAK 7
    Ens. John Iles   PT 125   OAK 38

Arrived on station at 2115. Left for base at 0430.
Account of the activities of these boats is contained hereafter
in paragraphs marked "4 (C)".

(B) GIZO STRAIT
    Lt. A. H. Berndston   PT 164   OAK 22
    Lt. (jg) E. McCauley   PT 168   OAK 28
    Lt. (jg) P. E. Potter   PT 169   OAK 31

Arrived on station at 2140. Left for base at 0415.
This section activities of the night is also taken up in paragraphs
marked "4 (C)".

(C) VANGA POINT AREA - WEST COAST OF KOLUMBANGARA ISLAND
    Lt. O. W. Hayes   PT 159   OAK 27
    Ens. W. F. Liebenow   PT 157   OAK 21
    Ens. O. H. P. Cabot   PT 160   OAK 30

Arrived on station at 2220. Left for base at 0400.
The above patrols were set in pursuance of an order directing
ComMTBRons, Rendova, to prevent the entry of any enemy forces into
Blackett Strait via its Western approaches. The PTs of the
Ferguson Passage to Kolumbangara patrol were placed at intervals
from close ashore the Northeast tip of Gizo Island to one mile off
Vanga Vanga, Kolumbangara. The Gizo Strait patrol was set to

MOTOR TORPEDO BOAT BASE, RENDOVA

File No.
Serial 0018 (I)
SECRET

Subject: PT Operations night 17-18 July 1943.
- -

detect and prevent any approach to Blackett Strait via either
Gizo or Wilson Strait. The Vanga Point - West Coast of Kolumbangara
patrol was set detect, attack and to decoy any enemy task force
South so that the PTs further South could hit it from two sides.
At 0128 while lying to off Vanga Point, Lt. Hayes' section sighted
six enemy destroyers approaching from 8 miles due North on course
200° T, speed 35-40 knots. Lt. Hayes radioed the remaining 9 PTs
that enemy destroyers were headed South and deployed his section
preparatory to attack. His boat was in the center with PT 160
to the South and PT 157 to his North. The destroyers continued
in a line abreast formation for 3-4 miles when two turned East;
to the North of the waiting PTs and ran close into shore of North
Kolumbangara. The other four destroyers changed to a column
formation and steamed South on course 180° T. Apparently the
destroyers had sighted the PTs and had sent the two sleepers to
box the PTs from the North. As the destroyers steamed Southward
they fired three Very signal lights - a white, one green followed
by another white. Whereupon, PT 159 fired all four of her torpedoes
with a wide spread and turned South to retire at high speed along
the west shore of Kolumbangara. PTs 157 and 160 followed suit.
However, PT 160's two starboard torpedoes failed to fire electrically.
As the torpedoman aboard the PT 160 started to fire the torpedoes
by hand, PT 159 cut between PT 160 and the target releasing a
puff of smoke which delayed the firing of the remaining torpedoes.
PT 160 then went through the smoke puff in an attempt to fire her
remaining two torpedoes. Heavy gun fire from the destroyers
prevented her from getting into firing position and forced her to
retire to the south behind PTs 159 and 157. She was slowed down
in her southward retirement when her center engine stopped. All
three PTs continued to release puffs of smoke to distract gun fire
of the enemy destroyers.

        All torpedoes were fired at the enemy destroyers at
a distance of 4000-5000 yards. All torpedoes fired ran true, and
all boats observed a torpedo hit on the leading destroyer just
abaft her bridge, amidships. PT 160, the last boat to retire
observed a torpedo hit a few seconds later on the second destroyer
in column.

        Simultaneously with the firing of the first torpedoes,
the destroyers opened up with starshells and gun fire on the PTs.

(2)

MOTOR TORPEDO BOAT BASE, RENDOVA

Serial 0018 (I)   18 July 1943
SECRET

Subject: PT Operations night 17-18 July 1943.
- -

An estimated 30-40 starshells illuminated the area of the PTs.
The destroyer gun fire appeared to be 40 mm. and 4.7 and seemed
to be directed at PT 159. No hits were scored on her although shells
fell so close that water was blown over her bow and stern. PT 157
received no hits from the enemy fire. PT 160 received one shrapnel
hit on her twin mount 50 cal. There was no damage to either boats
or personnel. The enemy destroyers continued shelling from Vanga
Point south to Merusu Cove. When Lt. Hayes encoded message was
received that enemy destroyers had been sighted, Lt. Cookman led
his six boats at slow speed toward the location of the sighting.
During his advance north, he had one radar contact which disappeared
when 1-2 miles distant from the location of destroyers given by
Lt. Hayes. No visual contact with the enemy was made by any of these
six boats. The three retiring PTs passed the six northbound boats
south of Merusu Cove. The latter six boats are certain that no
enemy shipping slipped by them into Blackett Strait.

        Lt. Berndtson's section closed from the southwest
toward the destroyers when summoned by Lt. Hayes. Although all
his boats observed the Very signals and the gun fire, they made
neither radar nor visual contact with the six destroyers. Lt.
Berndtson's and Lt. Cookman's sections made a thorough search of
Vella Gulf with negative results.

        It is believed that the destroyers sensed a trap and
steamed north out of Vella Gulf. During the retirement of PTs 159,
157 and 160, Lt. Hayes directed the nine other PTs toward the
chasing destroyers by means of plain English transmissions. The
possibility exists that the enemy destroyers intercepted these
messages, and decided that the best policy was to retreat to the
north. About 0615 while returning to base PTs received their
usual morning shelling from Munda Point shore batteries. Fire was
short and no damage was incurred.

        5.   COMMUNICATIONS: Satisfactory, although C/W jamming
was observed interfering with transmission from PT base to patrol boats.

        6.   At 1505 Lt. (jg)-R. W. Rome on PT 166 departed base
to investigate the feasibility of the use of Munda Bar by small
craft including PTs. Inspection seemed to indicate ample water with
little swell. No soundings were taken due to enemy fire. Lt. (jg)
E. Karuse aboard PT 163 followed to lend aid to PT 166 in event
of necessity. Shore batteries on Munda Point opened up and laid a
barrage across Munda Bar with no hits on PT 166.

(3)

MOTOR TORPEDO BOAT BASE, RENDOVA

Serial 0018 (I)   18 July 1943
SECRET

Subject: PT Operations night 17-18 July 1943.
- -

An artillery spotting plane happened to be overhead and directed
the shore batteries on Rendova to the Jap gun positions which
had fired on PT 166. It is believed that least one of these
guns was knocked out.

                                    T. G. WARFIELD
                                    Lt. Comdr., U.S.N.
                                    Commanding Officer

Copy to:
ComSoPac
ComMTBRons, SoPac
ComGen, Dowser
ComAG, AmpFor, New Georgia Area
ComMTBFlot One
Com Task For 31

MTBR/A16-3
Serial 0027
SECRET

27 July 1943.

From: The Commander, Motor Torpedo Boats, Rendova.
To :   The Commander in Chief, U. S. Fleet.
Via :   Official Channels.

Subject: PT Operations night 26-27 July 1943.

1.   FORCE: Six boats on patrol. Nine boats at base
        on alert as striking force.

2.   ENEMY CONTACTS: Six barges.

3.   WEATHER: Rain squalls until 2130. Clear thereafter
        with poor to fair visibility.

4.   PATROLS:

    (A) BLACKETT STRAIT AREA — SOUTH OF VANGA VANGA, KOLOMBANGARA
        Lt. A. H. Berndtson   PT 171   OAK 44
        Lt.(jg) R. E. Keresey   PT 105   OAK 7
        Lt.(jg) P. A. Potter   PT 169   OAK 31

    (B) BLACKETT STRAIT AREA — WEST OF MAKUTI ISLAND
        Lt.(jg) D. M. Payne   PT 106   OAK 10
        Ens. H. D. Smith   PT 154   OAK 12
        Lt.(jg) R. Hunt   PT 117   OAK 3

        Arrived on station at 2115. At 2325 PT 106's radar
picked up a small target, distance 2 miles, headed in a Westerly
direction toward Gizo Strait from the Southwest shore of Kolombangara.
Time was lost in informing senior section leader, as PT 106 transmitter was off frequency before investigating contact. PT 154 was
notified by means of megaphone to accompany PT 106. PT 117, the
remaining boat of section B, did not accompany her section leader
as she could not get the word. PT 106, with PT 154, closed slowly
on the target by means of radar until it became visible 1½ miles
North of the North central shore of Gizo Island. The target was seen
to consist of three barges, two small, about the size of a 35'
personnel barge, and the other a large barge similar in size to one
of our own LCMs. When the PTs closed to within 1 mile, the barges
in column formation changed course and headed toward the shore of
Gizo Island, where they lined up parallel to the shore line. PT 106
then started a strafing run from West to East, at a distance of 40
yards. All guns were concentrated on each individual barge as it
was passed. The first barge, a small one, was on the receiving end
of 60 rounds of 20MM and 300 rounds of 50 caliber, all of which appeared
to hit, but she was not seen to sink. One hundred fifty rounds of
50 caliber were fired at the center barge with no visible effect.

556637

MTBR/A16-3
Serial 0027
SECRET

27 July 1943.

Subject: PT Operations night 26-27 July 1943.

- -

Most all shots seem to ricochet harmlessly off it. PT 106 next poured 60 rounds of 20MM and 300 rounds of 50 caliber into the other small barge, which was last seen listing, with part of its superstructure under water and with but one foot of freeboard at the bow. PT 106 then pulled off to the North to circle for another run. Inability to distinguish between PT 154 and the barges prevented a second run. PT 106 was not fired upon.

PT 154 followed PT 106 in on the strafing run. She strafed the first barge seen and then lay to in order to pick out an individual target upon which to concentrate. She observed five barges lined up along the shore, all of which she described as about the size of our LCMs. She saw no small barges. Deciding to take the most Easterly barge she could see, she ran between it and the shore, firing 120 rounds of 20MM and 500 rounds of 50 caliber. Her fire was heard hitting the barge and was seen ricochet harmlessly in the air, leading to the belief that the barges were heavily armored. PT 154 then lay to in order to reload her guns. At this point a sixth barge from the East plus the barge she had fired upon opened fire on her. The other four barges, in the meantime, circled back to the East effectively boxing PT 154 between themselves and Gizo Island reefs. PT 154 backed out of the trap firing at her original target and proceeded North for a couple of minutes at slow speed, and again lay to in order to finish her reloading. When a barge approached and opened fire, she moved North a little farther. A barge again approached. This time she ran North for five minutes and lay to. One-half hour later at 0045, and after she had reloaded, a barge again approached but did not open fire. PT 154 was also unable to fire at the barge because it was between PT 154 and PT 117, which at that instant was engaged in firing at another barge. All PT 117's guns jammed after 100 rounds of 50 caliber had been fired at her target. The barge between PT 154 and PT 117 then opened fire on PT 117. PTs 117 and 154 retired to the North and further contact with the barges was lost. PTs 117 and 154 sustained many hits of 25 caliber and 7.7 fire from the barges. No casualties were sustained. One 7.7 penetrated a torpedo aboard PT 154. It was observed that as long as the PTs were firing, there was no return fire, but as soon as they stopped firing for any reason, the Japs immediately opened fire.

5.   COMMUNICATIONS: Satisfactory between boats except for PT 106, which could not be heard because her transmitter was off frequency. Satisfactory between boats and base, except for PT 171, which had difficulty receiving base radio. Jamming was

- 2 -

MTBR/A16-3
Serial 0027
SECRET

27 July 1943.

Subject: PT Operations night 26-27 July 1943.

- -

excessive.   It is believed boats are being located by Japanese RD/F.

6.   COMMENTS:

(a) It is believed that the use of IFF on Motor Torpedo Boats operating in this area would be highly beneficial in alleviating faulty identification between Motor Torpedo Boats and friendly air and surface craft.

(b) Tactics are under revision for barge strafing.

(c) Performance of PT 117's guns indicate poor supervision and incompetent gunnery upkeep.

T. G. WARFIELD

Advance Copy to:
    CTF 31
    Cincpac
Copy to:
    CMB, Dowser
    ComMTB, Russells
    ComAirSols
    ComAir,New Georgia
    ComGen,New Georgia.

MTBR/A16-3
Serial 0029 (I)

DECLASSIFIED - OPNAV INST 5500.30
BY *OR-08B9C* DATE *6 APR 61*

RECEIVED
CINCPAC
30 July 1943. 2 A.M.
63

From: The Commander.
To :   The Commander in Chief, U. S. Fleet.
Via :   Official Channels.
Subject: PT Operations night 27-28 July 1943.

1.   FORCE: Eight boats on patrol. Nine boats on alert
             at base as striking force.

2.   ENEMY CONTACTS: None.

3.   WEATHER: Scattered rain squalls in early evening.
               Overcast thereafter.

4.   PATROLS:

(A) TWO MILES NORTH OF GIZO STRAIT
    Lt. H. J. Brantingham   PT 159   OAK 27
    Lt.(jg) W. F. Liebenow   PT 157   OAK 21
    Lt.(jg) J. R. Lowrey   PT 162   OAK 36
    Lt.(jg) Jack Kennedy   PT 109   OAK 14
    Lt.(jg) S. Hamilton   PT 172   OAK 47

(B) GIZO STRAIT.
    Lt. G. C. Cookman   PT 107   OAK 13
    Lt.(jg) R. K. Roberts   PT 103   OAK 1
    Lt.(jg) R. D. Shearer   PT 104   OAK 4

All boats arrived on station at 2100. Section B
proceeded from its patrol station to the southeast coast of Vella
Lavella where at 0210 two men disembarked, and 17 men were taken
aboard for transportation to Rendova. Eleven of the seventeen were
survivors of a "Blackcat" forced down at sea on July 16 off northwest coast of Vella Lavella, while the other six were members of a
returning reconnaisance party. Previously at 2123, an aircraft
flare was sighted two miles south of Gizo Strait. This flare was
followed by another flare dropped over Gizo Passage illuminating
all PTs. Planes passed overhead of section B at 2154, 0003, 0025
and 0030, at which latter time a plane was clearly visible and
was described as being a single float monoplane. These planes
appeared to patrol from Wilson Strait to the northwestern tip of
Gizo Island. Boats departed stations at 0430, arriving at base
at 0700, where the reconnaisance party and the plane survivors
were safely landed.

5.   COMMUNICATIONS: No radio contact was had with the
"Blackcats". Communications between boats and base were generally
satisfactory. Much jamming of PT frequency was again experienced.
It is believed that a change in the frequency used by the PTs might

556377

MOTOR TORPEDO BOAT, RENDOVA

MTBR/A16-3
Serial 0030 (I)
SECRET

30 July 1943

From: The Commander.
To: The Commander in Chief, U. S. Fleet.
Via: Official Channels.

Subject: PT Operations night 29-30 July 1943.

1. FORCE: Eight boats on patrol. Eight boats on alert
    at base as striking force.

2. ENEMY CONTACTS: Three enemy barges.

3. WEATHER: Cloudy with frequent rain squalls.
    Visibility was poor.

4. PATROLS:

(A) WEST OF MAKUTI ISLAND.
    DIVISION B.
    Lt. H. J. Brantingham   PT 159   OAK 27
    Ens. W. C. Battle   PT 171   OAK 44
    Lt. (jg) J. R. Lowrey   PT 162   OAK 36
    Ens. W. F. Griffin   PT 174   OAK 50

(B) SOUTHEAST OF VANGA VANGA, KOLUMBANGARA.
    DIVISION C.
    Lt. G. C. Cookman   PT 107   OAK 13
    Lt. (jg) S. Hamilton   PT 172   OAK 47
    Lt. (jg) R. D. Shearer   PT 104   OAK 4-
    Lt. (jg) S. D. Hix   PT 108   OAK 16

        Arrived on station at 2130. Until 2400 a fire or light
which at times increased in intensity was seen on the West Coast of
Kolumbangara Island about 1 mile South of Vanga Vanga. At 2130,
PT 107's radar picked up a target North of Makuti Island, which was
westbound. Division C was at this time 2-3 miles to the Northwest
of the target. The target was slowly closed by Division C in
column formation to a point 2 miles North of the North Central shore
of Gizo Island, where it was first visually observed. It appeared
to be a very large barge, the size of an LCT. At 2215 the lead boat
of Division C opened fire at the target which was 50 yards off its
starboard beam. The other boats followed through on the strafing
run. PT 107 fired 350 rounds of 50 caliber and 20 rounds of 20MM;
PT 172, 120 rounds of 50 caliber and 20 rounds of 20MM; PT 104, 100
rounds of 50 caliber and 20 rounds of 20MM; and PT 108, 250 rounds
of 50 caliber and 60 rounds of 20MM. Numerous 50 caliber hits were
observed as well as a few 20's. As the boats turned for a second
strafing run, PT 108 rammed PT 107 with minor damage to both. The
column formation was thus broken up, and further attempts at

[55637]   1.

MOTOR TORPEDO BOATS, RENDOVA

DECLASSIFIED - OPNAV INST. 5500.30
BY *GRPIC* DATE *APR 61*

MTBR/A16-3
Serial 0031 (I)

31 July 1943.

From: The Commander.
To: The Commander in Chief, U. S. Fleet.
Via: Official Channels.

Subject: PT Operation night 30-31 July 1943.

1. **FORCE:** Eight boats on patrol. Eight boats at base as a striking force.

2. **ENEMY CONTACTS:** One 100' Japanese auxiliary sunk by machine gun fire.

3. **WEATHER:** Overcast; visibility poor.

4. **PATROLS:**

(A) WEST OF MAKUTI ISLAND.
DIVISION D.

Lt. (jg) D. M. Payne	PT 106	OAK 10
Lt. (jg) J. Kennedy	PT 109	OAK 14
Lt. (jg) R. K. Roberts	PT 103	OAK 1
Lt. (jg) R. E. Keresey	PT 105	OAK 7

On the way to station PT 109's rudder failed and it returned to base. On station at 2130, at which time PT 106's radar ceased to function. About 2240, recurring flashes, resembling gunfire were seen in the direction of Kula Gulf. Departed for base at 0330.

(B) SOUTH OF LINE, MERESU COVE TO GIZO ISLAND.
DIVISION A.

Lt. A. H. Berndtson	PT 170	OAK 34
Lt. (jg) W. F. Liebenow	PT 157	OAK 21
Lt. (jg) P. A. Potter	PT 169	OAK 31
Lt. (jg) R. Hunt	PT 117	OAK 3

Arrived on station about 2200. At 0155 a vessel about 100' long with quite high superstructure was picked up by radar about 2/3 mile Southwest of Meresu Cove. At 0150 it was attacked from a column formation proceeding North, firing to starboard at 50 yards range. PT 170 fired 120 rounds of 20MM, 100 rounds of 50 caliber and 50 rounds of 45 caliber. Almost all the shots appeared to be hits; very few ricocheted. PT 169 was next in column. It fired 60 rounds of 20MM and 300 rounds of 50 caliber. Those aboard the PT 169 believed the vessel was listing when they saw it. The following boats in the column could not find anything to shoot at, but those aboard PT 117 noted the odor of burnt wood and diesel oil. Another sweep and radar search was immediately made by the patrol, but nothing could be found. Left for base at 0400.

MTBR/A16-3
Serial 0032 (I)
SECRET

1 August 1943

From: The Commander.
To: The Commander in Chief, U. S. Fleet.
Via: Official Channels.

Subject: PT Operation night 31 July - 1 August 1943.

1.   FORCE: Eight boats on patrol. Nine boats on the
             alert at base as a striking force.

2.   ENEMY CONTACTS: 1 enemy 90' barge strafed at 100 yards
                       with 850 rounds 50 caliber and 220
                       rounds of 20MM.

3.   WEATHER: Clear, but dark. Visibility poor.

4.   PATROLS AREA - BAKER
      (DIVISION B AT THE NORTH END OF THE AREA)
      Lt. O. W. Hayes   PT 159   OAK 27
      Lt. (jg) J. R. Lowrey   PT 162   OAK 36
      Lt. (jg) S. Hamilton   PT 172   OAK 47
      Lt. (jg) N. D. McCarthy   PT 171   OAK 44

      (DIVISION C AT THE SOUTH END OF THE AREA)
      Lt. (jg) W. F. Barrett   PT 107   OAK 13
      Lt. (jg) R. D. Shearer   PT 104   OAK 4
      Lt. (jg) S. D. Hix   PT 108   OAK 16
      Ens. W. S. Whitney   PT 174   OAK 50

        Enroute to station at 2005, when South of
Ferguson Passage, two searchlights were seen in the direction of
Wilson Strait. Again at 2042 a searchlight was seen West of Gizo
Island and toward the North tip of Ganongga Island. A moment later
the radar picked up a plane on course 035° M, passing over Gizo
Island. About 2107 a steady bright red light shone for two or three
minutes from the center of the Eastern shore of Ganongga Island.
Arrived on station at 2125. At 2308 a bright white light was seen
for two minutes in Gizo Strait. From 2350 to 0015 flashes were
observed on the surface of Gizo Strait, a set of red and green
lights were seen, as well as tracer bullets coursing downward.
In addition there were three white flares over the Northwest tip
of Ganongga Island.

        At 0130 a large barge, about 90' long with about
12' freeboard, was contacted by radar and a moment later visually.
It was then about in the middle of Blackett Strait and 4 miles
South of Meresu Cove, course Southeast. It was attacked at 0111
by Division B in column on a Northwest course at a range of 100

SECRET

ACTION REPORT

COMMANDER SOUTH PACIFIC FORCE

SERIAL 002236   23 OCTOBER 1943

ACTION REPORTS: 1-31 AUGUST 1943, FORWARDING OF.

FORWARDS, WITH SUMMARY, ACTION REPORTS
OF PTS BASED RENDOVA AND LEVER HARBORS
ENGAGED, PRINCIPALLY, IN INTERCEPTION
OF SHIP REINFORCEMENTS TO VILA, RESULT-
ING IN BLACKETT STRAIT ENGAGEMENTS.

NAVAL HISTORY DIVISION

COMSOPAC FILE

A16-3/(90)
Serial 002236

SOUTH PACIFIC FORCE
OF THE UNITED STATES PACIFIC FLEET
HEADQUARTERS OF THE COMMANDER

2 3 OCT 194

From: The Commander South Pacific.
To :   The Commander in Chief, U. S. Pacific Fleet.

Subject: PT Action Reports - forwarding of.

Enclosure: (A) PT Operations night 1-2 August, 1943. (revised)
           (A1) PT Operations night 2-3 August, 1943.
           (B) PT Operations night 3-4 August, 1943.
           (C) PT Operations night 4-5 August, 1943.
           (D) PT Operations night 11-12 August, 1943.
           (E) PT Operations night 12-13 August, 1943.
           (F) PT Operations night 13-14 August, 1943.
           (G) PT Operations night 14-15 August, 1943.
           (G1) PT Operations night 14-15 August, 1943.
           (H) PT Operations night 15-16 August, 1943.
           (I) PT Operations night 16-17 August, 1943.
           (I1) PT Operations night 16-17 August, 1943.
           (J) PT Operations night 17-18 August, 1943.
           (K) PT Operations night 18-19 August, 1943.
           (K1) PT Operations night 18-19 August, 1943.
           (L) PT Operations night 19-20 August, 1943.
           (M) PT Operations night 20-21 August, 1943.
           (M1) PT Operations night 20-21 August, 1943.
           (N) PT Operations, Daylight Mission, 22 August, 1943.
           (O) PT Operations night 21-22 August, 1943.
           (P) PT Operations night 22-23 August, 1943.
           (Q) PT Operations night 23-24 August, 1943.
           (R) PT Operations night 24-25 August, 1943.
           (S) PT Operations night 25-26 August, 1943.
           (S1) PT Operations night 25-26 August, 1943.
           (T) PT Operations night 26-27 August, 1943.
           (U) PT Operations night 27-28 August, 1943.
           (V) PT Operations night 28-29 August, 1943.
           (W) PT Operations night 29-30 August, 1943.
           (W1) PT Operations night 29-30 August, 1943.
           (X) PT Operations night 30-31 August, 1943.
           (Y) PT Operations night 31 Aug - 1 Sept., 1943.
           (Z) Summary of PT - Barge Engagements in the
                KULA GULF Area during August, 1943.

    1.   Enclosures (A) to (Z) inclusive are forwarded herewith.

- 1 -

COMSOPAC FILE

A16-3/(90)
Serial 002236

SOUTH PACIFIC FORCE
OF THE UNITED STATES PACIFIC FLEET
HEADQUARTERS OF THE COMMANDER

2 3 OCT 1943

S-E-C-R-E-T

Subject: PT Action Reports - forwarding of.

- -

2.   The officers and men of the Motor Torpedo Boat Squadrons are deserving of high praise for the courage, resourcefulness and tenacity displayed during many days of hazardous and trying operations against strong enemy barge activity.

3.   Enemy losses cannot be assessed accurately. However, it is reasonable to assume that considerable disruption of enemy barge traffic resulted from these operations, and that numerous casualties were inflicted on the forces embarked.

4.   The principal barge route appears to have been from Choiseul Island across to the northern tip of Vella Lavella down the west coast through Wilson, Gizo and Blackett Straits to Vila on Kolombangara Island. Alternative routes appear to have been from Choiseul Island or the north tip of Vella Lavella to the northern tip of Kolombangara thence down the east coast as far as Vila.

5.   To interrupt this barge traffic PT boats in a coordinated effort with Black Cats and night fighters conducted nightly operations in assigned areas where barge traffic was reported concentrated. Cruiser or destroyer task units were only employed in sweeps to the north of Kolombangara and into Vella Gulf when large Jap units were suspected of covering such barge operations.

6.   Japanese counter measures were speedily and effectively adopted making maximum use of shore batteries and covering planes for added protection. This has forced PT squadrons to adopt "hit and run" tactics and a program of continuous experimentation and improvement.

7.   Enemy barges presently encountered are believed to be similar to those Japanese landing craft barges shown in ONI pamphlet 225-J. In addition there is perhaps a new series of steel, diesel-driven types similar to the 70 foot barge captured in the New Guinea area mounting 20mm guns. There is also some evidence that some barges have now been fitted with 40mm guns for the express purpose of convoying barge traffic through PT opposition. As a matter of interest tests were conducted on a Jap barge captured in New Georgia to determine the relative effectiveness of the different types of automatic weapon fire. These tests proved that penetration was effected by all types including .30 caliber.

- 2 -

COMSOPAC FILE
A16-3/(90)
Serial 002236

SOUTH PACIFIC FORCE
OF THE UNITED STATES PACIFIC FLEET
HEADQUARTERS OF THE COMMANDER

2 3 OCT 1943

S-E-C-R-E-T

Subject: PT Action Reports - forwarding of.
- -

8.   The use of PT boats as barge destroyers leaves much to be desired. Such employment in daylight or bright moonlight is distinctly hazardous and frequently expensive to an unacceptable degree but Commander South Pacific does not agree that PT boats in anti-barge operations are ineffective and costly under all conditions. However, steps have been taken locally to improve their effectiveness, when so employed, by equipping them with a 37mm or 40mm single AA gun. Work is now underway on the conversion of three 77 foot MTB's into motor gunboats by the removal of torpedo tubes and depth charges to provide space and weight compensation for an additional 40mm single AA gun and armor.

9.   Fundamentals in PT night patrol and combat doctrine are believed sound but errors in application are traceable to basic training. It is strongly recommended that the curriculum of the Motor Torpedo Boat School at Melville, R.I., be revised and expanded at once to cover possible short-comings in the present course. The principal deficiencies noted in action to date are:

    (a) Lack of knowledge of relative movement, the fundamentals of which are necessary for intelligent torpedo fire.

    (b) Lack of training in radar approach and attack.

    (c) Lack of indoctrination in communication security, discipline and form. Contact reports are frequently incomplete.

    (d) Lack of indoctrination in fire control. A large percentage of torpedoes are fired at ranges which preclude any possibility of obtaining a live hit.

    (e) Lack of indoctrination in the principles of multiple command and coordinated attack.

10.   It is the opinion of Commander South Pacific that barges have been adopted by the enemy as his primary form of inter-island supply, and that strenuous efforts will be required to throttle this traffic. SC and PC types are too slow, PTs are too vulnerable and lightly armed, and DDs are too large and valuable to perform the duties of barge destruction

- 3 -

COMSOPAC FILE

A16-3/(90)
Serial 002236

SOUTH PACIFIC FORCE
OF THE UNITED STATES PACIFIC FLEET
HEADQUARTERS OF THE COMMANDER

23 OCT 1943

S-E-C-R-E-T

Subject: PT Action Reports - forwarding of.

efficiently. Therefore, it is recommended that the development of a
motor gunboat be given urgent priority as it is believed that the use of
such a gunboat has a direct bearing on the rapidity of our movement forward. A suggested design has been submitted by this command in separate
correspondence. However, as a necessary expedient, four LCI's are being
converted into anti-barge boats and will mount one 3"/50, one 40mm AA
single, four 20mm and six to eight .50 caliber guns. Limited armor protection will be provided. In addition one LCS is being converted but
little success is anticipated with this type.

I. H. Mayfield
Acting Chief of Staff.

Copy to:
    CTF 31
    ComMTBRons Sopac
    ComMTBFlot ONE
    ComMTBRon NINE
    ComMTB's Rendova
    ComMTB's Lever Harbor

MOTOR TORPEDO BOATS, RENDOVA

MTBR/A16-3   21 August 1943
Serial 0034 (I)
SECRET

From: The Commander.
To: The Commander in Chief, U. S. Fleet.
Via: Official Channels.

Subject: PT Operations night 1-2 August 1943 (Revised).

1.   FORCE: All available boats (15) on patrol.

2.   ENEMY CONTACTS: Five enemy destroyers, attacked in
                        Blackett Strait, five or possibly
                        six torpedo hits scored.

3.   WEATHER: Overcast, visibility poor.

4.   PATROLS:

AREA B - (BLACKETT STRAIT)
DIVISION B - OFF VANGA VANGA
Lt. H. J. Brantingham   PT 159   OAK 27
Lt. (jg) W. F. Liebenow   PT 157   OAK 21
Lt. (jg) J. R. Lowrey   PT 162   OAK 36
Lt. (jg) Jack Kennedy   PT 109   OAK 14

DIVISION A - OFF GATERE
Lt. A. H. Berndtson   PT 171   OAK 44
Lt. (jg) P. A. Potter   PT 169   OAK 31
Lt. (jg) S. Hamilton   PT 172   OAK 47
Ens. E. H. Kruse   PT 163   OAK 19

DIVISION R - EAST OF MAKUTI ISLAND
Lt. R. W. Rome   PT 174   OAK 50
Lt. (jg) R. E. Keresey   PT 105   OAK 7
Lt. (jg) R. K. Roberts   PT 103   OAK 1

DIVISION C - SOUTH OF FERGUSON PASSAGE
Lt. G. C. Cookman   PT 107   OAK 13
Lt. (jg) R. D. Shearer   PT 104   OAK 4
Lt. (jg) D. M. Payne   PT 106   OAK 10
Lt. (jg) S. D. Hix   PT 108   OAK 16

INCOMING TOKYO EXPRESS.
All boats were on the stations above indicated by 2130.

        At 2400 Division B made radar contact indicating 5
craft approaching from the North close to the coast of Kolombangara
Island. Visual contact was made shortly thereafter, by PT 159 which
saw 4 shapes in column heading Southeast close into the coast at
15 knots. The PT 157 saw only two. The shapes were first believed
to be large landing craft. The PTs 159 and 157, after directing
the PTs 162 and 109 to lay to, began closing to make a strafing attack.

MOTOR TORPEDO BOATS, RENDOVA

MTBR/A16-3   21 August 1943
Serial 0034 (I)
SECRET

Subject: PT Operations night 1-2 August 1943.(Revised).
- -

In a moment the enemy opened fire with many large caliber guns,
which was continued for several minutes. PT 159 fired a spread of
4 torpedoes and the PT 157 2 torpedoes, all at a range of about
1800 yards. The torpedo tubes of the PT 159 flashed and one caught
fire. A large explosion was seen at the target by personnel on both
of these boats. They then retired to the Northwest laying puffs of
smoke and making frequent radical course changes, until they were
in Gizo Strait, where they lay to. It was decided that PT 157
should return to station and that the PT 159 should return to base,
as it was out of torpedoes, all of which was done. PTs 162 and 109
lay to as directed. When the firing began, there was so much and
over such a long stretch of coast, they thought shore batteries had
opened up and retired to the Northwest, but did not regain contact
with the other two boats. After the firing had ceased, they were
joined by PT 169 from Division A, and after receiving radio orders
to do so, took up station, but did not make contact with PT 157.
The PT 169 stayed with the PTs 162 and 109 on Division A's station
off Vanga Vanga.

       DIVISION A: Around 0004 Division A picked up 4
destroyers headed close in shore off Gatere. When PT 171 got in
position it was abeam the first destroyer. Estimating its speed
at 30 knots, the PT 171 closed to 1500 yards, at which point the
destroyers fired starshells and opened fire, straddling the PT 171
and splashing water on its deck. Fire was also opened with automatic
weapons and one destroyer turned on its searchlight but did not pick
up PT 171. The PT 171 let go 4 torpedoes at the second destroyer.
The tubes flashed and the destroyers turned directly toward it to
evade. One destroyer stood on South toward Ferguson Passage. The
last destroyer was seen to drop 2½ miles behind the others. The
PT 171 retired to the South laying smoke puffs and then getting out
from behind them to the right and left. Feeling that the first
destroyer might be blocking Ferguson Passage the PT 171 reversed
course and proceeded Northwest along the reefs to the East of Gizo
and out Gizo Passage departing for base, having expended all its
torpedoes. The other three boats, PTs 170, 169 and 172 did not
receive the contact report or any message to deploy for attack and
could not fire their torpedoes after the destroyers opened fire, as
PT 171 was in the way crossing their bows in its turn to the South.
Contact between PT 169 and the other 3 PTs was lost as it reversed
course to the Northwest after hearing radio message that destroyers
might be blocking Ferguson Passage. After proceeding some distance
North, (where it joined the PTs 159 and 157), the PTs 170 and 172
were straddled by the gunfire from the 2 destroyers, which they saw,
but could not fire at because PT 171 was in front of them, retired
zig-zagging and laying smoke puffs to the South thru Ferguson Passage.
Going thru they were attacked by 4 float planes which dropped 3
flares and 2 bombs, which missed.

                            (2)

MOTOR TORPEDO BOATS, RENDOVA

MTBR/A16-3   21 August 1943
Serial 0034 (I)
SECRET

Subject: PT Operations night 1-2 August 1943 (Revised).
- -
They proceeded to the South and East, but returned to station on
orders at 0255. Nothing further happened.

DIVISION C: When enroute to station Southeast of
Gizo Island this section was circled by planes. At 0005 2 ships
were picked up by the radar on the PT 107. No previous contact report
had been received, but a searchlight and gunfire had been seen to the
North. PT 107 proceeded at high speed thru Ferguson Passage to attack,
leaving the other 2 PTs behind. Inside of Ferguson Passage the PT
107 fired a spread of 4 torpedoes by radar. Shortly thereafter a
dull red flash was seen in the direction of the target. Course
was reversed and the PT 107, apparently undiscovered, proceeded
South thru Ferguson Passage, enroute to base, its fish expended.
PTs 104, 106 and 108 coming North thru the Passage were passed. In
Ferguson Passage all these boats were attacked by a plane, which
dropped flares and bombs and attempted to strafe the boats. There
were no injuries or damage by this attack. PTs 104, 106 and 108 had
no radar and saw nothing to fire at, however, they proceeded into
Blackett Strait where they saw an explosion East of Makuti Island.
They patrolled until ordered to resume their original station at
0137. The rest of their patrol was negative.

DIVISION R: At 0010 this division saw gun flashes to
the North which continued for about 10 minutes, 3 or 4 much larger
flashes were seen. A flare and bombs were dropped about a mile west
of them a moment later. At 0025 the shape of ship was seen by
PT 174 to the Northeast lying to or moving very slowly, about one
mile off the shore of Kolombangara Island and seemed to be guarding
the entrance to Blackett Strait from Ferguson Passage. She was
firing at something to the West using a searchlight, all of which
illuminated her. PT 174 fired 4 torpedoes at 1000 yards range and
two explosions were seen at the target. The PT 174 circled to the
right, passed behind Makuti Island and headed for Ferguson Passage.
The ship fired shells which passed overhead, so the PT 174 used
smoke puffs and put on speed. A plane also made a strafing run on it.
PT 174 then proceeded to base as it had expended all its torpedoes.
PT 103 sighted the destroyer when it turned on its searchlight. It
had no previous information of contact with the enemy. After the
PT 174 fired, the PT 103 also fired 4 torpedoes at a range of 2
miles. One flash was seen about 3 minutes later and possibly a
second. They retired at slow speed but when shells hit about 150'
behind they increased speed and used smoke puffs. They passed
out behind Makuti Island and headed for base, having fired all
torpedoes.

PT 105 sighted the destroyer when it turned on
searchlight and began firing to the West, but had received the
previous advice that the enemy was in the area. The destroyer

(3)

MOTOR TORPEDO BOATS, RENDOVA

MTBR/A16-3
Serial 0034 (I)
SECRET

1 August 1943

Subject: PT Operations night of 1-2 August 1943.(Revised)

was traveling east slowly but was already past the 105, which followed a short distance and fired two torpedoes in stern chase shot. Members of the crew on the stern saw a column of black smoke go up behind them. The 105 retired undetected south of Makuti Is. and out through Ferguson Passage. About 0130 orders were received to patrol Ferguson Passage.

OUTGOING TOKYO EXPRESS.
DIVISION R. As related PT 105 with two torpedoes was on duty at Ferguson Passage patrolling just inside on one engine. Just before 0230 a flame flashed up to the Northwest in the middle of Blackett Strait opposite Gatere. Gunfire immediately broke out about a mile to the North along the Kolombangara Coast. All of this showed the outling of a destroyer 200 yards away to the East moving slowly to the North at about 10 knots. PT 105 was abeam this vessel. Two torpedoes were fired, but no explosion was observed. The PT 105 retired to the South and radioed that a target was proceeding North. As the PT 105 passed thru Ferguson Passage heading for base, its fish expended, three PTs were seen headed North thru the Passage.

DIVISION C. PT 107 had left for base, all its torpedoes gone, PTs 104, 106 and 108 had resumed station south of Ferguson Passage. When the explosion and firing were seen to the North around 0215, these three PTs went back thru Ferguson Passage into Blackett Strait, but were unable to find anything.

DIVISION A. PTs 172 and 163 which had retired well to the South of Ferguson Passage did not resume station until after 0255 and were too late to make contact. PT 169 was with Division B to the North in Blackett Strait.

DIVISION B. As hereinbefore set out, PTs 162 and 109 of Division B with PT 169 of Division A were in Blackett Strait off Vanga Vanga, as was PT 157, which however, was not in contact with them. Around 0215 the first three were due East of Gizo Island headed South, in right echelon formation with PT 109 leading, PT 162 second and PT 169 last. PT 162 saw on a collision course, a warship headed Northward about 700 yards away. The PT 162 turned to fire its torpedoes, but they did not fire. The PT 162 finally turned to the Southwest upon getting within 100 yards of the warship to avoid collision. Personnel aboard the PT 162 saw 2 raded stacks, and at least 2 turrets aft, and possibly a third turret. At the time of turning, PT 109 was seen to collide with the warship, followed by an explosion and a large flame which died down a little, but continued to burn for 10 or 15 minutes. The warship fired 3 or 4 rounds, apparently not at the PT 162, which laid smoke for 1 minute and returned to the South. PT 169 saw the warship when it was about 3000 yards away headed toward them at high speed. The PT 169 stopped just before the warship hit PT 109, turned toward it and fired two torpedoes when abeam at 150 yards range. The destroyer straddled the PT 169 with shell fire, just after it collided with the PT 109, and then circled left toward Gizo Island at increased speed and disappeared.

(4)

MOTOR TORPEDO BOATS, RENDOVA

MTBR/A16-3   21 August 1943
Serial 0034 (I)
SECRET

Subject: PT Operations night 1-2 August 1943 (Revised).
- -

The PT 169 laid smoke screen and zigzagged to the southeast along
the reefs off Gizo Island. About 0245 a wake was seen coming up
from the near northwest and on a parallel course. The PT 169
swung around to the left toward the ship (a destroyer) and fired
port and starboard forward torpedoes at 2000 yards. The destroyer
turned to its port just in time for the starboard torpedo to hit
its bow and explode. The PT 169 continued its swing and retired
south through Ferguson Passage going at high speed for ½ mile laying
smoke and zigzagging and headed for base, all its torpedoes gone.

          PT 157 was farther north than the other 3 PTs.
About 0200 the PT 157 saw a ship close in shore off Kolombangara
due east of the center of Gizo Island and fired 2 torpedoes at
it, but no explosion was seen. The ship continued northwest at
about 5 knots, without firing and disappeared.

          No further contact was made with the express. The
boats remaining on station departed for base at 0400.

     5.   All times are Love.

     6.   COMMUNICATIONS: Communications with base were good,
however, several PTs failed to put out immediate intelligible
report of contact with the enemy, with the result that the others
had no chance to get into position for an attack.

                                        T. G. WARFIELD

Advance copy to:
     Cincpac
     CTF 31
Copy to:
     ComMTB, Russells
     CNB, Dowser
     ComAirSols
     ComAir, New Georgia
     ComGen, New Georgia

The MTB consolidated report on page 124 reports there were no reports for August 5-6 through 10-11, however this report for August 7/8 was found by Nathanial Smith's personal research at the NARA. This page, and the next (pg 134), provided first word by the Rendova PT commander, Lt. Cmdr Warfield, to C-i-C U.S Fleet about the rescue of the crew of the PT-109 by the PT-157.

MTBR/A16-3
Serial 0038 (I)
~~SECRET~~

DECLASSIFIED - OPNAV INST 5500.30
BY *CPBSIC* DATE *_____*

8 August 1943

From: The Commander.
To: The Commander in Chief, U. S. Fleet.
Via: Official Channels.

Subject: PT Operations night 7-8 August 1943.

1.   **FORCE:** Eight boats on patrol. Two boats on the alert at base.

2.   **ENEMY CONTACTS:** None.

3.   **WEATHER:** Overcast with occasional showers, visibility poor to fair.

4.   **PATROL:**

AREA K (EASTERN SIDE OF LOWER VELLA GULF)

DIVISION A

Lt. A. H. Berndtson	PT 171	OAK 44
Ens. W. F. Griffin	PT 168	OAK 28

DIVISION P

Lt. (jg) D. M. Payne	PT 106	OAK 10
Lt. (jg) R. D. Shearer	PT 104	OAK 4

DIVISION T

Lt. (jg) P. A. Potter	PT 169	OAK 31
Lt. (jg) J. E. McElroy	PT 161	OAK 33

DIVISION D

Lt. (jg) D. S. Kennedy	PT 118	OAK 6
Lt. (jg) H. D. Smith	PT 154	OAK 12

All boats arrived on station 2130, except PT 171 which waited to accompany PT 157 on the rescue mission hereinafter set out. No contacts or sightings were made during the night by radar or otherwise. Left for base at 0330. Enroute to base a raft with two Japs on it, made of two empty oil drums and planks, was found five miles West of Rendova Harbor. The Japs were taken prisoner and later delivered with all their gear to Army Intelligence, Commanding General, New Georgia.

5.   **COMMUNICATIONS:** Communications were good with base, but transmissions between some of the boats were weak.

+341

MTBR/A16-3
Serial 0038 (I)

8 August 1943.

DECLASSIFIED ~~SECRET~~

Subject: PT Operations night 7-8 August 1943.

- -

    6.   RESCUE MISSION: August 6, word was received from the Coastwatcher, and by Native messenger that eleven survivors of PT 109, sunk in a collision with an enemy destroyer on the morning of August 2, were alive and on a small islet near Cross Island on the West side of Ferguson Passage. Arrangements were made through the Offices of the Coastwatcher Organization for the rescue. Lt. (jg) W. F. Liebenow in PT 157, assisted by PT 171 of the regular patrol made the rescue. The Native messengers were taken along as guides and were most helpful in guiding the PT 157 through the reefs and in handling the small boats. Several trips from shore over the reef to the PT 157 were required to remove all the men, three of whom had been badly, but not critically burned. Everything went off smoothly. The natives had fed and done everything to make the men comfortable during their stay on the island. PT 157 returned to base at 0500.

    7.   All times are Love.

                                      T. G. WARFIELD

Advance copy to:
    Cincpac
    CTF 31
Copy to:
    ComMTB,Russells
    CNB, DOWSER
    ComAirSols
    ComAir,NewGeorgia
    ComGen,NewGeorgia

MOTOR TORPEDO BOATS, RENDOVA

MTBR/A16-3
Serial 0041 (I)
SECRET

12 August 1943

From: The Commander.
To: The Commander in Chief, U. S. Fleet.
Via: Official Channels.

Subject: PT Operations, Night of 11-12 August 1943.

1. FORCE: Eight boats on patrol. Eleven boats on the alert at base.

2. ENEMY CONTACTS: One large enemy barge, riddled and aground.

3. WEATHER: High, thin overcast; visibility good.

4. PATROL:

AREA G - (WILSON AND GIZO STRAITS)
(DIVISION B - Southwest)

Lt. H. J. Brantingham	PT 167	OAK 41
Lt. O. W. Hayes	PT 159	OAK 27
Lt.(jg) W. F. Liebenow	PT 157	OAK 21
Lt.(jg) J. E. McElroy	PT 161	OAK 33

(DIVISION T - Northeast)

Lt.Comdr. LeRoy Taylor	PT 184	OAK 52
Lt.(jg) R. E. Keresey	PT 105	OAK 7
Lt.(jg) S. D. Hix	PT 108	OAK 16
Ens. J. L. Iles	PT 125	OAK 38

Enroute to station between 2015 and 2040, when about five miles east of Gizo, two bombs were dropped at the boats but missed. A moment later the plane dropped a flare from 800 feet and made a strafing run from the starboard quarter. The fire was returned by three of the PTs. This plane was seen to be a twin float monoplane. When leaving the plane dropped a float light, possibly to mark the position. About this time a flashing light was seen about the middle of the east coast of Simbo Island. At 2109 a white flare one mile south of Vella Lavella. At 2124 one white and one green flare were dropped near the southeast tip of Gonongga Island. At 2126 a white flare dropped over Wilson Strait; tracer fire from a plane was also seen. Another white flare in the same place at 2134. Planes were heard going south over the middle of Gizo Strait at 2149. About 2216 a green flare was dropped over Gizo Strait by a plane going west. Two minutes later a white flare was dropped over Gonongga. Almost immediately a white flashing light was observed on the north end of Gononga Island and a white flare dropped over Gizo Strait. At

MOTOR TORPEDO BOATS, RENDOVA

MTBR/A16-3   12 August 1943
Serial 0041 (I)
SECRET

Subject: PT Operations, Night of 11-12 August 1943.
- -
2233 a flashing light was seen from the northwest end of Gizo. A
couple of minutes later a plane went north over Gizo Strait. Again
at 2240 more flashing lights were seen at the northwest end of Gizo
Island. A minute later a bomb hit in the water a half mile from
one of the boats and was followed by tracer fire which was about
a mile off the northwest end of Gizo. At 2249 a plane's running
lights were seen going northwest over the middle of Gizo Strait.
About 2315 it appeared that a shore battery on the north end of
Ganongga fired 4 to 6 shots from a medium calibre gun. At the
same time the flashing light on Gizo Island, which had been operating since 2230, went out. About this time a plane was seen giving
signals over the Biloa Mission Area of Vella Lavella, which signals
seemed to be directed at the ground. A few minutes later a large
barge or auxiliary about 80 feet long and with high bow and stern
was picked up three miles east of the south tip of Vella Lavella.
It was said to have somewhat the lines of a tug. The craft was
headed west. Division "T", patrolling in the area, made five runs
on it. Three torpedoes, set at two feet, were fired from 300 yards,
one, when the barge appeared to be aground, but none exploded. One
of the others was seen to go under the barge. The torpedo tubes on
PT 164 which fired two of the torpedoes flashed and one of them
caught fire. Two depth charges were dropped ahead of it, which
raised it up slightly out of the water. During the attacks there
was heavy return fire at first, coming mainly from the barges stern,
composed of .25 calibre and slightly larger than .50 calibre. The
PTs suffered no casualties, but bullets went through the starboard
gasoline tank and exhaust stack of PT 164 at 2355, releasing gasoline fumes in the engine room and causing it to return to base.
One or two of the other PTs were also hit by stray bullets, which
caused only minor damage. When the 164 had gone five miles south
a bomb dropped in the water nearby without effect. The other PTs
continued the attack, and a plane, seen to be a two engine bomber
flying at about 3000 feet, dropped two bombs very close by and
attempted to strafe the boats without effect. After the first run
the barge was dead in the water. There was no return fire after
the third run. When the attacks ceased at 0030 there were no signs
of life in the craft, which appeared to be on a reef about 100 yards
off Sumbulai Point, Vella Lavella.

       5.   COMMUNICATIONS: Satisfactory except for TBYs, several
of which failed unaccountably.

       6.   All times are Love.

                                                  H. FARROW

Advance copy to: Cincpac
                 CTF 31
Copy to: ComMTB, Russells ComAir, New Georgia
         CMB, Dowser   ComGen, New Georgia
         ComAirSols

MOTOR TORPEDO BOATS, LEVER HARBOR.

MTBLH/A16-3
Serial 002
SECRET

16 August 1943.

From: The Commander, Motor Torpedo Boats, Lever Harbor.
To :   The Commander in Chief, U. S. Fleet.
Via :   Official Channels.

Subject: PT Operations night 14-15 August 1943.

  1.   FORCE: Ten boats on patrol. None at base.

  2.   ENEMY CONTACTS: None.

  3.   WEATHER: Bright moon. Visibility excellent, 3-4 miles.

  4.   PATROL:

MAINTAIN PICKET LINE FROM BOKO POINT, VELLA LAVELLA TO FIVE MILES EASTWARD FROM 2100 TO 0600.

A.	PT 160	Lt. Cdr. R. B. Kelly
	PT 162	Lt.(jg) J. R. Lowrey
	PT 156	Lt.(jg) R. E. Schneider
	PT 161	Lt.(jg) J. E. McElroy
B.	PT 159	Lt. H.J. Brantingham
	PT 157	Lt.(jg) W. F. Liebenow
	PT 154	Lt.(jg) H. D. Smith
C.	PT 126	Lt. C. Smith
	PT 116	Lt.(jg) R. G. Anne
	PT 115	Lt.(jg) R. North

Departed base 1815. At 1950 and 2050 observed A.A. fire over Vila. At 2035 arrived on station.

At 2158 observed 3 float flares in central Vella Gulf distance 3-4 miles. Lights burned until 2212. PTs did not investigate since it was believed that this was probably a ruse to locate the position of the boats. At 2220 one bomb explosion heard in vicinity of where the float flares had last been seen.

At 2240 a large twin float single engine monoplane passed directly over the PT 160, altitude 300-500 feet, apparently did not see the boats which were all lying to on a picket line. The plane circled over towards Kolombangara and dropped two more float flares near North tip of Kolombangara. At 2255 the same plane returned on an East to West course approximately one mile North of our picket line firing short bursts of tracers at the water.

MTBLH/A16-3
Serial 002
SECRET

16 August 1943

Subject: PT Operations night 14-15 August 1943.
- -

At 0600 boats departed for base. Planes were heard over PT Base intermittently throughout the night.

5.   COMMUNICATIONS: Radio silence maintained.

R. B. KELLY.

Advance copy to:
    Cincpac
    CTF31
Copy to:
    ComMTBFlotOne

MOTOR TORPEDO BOATS, LEVER HARBOR.

MTBLH/A16-3
Serial 003
SECRET

16 August 1943.

From: The Commander, Motor Torpedo Boats, Lever Harbor.
To :   The Commander in Chief, U. S. Fleet.
Via :   Official Channels.

Subject: PT Operations night 15-16 August 1943.

1.   FORCE: Four boats on patrol. Seven boats on
            alert at base as a striking force.

2.   ENEMY CONTACTS: Two plane attacks.

3.   WEATHER: Clear, visibility excellent.

4.   PATROLS:

   A.   OPERATE AGAINST BARGES IN SOUTH KULA GULF
            PT 159   Lt. H. J. Brantingham
            PT 161   Lt.(jg) J. E. McElroy

   B.   ESCORT APc 25 AND TWO LCT'S FROM VISU VISU POINT
        TO ENOGAI
            PT 157   Lt.(jg) W. F. Liebenow
            PT 154   Lt.(jg) H. D. Smith

Section A departed from base at 1800, arriving on station at 2015. At 2058 observed four flares; green, red, green, white, South of Ferguson Passage. At 2120 four more flares; white, green, green, white, same location. At 2129 two more flares, red and white. At 2150, three white flares same general direction.

At 2200 this section headed North to take screening position five miles West of BOLY POINT, arriving at 2400. Departed for base at 0630.

Section B departed from base at 2100. Picked up APc 25 and two LCT's off entrance to Lever Harbor at 2105. At 2200 one plane flew over formation. At 2310 a plane flew over formation off VISU VISU POINT and dropped one bomb 300 yards from the APc 25. The PT's created a diversion by zig-zagging at high speed and making puffs of smoke. This plane then attacked them dropping two bombs after which it departed. The PT's then returned to their original position.

MTBLH/A16-3
Serial 003
SECRET

16 August 1943.

Subject: PT Operations night 15-16 August 1943.

- -

At 0215, while approaching Rice Anchorage, three planes were seen overhead. The PT's again diverted attention of planes from the convoy to themselves as previously mentioned. The planes dropped eight or nine bombs on the boats, none near the convoy and attempted unsuccessfully to strafe the PTs. One bomb landed within 50 yards of the PT 157. The convoy successfully reached Enogai while the planes were pressing home their attack on the PTs. The PTs then screened the approaches to ENOGAI until 0500 when this section departed for its base.

At 2155 a double float single engine monoplane circled the PT base, proceeded to Lever Harbor where it circled for ten minutes before making another circle over this harbor. At 2240 a plane passed low over the native village where the APc is moored and then circled over the lagoon to Eastward, firing several short bursts at the water. It then passed over one of the nests, circled over Lever Harbor and disappeared. At 0210 a plane returned, circled both this harbor and Lever Harbor, dropping a flare over the native village at Lever. A few nights previously a bomb was dropped at this same location.

It appears obvious that the enemy is trying to locate this base but is apparently having difficulty. It is felt that a daylight raid may be expected in the near future. Boats are rather well dispersed. However, it is somewhat difficult to provide adequate protection for more than one APc at a time.

In view of the attack on last nights convoy, it is recommended that future runs into ENOGAI be made during daylight. The LCT's make excellent targets on bright moonlight nights and it is not felt that the PT's can afford them adequate A.A. protection.

Conferences with Marine Observers at ENOGAI have disclosed a new barge route now in operation from Sunday Inlet to Bairoko. Apparently the barges have been run in about 2300 on the nights that the PT's have had to depart early in order to screen movements to ENOGAI. A series of signals has been arranged with the Marine Observation Post which may enable the PT's to be more effective in disrupting this traffic.

5.   COMMUNICATIONS: Poor between sections.

R. B. KELLY.

Advance copy to:
  Cincpac
  CTF31

Advance Copy

As Orig. 6-11-51 OIN

MOTOR TORPEDO BOATS, LEVER HARBOR

MTBLH/A16-3
Serial 004
SECRET

17 August 1943.

From: The Commander, Motor Torpedo Boats, Lever Harbor.
To : The Commander in Chief, U. S. Fleet.
Via : Official Channels.

Subject: PT Operations night 16-17 August 1943.

1.   FORCE: Four boats on patrol. Six boats at
base on alert as striking force.

2.   WEATHER: Slight overcast. Visibility good,
full moon. Sea calm.

3.   ENEMY CONTACTS: Four barges off Bairoko.

4.   PATROLS:

DIVISION A
OPERATE AGAINST POSSIBLE BARGE ACTIVITY, BAIROKO-
ARUNDEL AREA
    PT 155   Lt. Comdr. R. B. Kelly
    PT 160   Lt.(jg) O.H.P. Cabot

DIVISION B
ESCORT APc 25 PLUS TWO LCT'S FROM ENOGAI TO
LEVER HARBOR
    PT 156   Lt.(jg) R. E. Schneider
    PT 162   Lt.(jg) J. R. Lowrey

Section A departed base 1830 and arrived on station
1½ miles West of ENOGAI at 2000. At 2130 observed pre-arranged
signal (green parachute flare) from Marine Observation Post at
Enogai Point indicating barges entering BAIROKO. Section got
underway and proceeded to position 1500 yards North of MAHAFFY
Island, arriving at 2140. No barges could be detected visually
or by radar in spite of full moon. This section then proceeded
to a position 600 yards off the entrance to Bairoko. Although
no barges were visible a stake marking reef at harbor entrance
could be seen. At 2325 retired to the Northward to await develop-
ments.

At 0048 a flare signal was seen indicating barges
departing from Bairoko. Visual contact was made at 0055, their
wakes being faintly visible through binoculars. They appeared
to be making approximately 15 knots and were just clearing the
harbor entrance, range 1200 yards. At 0100 the barges opened
fire at the PT's with what appeared to be 40MM high explosive

141

MTBLH/A16-3
Serial 004
SECRET

17 August 1943.

Subject: PT Operations night 16-17 August 1943.

--- --- --- --- --- --- --- --- --- --- --- --- --- --- --- --- --- ---

shells with excellent accuracy. The PT's were silhouetted by
the moonlight but the barges, now at about 1000 yards, could
not be seen without using binoculars. Both PTs opened fire
aiming at the gun flashes and the tracers but gunners could
seldom see any targets. In the meantime 40MM and / or 20MM
shore batteries opened fire from Bairoko, Mahaffy Island, and
Arundel Island. Machine guns were now being fired from the
barges and from several shore positions on Mahaffy Island. At
0110 the boats retired under smoke and lay to two miles off shore.
The shore batteries continued to fire at random and the barges
appeared to be firing both at each other and in the air. Another
firing run was made at 0116 but the fire power from ashore was
too heavy to close the range decisively. At 0123 two of the barges
were seen to round Mahaffy Island and head down Hathorn Sound.
Several rounds were fired at them using the 37MM on the PT 155
but no hits were observed. This section remained two miles off
the tip of Mahaffy Island until 0300, but no other barges were
seen to round the point. Departed for base at 0520.

Results of this attack are as yet indeterminate.
However, it is doubted if more than slight damage was done to
the barges. Since the successful attack on enemy barges in
Hathorn Sound on August 3-4 shore batteries have been installed
covering the routes and the armament on the barges has been greatly
increased. It is considered that this use of PT's to combat barges
is both ineffective and costly. It is recommended that LCM's
equipped with 20 and 40MM's, 50 caliber machine guns and FM smoke
be employed as "barge destroyers".

Section B underway 1900. Escorted APc 25 from
Lever Harbor to ENOGAI arriving at 2000. At 2235 picked up the
APc 25 and two LCT's off the entrance to ENOGAI and escorted them
as far as Lever Harbor, return to base at 0115.

5.   COMMUNICATIONS: Very unsatisfactory. Due to the
constant use of this circuit by Oak Ø , it was impossible to give
any orders to the PT 160 prior or during the barge attack. When
the PT 160 had engine trouble 1000 yards off the entrance to
BAIROKO earlier in the evening it was equally impossible for her
to contact the PT 155 for over ½ hour due to the congestion on
this circuit.

R. B. KELLY.

Advance copy to:
    Cincpac
    CTF31

MOTOR TORPEDO BOATS, LEVER HARBOR

MTBLH/A16-3
Serial 005
SECRET

18 August 1943.

From: The Commander, Motor Torpedo Boats, Lever Harbor.
To :   The Commander in Chief, U. S. Fleet.
Via : Official Channels.

Subject: PT Operations night 17-18 August 1943.

1. FORCE: Four boats on patrol. Six boats at base on alert as striking force.

2. ENEMY CONTACTS: Eight enemy barges off Arundel Island. Two enemy planes South Kula Gulf.

3. WEATHER: Heavy overcast prior to midnight, light overcast thereafter. Full moon, calm sea.

4. PATROLS:

INTERCEPT BARGE TRAFFIC IN THE BAIROKO - ARUNDEL - VILA AREA

SECTION A
  PT 159*   Lt. H. J. Brantingham
  PT 157   Lt.(jg) W. F. Liebenow

SECTION B
  PT 126*   Lt. C. Smith
  PT 116   Lt. (jg) R. Amme

*Radar equipped

Both sections departed from base at 1830 and arrived on station at 2100. Section A took station 1 - 1½ miles off ENOGAI. Section B took station 2 miles Northwest of TUNGUIRILI POINT (Mahaffy Island) and 2 miles Northeast of Arundel Island.

At 2052 observed large explosion with continuing smoke and fire on KOLOMBANGARA apparently near the OKOPO RIVER.

At 0200 Section A observed 3-4 barges passing TUNGUIRILI POINT headed West. PT 159 radioed contact to other boats. Section A proceeded to make interception. At this time barges were making about 10 knots and appeared to be unaware of location of PTs. About 0215 the barges appeared to change course and proceed up coast of Arundel Island. Section B was so notified in accordance with previously arranged plan and Section A returned to station. Section B immediately headed Southeast towards barges. At 0220 Section B made

MTBLH/A16-3
Serial 005
SECRET

18 August 1943.

Subject: PT Operations night 17-18 August 1943.
- -

radar contact with targets off SASAMBOKI Island and suspecting a trap reversed course to attack "sleepers". Meanwhile original targets speeded up heading for Vila, hugging the coast of Arundel. At 0230 radar contact was lost with the "sleepers" and Section B again reversed course in order to attack original targets. At 0235 contact was made approximately 1½ miles South of Vila. Eight barges were now seen (three large and five medium size) distance 400 yards, speed 15 knots. Section B now attacked making two firing runs. 2200 rounds of 50 caliber and 200 rounds of 20MM were fired. However, none were seen to sink. Heavy return fire was encountered from the barges and shore batteries on Arundel Island. The large barges carried automatic 40MM guns with full arc of train, firing in clips of four rounds, in addition to their machine guns. The medium barges carried machine guns and rifles only. Vila opened fire on Section B as it was retiring. There appeared to be three guns located near Vila plantation and 25-30 rounds were fired, several landing very close to the boats covering them with spray.

The PTs were well cognizant of the existance of the shore batteries at Vila and Arundel. Lt. Smith and Lt.(jg) Amme are commended for their audacious and effective attack against greatly superior enemy forces.

At 0245 Section B retired under smoke towards ENOGAI. At 0256 two very large bombs were dropped 300 yards to starboard of these boats by a heavy bomber. Planes were in vicinity remainder of night.

Section A returned to station remaining until 0445 at which time it strafed the shore batteries off Bairoko entrance with 50 caliber. There was no return fire.

Both sections departed for base at 0500.

5.   COMMUNICATIONS: Excellent between boats and section.

R. B. KELLY.

Advance copy to:
    Cincpac
    CTF31

Ar Orig. 6-11-51 OJW

MOTOR TORPEDO BOATS, LEVER HARBOR AND
MOTOR TORPEDO BOAT SQUADRON NINE

MTBLH/A16-3
Serial 008
SECRET

21 August 1943.

From: The Commander.
To :   The Commander in Chief, U. S. Fleet.
Via :   Official Channels.

Subject: PT Operations night 19-20 August 1943.

1.   FORCE: Four boats on patrol. Six boats on alert
              at base as striking force.

2.   ENEMY CONTACTS: Five barges.

3.   WEATHER: Sea calm. Full moon, slight overcast.

4.   PATROL:

DISRUPT BARGE TRAFFIC BAIROKO - ARUNDEL - VILA AREA

SECTION A
    PT 126   Lt. C. Smith
    PT 116   Lt.(jg) R. Amne

SECTION B
    PT 156   Lt.(jg) R. E. Schneider
    PT 160   Lt.(jg) O.H.P. Cabot

        Both sections departed from base at 1817 and
arrived on station at 2040. Established a picket line 2 miles
Northeast of Mahaffy Island with boats at 1000 yard intervals
from TUNGUIRILI POINT toward BAIROKO.

        At 2145 Marine Observation Post #1 (Enogai)
heard barge motors entering Bairoko and gave signal (amber cluster
flare) to PTs. PTs closed in toward Mahaffy Island. At 2154
PT 160 was within 500 yards of entrance to Bairoko. No barges
could be seen. All boats returned to original station at 2215.

        At 0205 enemy planes heard and seen overhead. At
0215 Marine Observation Post #1 observed five barges leaving
Bairoko harbor. Signalled PTs (amber parachute flare). Due to
presence of plane overhead PTs had to move slowly. At 0232 PT 160
PT 156 engaged two barges at about 1000 yards half way between
Bairoko and Tunguirili Point. At 0241 both PTs retired from attack.
At 0242 the PT 126 having closed to 1500 yards fired on the barges
as they rounded Tunguirili Point and began heading down Hathorn
Sound. A total 1250 rounds of 50 caliber and 420 rounds of 20MM
were fired. Results could not be observed. Return fire from
barges brisk. PTs were also fired on by the usual shore
batteries at Bairoko entrance and on Arundel Island.

MTMB/A16-3
Serial 006
SECRET

21 August 1943.

Subject: PT Operations night 19-20 August 1943.
- -

        A recent conference with the Commanding Officers of the First and Fourth Marine Raider Battalions at Enogai revealed that during the period 14-19 August twenty-eight barges have been observed by their Observation Post to enter and leave Bairoko. On three of these nights the PTs have attacked a total of seventeen barges leaving Bairoko. On each occasion the return fire from the barges and shore batteries has been so heavy that the PTs have been unable to close to effective range. Only two barges were seen to be damaged and none are believed to have sunk or been seriously disabled. Without illumination it is impossible for the PTs to see the barges which closely hug the shore. However, the PTs themselves are clearly visible against the horizon in the moonlight. Heavily armored large barges with 40MM and machine guns escort the medium barges which carry only machine guns and / or 20MM. In order to sink a barge, the range must be closed well within 100 yards and more than 1000 rounds of 50 caliber and 500 rounds of 20MM are required. (Based on engagement of August 3-4 in Hathorn Sound). This requires laying to at point blank range of shore batteries and barges for approximately ten minutes which is tantamount to sacrificing the PT boat. It is therefore believed that the only practical solution for combatting this barge traffic would be to employ similarly armored barges of our own or to install appropriate shore batteries capable of interdicting the barge route. In the case of ENOGAI, the latter could be accomplished effectively by a half track 75MM and a battery of pack howitzers. The range to Bairoko harbor is approximately 3700 yards and Marine Observation Post #1 is equipped with a pair of 20 power Jap binoculars which can easily cover from the harbor entrance to TUMGWIRILI POINT.

    5.   COMMUNICATIONS: Satisfactory.

                            R. B. KELLY.

Advance copy to:
    Cincpac
    CTF 31
Copy to:
    C.O., Enogai

MOTOR TORPEDO BOATS, LEVER HARBOR AND
MOTOR TORPEDO BOAT SQUADRON NINE

MTBLH/A16-3
Serial 0010
SECRET

22 August 1943.

From: The Commander.
To :   The Commander in Chief, U. S. Fleet.
Via :   Official Channels.

Subject: PT Operations night 20-21 August 1943.

1.   FORCE: Four boats on patrol. Six boats at
base on alert as striking force.

2.   ENEMY CONTACTS: Six to eight barges en route
Bairoko to Vila.

3.   WEATHER: Overcast and occasional rain squalls
until mid-night. Bright moonlight thereafter. Sea calm.

4.   PATROL:

DISRUPT BARGE TRAFFIC BAIROKO - ARUNDEL - VILA AREA

SECTION A
PT 159   Lt. H. J. Brantingham
PT 161   Lt.(jg) J. E. McElroy

SECTION B
PT 157   Lt.(jg) W. F. Liebenow, Jr.
PT 154   Lt.(jg) H. D. Smith

Both sections departed from base at 1755, arriving on station at 2005. Boats were stationed on a picket line at 1000 yards intervals approximately 1 - 1½ miles off shore of Mahaffy Island. Order of boats from East to West: PT 154, 157, 161 and 159; the PT 159 being off TUNGUIRILI POINT.

At 0200 Marine Observation Post #1 at Enogai signalled PTs that barges were leaving Bairoko Harbor (Green cluster flare). At 0210 the PT 159 sighted wakes of barges near entrance to Bairoko Harbor. The other boats did not see the barges at this time. At 0215 both the PT 157 and 159 saw the barges off Tunguirili Point. The PT 159 attacked first from about 600 yards and received very heavy return fire. The PT 157 next made a firing run using 50 caliber and 20MM from 800 yards. The PT 157 then pursued the barges as they proceeded towards Vila firing 33 rounds of 37MM range 1500 yards, as they crossed Blackett Straits. The PT 159 joined in the latter portion of this attack firing 6 rounds of 37MM at the barges. The other boats were unable to gain positions to make firing runs.

MTBLH/A16-3
Serial 0010
SECRET
                                                    22 August 1943.

Subject: PT Operations night 20-21 August 1943.
- -

        It is believed that hits were scored by the
PT 159 with 50 caliber and 20MM on two barges and that the
PT 157 obtained some hits on one or more barges with its 37MM
gun. Results were indeterminate since all barges appeared to
reach Vila.

        The PT 159 was hit by light machine gun fire
close to its gas tanks and one bullet pierced the warhead
of the starboard after torpedo.

        At 0315 the boats returned to station and
departed for base at 0430.

        Ammunition expended: 240 rounds 20MM, 550
rounds 50 caliber, 39 rounds 37MM.

    5.   COMMUNICATIONS: Satisfactory.

                                R. B. KELLY.

Advance copy to:
    Cincpac
    CTF 31

As Orig. 6-11-57 osw

Source Copy

Serial 0011

SECRET

22 August 1943.

From: The Commander.
To :   The Commander in Chief, U. S. Fleet.
Via :   Official Channels.

Subject: PT Operations night 21-22 August 1943.

    1.   FORCE: Four boats on patrol. Four boats at base on alert as striking force.

    2.   ENEMY CONTACT: Two groups 5-6 barges each.

    3.   WEATHER: Heavy overcast, visibility fair. Calm sea, occasional squalls.

    4.   PATROLS:

DISRUPT BARGE TRAFFIC BAIROKO - VILA - ARUNDEL AREA.

SECTION A
PT 155   Lt. Comdr., R. B. Kelly
PT 160   Lt. (jg) O.H.P. Cabot

ESCORT APc 24 FROM LEVER HARBOR TO ENOGAI AND BACK

SECTION B
PT 156   Lt. (jg) R. E. Schneider
PT 162   Lt. (jg) J. R. Lowrey

Section A departed from base at 1815 and arrived in South Kula Gulf at 1950. At 2015 on station as follows: PT 159, 1500 yards North of TUNGUIRILI POINT; PT 160, 1200 yards Northwest of BAIROKO HARBOR entrance. At 2035 the PT 155 developed engine trouble in its center engine and withdrew to a position 3 miles North of Tunguirili Point to repair same notifying T 160.

At 2116 received message from PT 160 that six barges were rounding TUNGUIRILI POINT. PT 155 endeavored unsuccessfully to close in for attack on two engines. At 2120 the PT 160 engaged the barges at 500 yards, range ½ mile off Baiyoko Harbor chasing them to the entrance. Obtained several hits on second and last barge. Return fire was very heavy. PT 160 then retired under smoke to avoid shore batteries shortly thereafter taking station one mile off Bairoko. At 2208 the PT 155 completed repairs on center engine and proceeded to new

MTBLN/A16-3
Serial 0011
SECRET

22 August 1943.

Subject: PT Operations night 21-22 August 1943.

- -

station inside HATHORNE SOUND 1000 yards from Mahaffy Island.

At 0033 sighted signal from ENOGAI indicating barges leaving BAIROKO. Barges apparently proceeded at very slow speed to avoid wake and closely hugged the shore of Mahaffy Island for PT 160 was unable to see them. At 0045 a column of barges was seen to round Tunguirili Point heading West to North of the PT 155. At 0050 the PT 155 attacked from 400-500 yards distance using its 37MM and 20MM on the leading barges. For the first time barges appeared to scatter in all directions. For the next twenty minutes a wild melle ensued. The return fire was heavily concentrated on the PT 155 whose smoke puffs were riddled with holes. Two shore batteries on Arundel, one on Vila, one on Mahaffy and one at Bairoko continued their bombardment for approximately ½ an hour. One barge turned around and headed for Bairoko at full speed (15-17 knots) with the PT 160 in pursuit. The others apparently escaped to Vila and Hathorn Sound. It is believed that at least one barge was badly hit.

The PTs retired to vicinity of ENOGAI after this engagement and remained there until 0515 when they departed for their base.

Ammunition expended:

1st engagement	180 rounds	20MM
	400 rounds	50 caliber
2nd engagement	240 rounds	20 MM
	650 rounds	50 caliber
	40 rounds	37MM

Section B departed from base with the APc 24 at 1930 arriving at ENOGAI at 2330. They departed from Enogai at 0015 and arrived at the PT base at 0315.

5.   COMMUNICATIONS: Excellent reception.

R. B. KELLY.

Advance copy to:
    Cincpac
    CTF 31

MOTOR TORPEDO BOATS, LEVER HARBOR AND
MOTOR TORPEDO BOAT SQUADRON NINE

MTBLH/A16-3
Serial 0012
SECRET

23 August 1943.

From: The Commander.
To :   The Commander in Chief, U. S. Fleet.
Via :   Official Channels.

Subject: PT Operations night 22-23 August 1943.

  1.   FORCE: Four boats on patrol. Three boats at
                base on alert as striking force.

  2.   ENEMY CONTACTS: Five enemy barges leaving Bairoko.

  3.   WEATHER: Overcast and rainy most of night. Fair
visibility during engagement. Sea calm.

  4.   PATROL:

DISRUPT BARGE TRAFFIC BAIROKO - ARUNDEL - VILA AREA

Section A
    PT 159*   Lt. H.J. Brantingham
    PT 154   Lt.(jg) H. D. Smith

Section B
    PT 157*   Lt.(jg) W. F. Liebenow, Jr.
    PT 161   Lt.(jg) J. E. McElroy

        * Equipped with "jury-rig" 37MM bow mount

        Sections A and B departed from base at 1750
arriving on station at 2000. Section A one mile Northwest of
Tunguirili Point. Section B 1500 yards off Bairoko Harbor entrance.

        At 0016 shore batteries at Bairoko opened fire on
Section B which made a puff of smoke and retired 1000 yards. The
PT 157 then returned to station and fired on the shore battery
with its 37MM gun using the smoke puff as a screen. The firing
then ceased from the shore battery and both boats remained on
station.

        At 0155 received signal from the Marine Observation
Post at Enogai (green flares) indicating barges leaving Bairoko.
The wakes of the barges were noted by Section B a few moments
later. At 0200 Section B commenced its attack, the PT 157 firing
with its 37MM and 20MM forward turret, while closing the range to
500 yards. At this point the return fire from the barges and shore
batteries on Bairoko and Mahaffy was extremely heavy. Speed was

MTBLM/A16-3
Serial 0012
SECRET

23 August 1943.

Subject: PT Operations night 22-23 August 1943.
- -

increased and five starboard firing runs were made at 500-600
yards range. The barges scattered becoming separated in two
groups. Section A attacked the leading group, PT 159 firing
its 37MM until range was closed to approximately 800 yards.
At this time the return fire from the barges plus the shore
batteries on Mahaffy and Arundel Islands became very heavy.
A starboard firing run was then made by both boats at high
speed before retiring.

        The barges had now passed Tunguirili Point and
were heading towards Vila along the coast of Arundel. Both
sections kept up a running attack on the barges using their two
37MM bow guns.

        Action was broken off at 0245 when approximately
two miles from Vila because of very heavy automatic fire from
Arundel and the increasing accuracy of the fire from the large
caliber batteries at Vila.

        At least two 37MM hits (A.P.) were observed on
one barge although it did not slow down. Some hits were made by
20MM and 50 caliber fire.

        An increasing number of shore batteries are springing
up along the entire barge route from Bairoko to Vila. It is
interesting to note that this was the first attempt by the shore
batteries to drive off the PTs before sending the barges across.
This is the second night that the PTs have caused the barges to
scatter. However, it is believed that the effectiveness of these
PT attacks is strictly limited to harassing action.

        Ammunition expended: 78 rounds   37MM
                                1050 rounds   20MM
                                1450 rounds   50 caliber

        Both sections returned to their stations at 0315
remaining there until 0430 when they departed for their base.

    5.   COMMUNICATIONS: Satisfactory.

                                    R. B. KELLY.

Advance copy to:
    Cincpac
    CTF 31

Original

MOTOR TORPEDO BOATS, LEVER HARBOR AND
MOTOR TORPEDO BOAT SQUADRON NINE

MTBLH/A16-3
Serial 0013
SECRET   24 August 1943.

From: The Commander.
To :   The Commander in Chief, U. S. Fleet.
Via :   Official Channels.

Subject: PT Operations night 23-24 August 1943.

1.   FORCE: Three boats on patrol. Three boats at
                base on alert as striking force.

2.   ENEMY CONTACTS: None.

3.   WEATHER: Cloudy with intermittent rain squalls.
                  Visibility fair.

4.   PATROL:

        INTERCEPT POSSIBLE BARGE TRAFFIC TO NORTHERN
        KOLOMBANGARA FROM CHOISEUL

            PT 162   Lt. Comdr. R. B. Kelly
            PT 156   Lt.(jg) R. S. Schneider
            PT 160   Lt.(jg) O.H.P. Cabot

        Departed from base at 1850. At 1935 the PT 160
developed engine trouble in its port engine and returned to base.
At 2100 remainder of patrol arrived on station two miles Northeast
of REI Cove. At 0100 changed position to 1½ miles North of LUKI
POINT. At 0530 departed for base. Results negative.

5.   COMMUNICATIONS: Satisfactory.

                                        R. B. KELLY.

Advance copy to:
    Cincpac
    CTF 31

ADVANCE COPY

MOTOR TORPEDO BOATS, LEVER HARBOR AND
MOTOR TORPEDO BOAT SQUADRON NINE

MTBRN/A16-3
Serial 0014
SECRET

25 August 1943.

From: The Commander.
To :   The Commander in Chief, U. S. Fleet.
Via :   Official Channels.

Subject: PT Operations night 24-25 August 1943.

   1.   FORCE: Six boats on alert at base as
                     striking force.

   2.   There were no Motor Torpedo Boat Operations
this date. All boats were ordered by Commander, Task Force
Thirty-One to remain at base.

                          R. B. KELLY.

Advance copy to:
  Cincpac √
  CTF31

MOTOR TORPEDO BOATS, LEVER HARBOR AND
MOTOR TORPEDO BOAT SQUADRON NINE

MTBLH/A16-3
Serial 0015
SECRET

26 August 1943.

From: The Commander.
To :   The Commander in Chief, U. S. Fleet.
Via :   Official Channels.

Subject: PT Operations night 25-26 August 1943.

1.   FORCE: Three boats on patrol. Three boats
                at base on alert as striking force.

2.   ENEMY CONTACTS: None.

3.   WEATHER: Heavy overcast, visibility fair,
                calm sea.

4.   PATROL:

ESCORT APc 25 FROM LEVER HARBOR TO ENOGAI AND
RETURN

        PT 157   Lt. H. J. Brantingham
        PT 154   Lt.(jg) H. D. Smith
        PT 161   Lt.(jg) J. E. McElroy

        Departed from base at 1815, arriving at Enogai
at 2130. Departed from Enogai at 2300 returning to base at
0350.

5.   COMMUNICATIONS: Satisfactory.

                            R. B. KELLY.

Advance copy to:
    Cincpac
    CTF 31

ADVANCE COPY - Cincpac

To be ~~carded~~ 6-12-51 OSW

RECEIVED SEP 5 1943 CINCPAC

A-16-3/Bu4

MOTOR TORPEDO BOATS, LEVER HARBOR AND
MOTOR TORPEDO BOAT SQUADRON NINE

MTBLH/A16-3
Serial 0012
SECRET

27 August 1943.

From: The Commander.
To :   The Commander-in-Chief, U. S. Fleet.
Via : Official Channels.

Subject: PT Operations night 26-27 August 1943.

1. SIZE: Four boats on patrol. Three boats at base on alert as striking force.

2. ENEMY CONTACTS: None.

3. WEATHER: Calm sea. Visibility good.

4. PATROLS:

THE SHORE AREA OF LUKI POINT, KOLOMBANGARA

SECTION A - Lt. Comdr. R. B. KELLY in PT 160

PT 160   Lt.(jg) D.H.F. Cabot
PT 161   Lt.(jg) J. R. McElroy

THE SHORE AREA OF BAMBARI HARBOR, KOLOMBANGARA

SECTION B - Lt.(jg) R. E. SCHNEIDER in PT 156

PT 156   Lt.(jg) R. E. Schneider
PT 162   Lt.(jg) J. R. Lowrey

Both sections departed from the base at 1815. Section A arrived on station 1½ to 2 miles North of LUKI POINT at 2006. At 2007 an unidentified plane passed overhead from East to West at 2-3000 feet altitude, circled area and headed Southeast over Kolombangara. 2117 unidentified plane overhead. At 2216 sighted flare bearing 290° T distance five to six miles. At 0700 departed for base. At 0520 observed A/A fire over Vella la Vella and Munda. 0525 bomb flashes vicinity of Munda. 0555 more A/A fire over Vella la Vella.

Section B arrived on station at 1936 1½ to 2 miles off Bambari Harbor. At 2002 and 2120 unidentified planes overhead. At 0221 observed bomb flash or large explosion near Vila. At 0540 four bombs appeared to land on shore line just North of Rice Anchorage. 0602 departed for base.

5. COMMUNICATIONS: Satisfactory.

6. All times are Love.

R. B. KELLY.

Cincpac

ADVANCE COPY

To be c[...] 6-11-51 oon

#16-3/Aug
SEP 5 [...]
CINCPAC
030

MOTOR TORPEDO BOATS, SOUTH PACIFIC FORCE
MOTOR TORPEDO BOAT Squadrons NINE

MTBRON/A16-3
Serial 0017
SECRET

28 August 1943.

From: The Commander,
To :   The Commander-in-Chief, U. S. Fleet.
Via :   Official Channels.

Subject: PT Operations night 27-28 August 1943.

    1.   FORCE: Three boats on patrol. Five boats at base on alert as striking force.

    2.   ENEMY CONTACTS: None.

    3.   WEATHER: Calm sea. Visibility fair, extremely dark; no moon.

    4.   PATROL:

SECTION A - ONE MILER NORTH OF LUKI POINT

(Intercept suspected barge traffic from Choiseul to Kolombangara)

Lt. H. J. BRANTINGHAM in PT 157

PT 157   Lt.(jg) W. F. Liebenow, Jr.
PT 154   Lt.(jg) E. D. Smith
PT 115   Lt.(jg) R. North

    Patrol departed from base at 1845, arriving on station at 2033. At 2041 unidentified plane overhead from Northwest. At 2146 sighted flare, distance 5-10 miles, to Southwest. Another flare, same location sighted at 2155.

    At 2200 base received word from Commander, Task Force Thirty-One, that patrol must be back at their base prior to 0500 to avoid making contact with our own task force en route Vella La Vella. This information was relayed to the boats on patrol.

    At 2330 the patrol departed for base at slow speed arriving at 0204.

    5.   COMMUNICATIONS: Between boats good. Impossible contact patrol by voice radio from base due to being land locked.

    6.   All times are Love.

                                     R. B. KELLY.

advance copy   THIRD

MOTOR TORPEDO BOATS, LEVER HARBOR AND
MOTOR TORPEDO BOAT SQUADRON NINE

MTBLN/A16-3
Serial 0018
AUGUST

29 August 1943.

From: The Commander,
To :   The Commander-in-Chief, U. S. Fleet.
Via :   Official Channels.

Subject: PT Operations night 26-27 August 1943.

   1.   FIRST: Seven boats at base on alert as
                    striking force.

   2.   There were no Motor Torpedo Boats on patrol
this date. The Commander, Task Force Thirty-One, ordered all
boats to remain at base.

                                   R. B. KELLY.

Advance copy to:
     Cincpac ✓
     CTF 31
Copy to:
     ComMTB,Cleanslate

30 August 1943.

From: The Commander,
To   :   The Commander-in-Chief, U. S. Fleet.
Via :   Official Channels.

Subject: PT Operations nights 29-30 August 1943.

1.   FORCE: Four boats on patrol. Four boats at
      base on alert as striking force.

2.   ENEMY CONTACTS: One large barge. Enemy planes.

3.   WEATHER: Prior 0100 visibility poor to fair;
      fair to good thereafter. Sea calm.

4.   PATROLS:

(Disrupt suspected barge traffic to North Kolombangara)

SECTION A - THE MINE NORTHWEST BELCOED

Lt. Comdr. R. B. KELLY, USN, in PT 160

PT 160   Lt.(jg) O.E.P. Cabot
PT 161   Lt.(jg) J. V. McElroy

SECTION B - TWO MILES NORTH TOKI POINT

Lt.(jg) R. L. SCHNEIDER in PT 156

PT 156   Lt.(jg) R. L. Schneider
PT 162   Lt.(jg) J. R. Lowry

        Both sections departed from the base at 1755.
Section B arrived on station at 1917. Section A was on station
at 1928. The locus of series of flares or explosions was observed
Northeast of Vella La Vella from 1935 to 2120.

        At 2130 Section A sighted an enemy barge as it
came out of a rain squall. Apparently it had crossed from Vella
La Vella and was heading for the North tangent of Kolombangara.
As this section maneuvered to close the range for attack it was
seen by the barge which increased speed and turned towards the
land. At 2144 Section A opened fire at about 400 yards while
still closing as the barge was fast blending into the shore line.
The PTs and the barge then continued on a parallel course some
300 yards abeam, at eleven knots until 2155 when action was
broken off and contact lost due to entering a rain squall. The
return fire was somewhat less than usually encountered but more
accurate. The barge appeared to be firing at least one 90 caliber

159

MENIS/A16-3
Serial 0013
SECRET

30 August 1943.

Subject: PT Operations night 29-30 August 1943.

- -

machine guns, one light machine gun, many rifles, and possibly a 20MM.

At 2400 Section B was notified by radio that an enemy barge was probably heading towards it and to stand by to make an interception. Section B then moved to a new position about ½ mile off Tuki Point. At 0015 both sections observed tracer fire in the air from off shore Kolombangara, West of Tuki Point. At 0019 Section B observed the barge and attacked same making four slow-speed firing runs at 200-300 yards distance, between 0021 and 0110. By this time the forward 20MM mount on the PT 156 had been hit and one man wounded, and other guns were low on ammunition. The 50 caliber turret on the PT 162 had also been hit and its after 20MM had jammed. Action was therefore broken off. The PT 156 was directed to return to the base and arrived at 0245. Other boats remained on station until 0530. From 0040 to 0053 an enemy plane was in the vicinity and was seen to drop two bombs well clear of Section B at 0245. At 0129 another unidentified plane passed overhead.

Numerous hits on the barge especially 20MM were observed by both sections. However, they appeared to have little effect in sinking or stopping same.

From 0512 to 0533 observed intermittent heavy tracer fire about five miles to the Northward. Radio intercepts indicated that this was a section of the Rendova based PTs attacking a barge well off the coast and East of Vella La Vella.

Ammunition Expended:

PT 160	775 rounds 50 cal.	180 rounds 20MM
PT 161	60 rounds 50 cal.	65 rounds 20MM
Section A	835 rounds 50 cal.	245 rounds 20MM
PT 156	550 rounds 50 cal.	350 rounds 20MM
PT 162	700 rounds 50 cal.	200 rounds 20MM
Section B	1250 rounds 50 cal.	550 rounds 20MM

5. COMMUNICATIONS: Satisfactory.

6. All times are Love.

R. B. KELLY.

Advance copy to:
  Cincpac
  CTF 31

Copy to:

Original pg.

A

MOTOR TORPEDO BOATS, LEVER HARBOR AND
MOTOR TORPEDO BOAT SQUADRON NINE

MTBLH/A16-3
Serial 0020
SECRET

31 August 1943.

From: The Commander,
To :   The Commander-in-Chief, U. S. Fleet.
Via :   Official Channels.

Subject: PT Operations night 30-31 August 1943.

    1.   FORCE: Four boats on patrol. Four boats at
                        base on alert as striking force.

    2.   ENEMY CONTACTS: None.

    3.   WEATHER: Visibility good except for dark clouds
                        on horizon. Sea calm.

    4.   PATROL:

(Disrupt suspected barge traffic to Northern
Kolombangara)

SECTION A - TWO MILES NORTH OF REI COVE

Lt. H. J. BRANTINGHAM, USN, in PT 157

PT 157   Lt.(jg) W. F. Liebenow, Jr.
PT 115   Lt.(jg) R. North

SECTION B - THREE MILES NORTH OF DOSORIANA ISLAND

Lt. O. W. HAYES, USNR, in PT 159

PT 159   Lt. O. W. Hayes
PT 154   Lt.(jg) H. D. Smith

        Both sections departed from the base at 1814.
Section B arrived on station at 2000. Section A was on station
at 2043.

        At 2210 A/A fire was observed over Vella la Vella
in the vicinity of BARAKOMA. An unidentified plane passed over
Section B at 2222 and over Section A at 2238. Unidentified
planes passed over Section B at 0125, 0200 and 0330. At 0430
Section A departed for base at slow speed. Section B left station
and headed for the base at 0530.

    5.   COMMUNICATIONS: Satisfactory.

    6.   All times are Love.

Advance copy:
    Cincpac
    CTF 31

                               R. B. KELLY.

A P P E N D I X D

RON-9 COMMANDER KELLY'S 'SUMMARY OF PT – BARGE ENGAGEMENTS IN THE KULA GULF AREA DURING AUGUST 1943'

All of the pages in this section these reports, requested by the author from the National Archives and Records Administration [NARA] were provided from NARA were in digital format. This has allowed the author to make some adjustments to help in their readability.

ALL pages in this section are declassified

Appendix

MOTOR TORPEDO BOAT SQUADRON NINE
% FLEET POST OFFICE, SAN FRANCISCO, CALIFORNIA.

FC8-9/A16
Serial 0012
SECRET

8 September 1943.

From: The Commander.
To :   The Commander, South Pacific.
Via :   Official Channels.

Subject: Summary of PT - Barge engagements in the Kula Gulf Area
during August 1943.

Enclosure: (A) Tabulation barge encounters Kula Gulf Area
during August 1943.
(B) Sketches and descriptions enemy barge types
encountered.
(C) Copy of CoMTBLever Harbor ltr. MTBLH/A3, Serial
001, to CTF-31 dated 14 August 1943, re Recommendation
conversion LCM to "Barge Destroyers".

    1.   During the month of August 1943, the Motor Torpedo Boats
under this command at Lever Harbor, New Georgia, B.S.I., attacked 43-44
enemy barges in the Kula Gulf Area in a series of ten engagements. Two
barges were seen to be sunk, one forced to be beached, and eight to
sixteen hit with possible minor damage. Five PTs were hit with minor
injuries to boats and personnel.

    2.   Enclosure (A) is a tabulation summarizing these
engagements. Enclosure (B) is considered to be a reasonably accurate
description of enemy barge types and is based on both the observation
of the writer and the PT Boat Captains under his command. Enclosure (C)
is a copy of this writers recommendation for the construction of
"jury-rig" anti-barge boats from LCM'S.

    3.   Although all these engagements, with exception of the
first, took place close off-shore along a barge route heavily protected
by shore batteries of automatic weapons and heavy caliber guns (3" and
5.7") it is believed that the results except for the extremely light
casualties, are representative of what may be expected in future barge -
PT encounters. In most instances the fire power from each barge appeared
to be equal to or greater than that of any individual PT boat. The
armament of the PTs were 2 - 20MM's and 3 - 50 caliber machine guns,
except for three boats on which a 37MM field piece was substituted for
the forward 50 caliber machine gun.

    4.   The majority of these engagements were observed by the
First Marine Raiders Observation Post at ENOGAI. Evaluation of damage
inflicted and relative fire power was largely based on their reports.

FC8-9/A16
Serial 0012
SECRET

8 September 1943.

Subject: Summary of PT - Barge engagements in the Kula Gulf
             Area during August 1943.

- -

　　　5.　　　It will be noted that their universally low freeboard
and sturdy steel hulls make all type Japanese barges a most difficult
target to sink, or even hit, except by prolonged fire at extremely
close range (50 - 100 yards). The inherent characteristics of PT boats
normally preclude such tactics without the certain sacrifice of boats
and even then with no reasonable assurance of defeating the barge, or
barges, encountered. Accordingly, a system of "hit and run" measures
has of necessity been resorted to. When it is possible to engage the
enemy well off shore, the defeat of the barge is possible. Under other
conditions only a harassing effect is obtained - probably resulting in
slowing down, but not stopping, the barge traffic.

　　　6.　　　Because of the inherent structural characteristics
of Motor Torpedo Boats, it is not believed that they are adaptable
to conversion to motor gun boats able effectively to engage barges
at the necessary extremely short ranges at the same time withstanding
the resultant return fire. It is realized that this use of PTs has
been only to provide a very necessary "stop - gap". It has therefore
been requested that this command be authorized to conduct experiments
in the construction and operation of a "barge destroyer" of the type
outlined in enclosure (C).

                              R. B. KELLY.

Advance copy to:
    CTF 31
    MTBSTC, Melville
    CoMTBFlotOne
    MTB Base, Dowser

NOTES:

1.   All but two of the above engagements were fought close off shore along a barge route well protected by shore batteries (light and heavy machine guns, 20 and 40 MMs, 3" and 5.7" guns).

2.   The barges themselves carried various combinations of light and heavy machine guns, 20MMs and occasional 40MMs plus riflemen.

3.   The inaccuracy of fire from the barges' automatic weapons was probably largely due to their portable mounts and the inexperience of the gun crews in firing from an unstable and moving platform. In most instances, the rifle fire was quite accurate.

- 2 -   ENCLOSURE A

TABULATION OF BARGE ENCOUNTERS KULA GULF AREA – AUGUST 1943

DATE	NUMBER BARGES SEEN	TYPE	NUMBER DESTROYED	MINOR DAMAGE (KNOWN HITS)	PROBABLE HITS (ADDITIONAL)	RANGE (YARDS)	50 CAL	20MM	37MM	EST. BARGE SPEED (KNOTS)	NUMBER OF PTS IN ATTACK	NUMBER OF PTS HIT
August 3	3	C	2		1	75-100	1400	840	8	8	1	1
16	4	D		1		800-1000	650	240		10-15	2	
17	8	3-D 5-A		2		400-500	2200	200		10-15	2	1
19	5	?				1000-1500	1250	420	39	8	3	1
20	6	A or D		1	2	600-800	550	240		8-10	2	
20	6	D		1	2-3	400-500	400	180		8	1	
21	6	D		1	2	500-800	650	240	40	8-	1	
21	5-6	D		1		500	1450	1050	78	10	4	
22	5	A & D	1*	1	7-8	300	1450	1050	78			1
29	1#	D		1#		200-400	635	245		10	2	
29	1#	D		1#		300	1250	550		10	2	2
TOTALS	43-44		3	8	7-8		10535	4205	165			5

* Forced Aground
\# Same Barge

- 1 -

ENCLOSURE A

DETAILS OF JAPANESE LANDING AND CARGO BARGES

1.   TYPES A1 AND A2 - "DAIHATSU" Large MLC - Two variations of this type were recently examined at BAIROKO, New Georgia, B.S.I. Type A1, had been completely stripped. However, Type A2 was in tact except that guns and cargo had been removed.

Both barges were about 49' long with 11' 7" beam and 1½' to 2' free board amidships. They were equipped with hoisting slings similar to those used on our ML's. Speed appears to be about 8 knots except for short spurts when what seemed to be 10-11 knots has been observed.

There was no evidence of fixed gun mounts on either of these barges. However, heavily concentrated 20MM or 51 caliber machine gun plus rifle fire has always been encountered when engaging them. The portable mounts used for these automatic weapons probably explain to a large degree their inaccuracy of fire.

2.   TYPE B - This type barge was encountered by the writer during the Philippine Campaign. It is probably now obsolete. Only light automatic weapons and rifles were carried. Speed was about 15 knots, length 35' - 40', beam 10'.

These barges were of the usual rugged steel hull with heavy wood gunwales. There was a rounded steel canopy aft with small gun ports or slits. A diesel engine was located amidships. There was dual steering control - amidships and at armored conning position.

3.   TYPE C - "SAMPAN" Model - Barges of this variety encountered all appeared to carry heavy caliber fixed machine guns aft in addition to the usual miscellaneous light guns amidships. The accuracy of their fire has been vastly superior to that of the other types.

This type barge appears to be 50' - 60' in length. Its free board is about 3½' forward, 2½' amidships and 6' - 8' aft. Speed is about 8 - 10 knots. The hull is of heavy steel plating.

4.   TYPE D - Because of its extremely low freeboard (1½ to 2') it is difficult accurately to determine its length. However, it appears to be about 80' - 90'. In all encounters to date, it has mounted a 40MM gun. Usually this is located forward and can be trained only by pointing the barge. However, on one instance an automatic 40MM with full arc of train appeared to be located aft. In addition, a variety of 20MMs, riflemen, and machine guns are carried. Speeds in excess of 10 knots have been estimated for this type. Hull appears to be of steel plating.

-1-   ENCLOSURE B

SKETCHES OF JAPANESE CARGO AND LANDING BARGES ENCOUNTERED

BY MOTOR TORPEDO BOATS

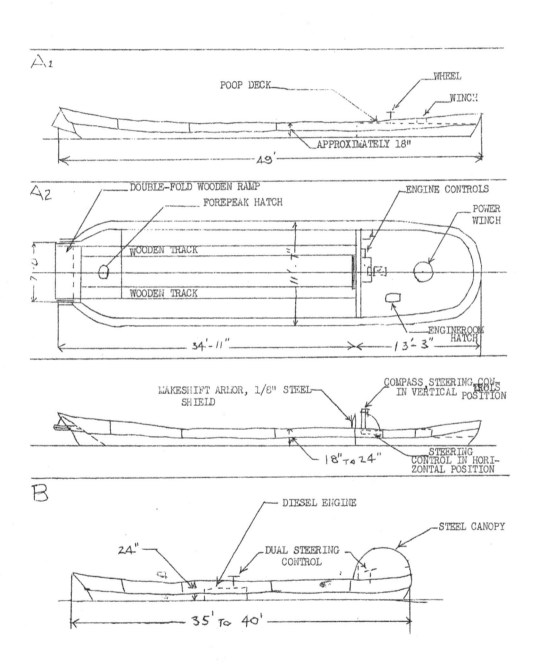

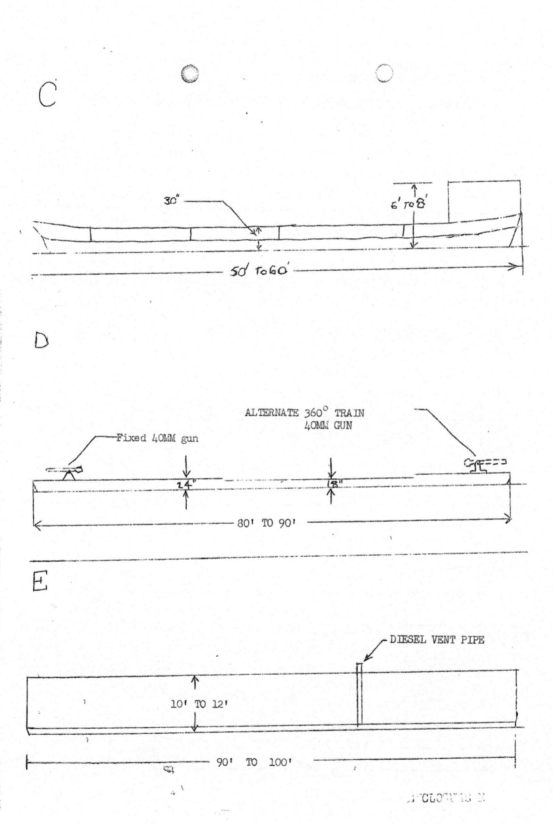

C

30"

6' TO 8'

50' TO 60'

D

ALTERNATE 360° TRAIN
40MM GUN

Fixed 40MM gun

24"

18"

80' TO 90'

E

DIESEL VENT PIPE

10' TO 12'

90' TO 100'

MOTOR TORPEDO BOATS, LEVER HARBOR.

MTBLH/A3
Serial 001
SECRET

14 August 1943.

From: The Commander, Motor Torpedo Boats, Lever Harbor.
To :   The Commander, Task Force Thirty-One.

Subject: Recommendation for conversion of LCM's to
            Barge Destroyers.

    1.   Results of recent operations tend to indicate the inability of Motor Torpedo Boats to cope with heavily armed and armored enemy barges. It is believed that satisfactory "Barge Destroyers" could very easily be constructed from LCM's as follows:

(a) Sand bag or armor engine and fuel tanks
(b) Add flotation tanks forward, aft and amidships
(c) Mount rapid fire 40MM forward, sand bagging position,
    cutting gun ports as necessary in ramp and sides
(d) Mount two 20MM on each side amidships on trunion or
    scarf ring mount
(e) Sand bag or armor conning position
(f) Retain 50 caliber machine guns now located aft
(g) Mount flask of FM smoke on stern
(h) Muffle engine exhaust
(i) Carry "Walkie Talkie" radio

    2.   Because of their size and draft, these craft could base at our most advanced positions - closest to the scene of enemy barge activity. They could be escorted nightly to the scene of operations by Motor Torpedo Boats, which would then retire to seaward protecting their flank from DDs. The Motor Torpedo Boats would escort them to their base each morning prior to dawn.

    3.   The FM smoke could be used in retiring from enemy shore battery fire, or plane attacks. The "Walkie Talkie" would be used for communications between LCM's and Motor Torpedo Boats.

    4.   A craft of the above type would have been invaluable for operations in Kula Gulf. Basing at Enogai it could easily cover the barge route off Arundel Island from dusk to dawn effectively blocking it.

    5.   Although time may not permit the conversion of such craft prior to the completion of present operations, it is felt that these barge destroyers will be necessary for future operations and experiments along this line should be made.

                             R. B. KELLY.

Copy to:
  ComSoPac
  ComMTBRons,SoPac
  ComTBFlotOne
  CoMTBS,Rendova

                          ENCLOSURE C

FD8-1/A16
Serial 272

SECRET

1st Endorsement to ComTBRon-9 ltr.
FC8-9/A16 serial 0012 of 9-8-43
MOTOR TORPEDO BOAT FLOTILLA ONE
16 September 1943

From: Commander, Motor Torpedo Boat Flotilla ONE.
To :   Commander South Pacific.
Via :   Commander, Motor Torpedo Boat Squadrons, South Pacific.

SUBJECT: Summary of PT - Barge engagements in the Kula Gulf Area during
            August 1943.

   1.   Forwarded.

A. P. CALVERT

Copy to: ComTBRon-9

- -

SECOND ENDORSEMENT
CMTB/A16

September 21, 1943.

SECRET

From: The Commander Motor Torpedo Boat Squadrons,
             South Pacific Force.
To: Commander South Pacific.

   1.   Forwarded.

E.J. MORAN.

Copy to:
   Com MTB Ron 9

Enclosure (Z) to COMSOPAC
Secret Serial 002236

APPENDIX E

MEMOS TO/FROM RON-9 COMMANDER ROBERT B. KELLY ON THE 'EXPERIMENT' TO OUTFIT RON-9 WITH 20MM OERLIKON IN THE FORWARD TURRET

All pages in this section are due to the personal research efforts of Nathanial Smith, the son of the Skipper of the PT-154 Hamlin D. Smith, while at the National Archives and Records Administration [NARA].

All Documents in the section are declassified

Appendix

B

C

Ad

Re

Fi

Mn

Pr

DEC 21 1942

X
PT/29
S74 (20mm)

From: The Chief of the Bureau of Ordnance
To: Commandant, Navy Yard New York

Subject: Motor Torpedo Boat Squadron NINE (PT'S 151-162,
           inclusive) - Experimental Installation of 20 mm
           Antiaircraft Gun Mounts

    1.   It is understood that the Navy Yard New York
has developed a design and has built two experimental prototypes of a single 20 mm scarff ring mount suitable for use
in lieu of the present twin .50 caliber mount Mark 17 and that
one of the prototype 20 mm mounts has been tested in a motor
torpedo boat.

    2.   The manufacture of 11 additional single 20 mm
scarff ring mounts has been authorized and a project order,
No. 300200-Ord. has been issued for this purpose. Including
the two mounts already built, the total of 13 mounts will be
sufficient to permit installation of one mount each in place
of the starboard forward caliber .50 mount in each of the
vessels of Motor Torpedo Boat Squadron NINE. The one mount
authorized in addition to the 12 required for Motor Torpedo
Boat Squadron NINE is intended for such installation and further
test as may be directed when this mount becomes available.

    3.   It is desired that the displaced caliber .50
machine guns and associated equipment be allowed to remain on
board the vessels of Motor Torpedo Boat Squadron NINE until
the reliability of the 20 mm mounts has been verified.

    4.   The Commandant is requested to issue one 20 mm
antiaircraft gun Mark 4, less mount, complete with spare parts
and accessories, including a total of 8 - 20 mm magazines per
gun to each of the vessels of Motor Torpedo Boat Squadron NINE
from the 20 mm antiaircraft gun pool at the Navy Yard New York
for use with the subject experimental mounts.

                              W. H. P. BLANDY
                              A. D. Blackburn
                              By Direction

A/eom
Copy to:
VOFNAV
COMINCH
BUSHIPS   Mn1, Re5, PL2, Re1, PLb   122142 90069

CONFIDENTIAL

174

PT/374

(Re5d)

30 DEC 1942

From: The Chief of the Bureau of Ordnance.
To: The Commandant, Navy Yard, New York.

Subject: Motor Torpedo Boat Squadron NINE
(PT's 151-162, inclusive) — Experimental
Installation of 20 mm. A. A. Gun Mounts,
Test of.

Reference: (a) NYd NY ltr PT161/374(L-79-70-73) to
BuOrd dated 14 Dec 1942.
(b) MTBRonNINE ltr FC8-9/S74 Serial 65 to
BuOrd dated 15 Dec 1942.
(c) BuOrd ltr PT/S74(Pr5d) to Comdt. New
York Navy Yard dated 21 Dec 1942.

1.   Reference (a) forwarded to the Bureau of Ordnance
photographs of a 20 mm. gun mount design (scarf ring type),
installed in a PT boat, in lieu of the caliber .50 twin mount.
Reference (a) also pointed out the advantages of such a design
and informed the Bureau the drawings of the proposed mount
were being corrected and would be forwarded to the Bureau in
a few days.

2.   Reference (b) requested the Navy Yard, New
York, be authorized to manufacture eleven of the subject
mounts, to be used interchangeably with the starboard caliber
.50 mounts on the boats of Squadron NINE.

3.   Reference (c) authorized the manufacture of
eleven single 20 mm. scarf ring mounts in addition to the two
mounts already built and assigned project order No. 300200-Ord,
for this purpose. Reference (c) also stated the total of
thirteen mounts would be sufficient to permit installation of
one mount each in place of the starboard forward caliber .50
mount in each of the vessels of Motor Torpedo Boat Squadron
NINE; the one mount authorized in addition to the twelve requested was to be for such installation and further tests as
may be directed when this mount became available.

4.   In order to expedite further tests of subject
mount, it is requested the Commandant install on one of

-1-

123042 50027

122142 00054

PT 874
(Re5d)

of the Motor Torpedo Boats outfitting in the Navy Yard, New York, one of the prototypes of subject mount. It is desired to give this mount tests by firing at surface targets and balloons. It would also be desirable to subject the mount to rough weather and handling operations both before and after the tests. Inspection of the roller paths and bearings should be made subsequent to tests.

5.   It is further requested the Commandant inform the Bureau when subject mount will be available so that the Bureau may have representatives present for the tests.

W. H. P. BLANDY

F. F. Foster
By direction

RDR/Jec
Copy to:
  Re15d

MS042 50027

-2-

122142 00054

Auth... **NND 755011**
By **MH** NARA Date **4/5/01**

MOTOR TORPEDO BOAT SQUADRON NINE
% FLEET POST OFFICE, NEW YORK, N. Y.

FC8-9/7
CONFIDENTIAL

27 March 1943.

From: The Commander.
To :   The Chief of the Bureau of Ordnance.

Subject: Experimental 20MM anti-aircraft gun
            scarf ring mounts, report on.

Reference: (a) BuOrd ltr PT/S74(Pr 5d) of
                December 21, 1942.

    1.   Reference (a) authorized the manufacture of eleven 20MM scarf ring mounts by Navy Yard, New York, for experimental installation in the forward turrets of the boats of Motor Torpedo Boat Squadron NINE. However, these mounts were not received in time to conduct test firings on more than three boats.

    2.   An average of four practices were fired by each boat at a towed sleeve. All runs were made on the beam at approximately 1500 feet altitude. During each practice there were approximately three firing runs made and a total of 60 rounds fired per gun.

    3.   Average weather conditions were experienced so that opportunity was offered to observe firings as follows:

    (a) No wind, calm sea
    (b) Light winds, slight chop (heavy spray)
    (c) Light rains (squalls)
    (d) Firing directly into the sun

    4.   Results of the above firings are not considered to be conclusive. However, the apparent advantages and disadvantages of subject mount may be summarized as follows:

Advantages
    (a) Less vibration than .50 caliber scarf ring
    (b) Heavier fire power forward
    (c) Essentially a more reliable gun
    (d) Easier to maintain and service
    (e) More effective A. A. gun

Disadvantages
    (a) Somewhat more difficult to train
    (b) Slightly unbalanced
    (c) "Empty brass" bag not satisfactory
    (d) Depression stop bracket not sufficiently rugged
    (e) No sight available
    (f) Depression rail inadequate

CONFIDENTIAL   040040 40288

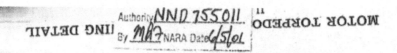

MOTOR TORPEDO
...ING DETAIL

FC8-9/7
CONFIDENTIAL   27 March 1943.

From: The Commander.
To :   The Chief of the Bureau of Ordnance.

Subject: Experimental 20MM anti-aircraft gun
                scarf ring mounts, report on.

- -

    5.   The 20MM scarf ring was found to be somewhat
more difficult to train than the original .50 caliber mount.
The back rest (NYd. NYk. Sketch 110659 - piece No. 5) was
modified so that side measurement is now 6.50", thus giving
the gunner greater leverage.

    6.   This mount was designed for the MK2 gun.
However, MK4 guns were issued this command. The back plate
on the MK4 gun is heavier than that on the MK2. This causes
the cradle to be breach heavy thus somewhat destroying the
designed balance.

    7.   The cartridge bag (NYd. NYk. sketch 110689 -
assembly) has not proven practical and has been removed.
The bag was too small to hold enough "empty brass". It was
also found that the weight of the empty cartridges destroyed
the balance of the mount.

    8.   The depression stop bracket (NYd. NYk. sketch
110791 - Piece 1) is not of sufficiently rugged construction
and requires stiffeners. This piece is easily bent against
the depression rail and catches in the spring bracket of the
gun preventing cocking.

    9.   The MK2 and MK4 sights are too cumbersome
for use on this mount. Due to this squadron's early departure
from New York, the sight brackets being manufactured by the
Navy Yard, New York, have not been received. This bracket
was designed to accommodate the experimental optical ring
(polaroid) sight which is expected to be satisfactory. At
present only tracer control can be used.

    10.   The depression rail requires slight modification
to prevent hitting the radar installation, searchlight and bow
gunner.

    11.   In order to provide adequate stowage for
magazines, a rack has been built abaft the turret on the
starboard ledge of the canopy. This contains four magazines
in addition to three normally stowed in the turret ammunition
locker.

CONFIDENTIAL   40288

FC8-9/7
CONFIDENTIAL

27 March 1943.

From: The Commander.
To :   The Chief of the Bureau of Ordnance.

Subject: Experimental 20MM anti-aircraft gun
          scarf ring mounts, report on.

- -

   12.   This command considers this mount superior
to the .50 caliber scarf ring for use in the forward turret
and is installing same on all boats for service in the
combat area.

                              R. B. KELLY.

Copy to:
    Cominch (Readiness)
    C.O. MTBSTC (Melville)
    NYd., N. Y.

CONFIDENTIAL

DECLASSIFIED
Authority NND 755011
By MAP NARA Date 6/5/01

MOTOR TORPEDO BOAT SQUADRON NINE

FILE NO.   FIRST POST OFFICE, SAN FRANCISCO, CALIFORNIA.

FC9-9/ S73
Serial 013
CONFIDENTIAL   10 June 1943.

From: The Commander.
To :   Commander, Motor Torpedo Boats, South Pacific.
Via :   Commander, Motor Torpedo Boat Flotilla One.

Subject: 20MM scarf ring mount - Report on.

Reference: (a) Squadron 9 conf. ltr. FC9-9/7 of 27 March 1943.

Enclosure: (A) Copy of Reference (a).

    1.   Reference (a) appended herewith as Enclosure (A), describes
subject installation. Since the writing of Reference (a), additional
opportunity has been afforded for further testing the 20MM scarf ring mount
and it is considered entirely satisfactory. In the past two months these
boats have been extensively employed in maintaining routine patrols in the
combat zone. This installation has been subjected to extensive test firing
on all boats in addition, to occasional firing practices using towed sleeve,
balloons and surface targets.

    2.   As a result of the past two month's experience, the vast
majority of the disadvantages listed in Reference (a), have been overcome
and some additional advantages are now apparent.

    3.   The modified back rest described in paragraph 5 of Reference
(a), has overcome the original difficulty in training.

    4.   All guns have now been fitted with an experimental polaroid
optical ring sight using a modified MK IV sight bracket and this has proved
very satisfactory.

    5.   The 20MM scarf ring mount has proved to be rugged and depend-
able under all operating conditions. Most gunners prefer the scarf ring
mount to the present 20MM mount located aft, as it is easier to handle.
Results of firing show it to be equally accurate.

    6.   The subject mount is considered more effective and reliable
than the former .50 caliber installation. An ideal combination of armament

BUREAU OF ORDNANCE

070142 40227.

180

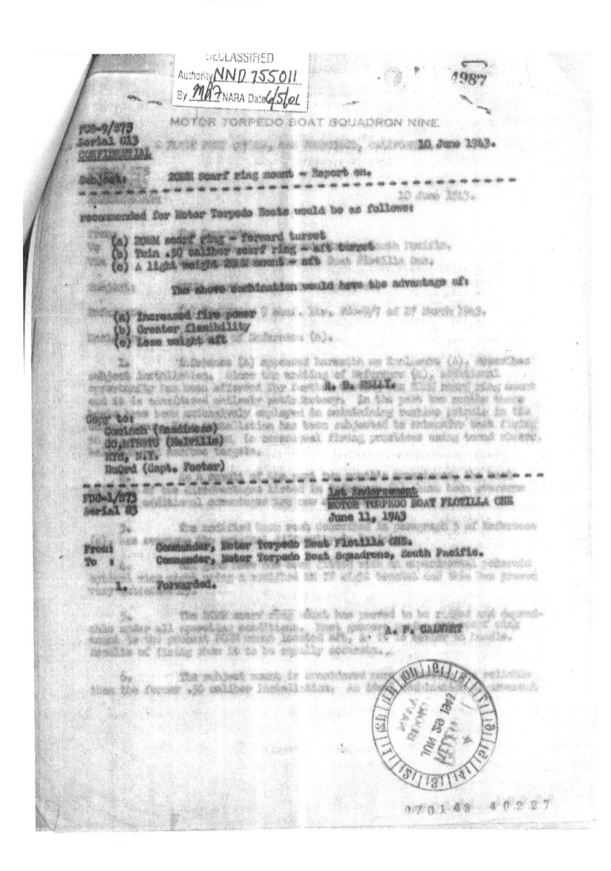

CREDITS, COMMENTS AND UPDATES

Bibliography:

At Close Quarters: PT Boats in the United States Navy   by Robert J. Bulkley Jr.
Marine Combat Correspondent   by Samuel E. Stavisky
History of United States Naval Operations in World War II   by Samuel Eliot Morison
Audio Tapes of interview with William F. Liebenow (1994-95) by Frank Andruss
American PT Boats of World War II, Volume II by Victor Chun
Correspondences from 2001 with PT-157 crewman William Liebenow, Ted Aust and Raymond Macht
        by Alex Johnson
Website: http://pt-king.gdinc.com/Torpedo.html

Photos:

U.S. National Archives and Research Administration [NARA] pages: 10, 11, 12, 19, 24, 25, 77
        Many NARA photos brought to the author's attention by review of Waldo DeWilde's photo
        collection provided by Peter DeWilde
Courtesy of William F. Liebenow: 13, 74, 68 (digitized by Nathaniel Smith)
Courtesy of Welford H. West: 13
Courtesy of Martha Ratchford (Tucker): 59
Courtesy of Peter DeWilde (originally from his father, PT-157 Q/M Waldo DeWilde): 77
U.S. Naval History and Heritage Command, Photo No. NH 96395: 63
Courtesy of PT Boats Museum, Fall River, Massachusetts: 71 (including hand written description). Brought
        to the author's attention by Ted Walther: 71
Courtesy of Gene Koury (nephew of Sam Koury), 71
PT-157 profile and deck drawings, created by and with permission of Dick Washichek: 8, 9

Maps:

Created by Author (using Google Satellite photos as the base) on pages: 30, 31, 32
U.S. National Archives and Research Administration [NARA] pages: 33, 34

Documents:

All documents obtained either directly from the U.S. National Archives and Research Administration
[NARA] or provided to the author by Nathanial Smith and all declassified. The only document that is not
from NARA is the following:
Citation, Silver Star: 74

Resources:

The active and knowledgeable participants of the PT Forum on www.PTBOATS.org website

Comments and updates:

You maybe contact the author at his email address of **bridge@PT-157.com**
The author will be posting any substantive update notices on the website **www.PT-157.com**.

INDEX

Notes:

- Index does not include references in any photos, plates or document reproductions.
- Due to the frequency of occurrences references to the crewman of the PT-157, the PT-157 and geographic locations are not included in this index.

ABOUT THE AUTHOR

Bridgeman (Bridge) Carney grew up in Bucks and Chester counties of Pennsylvania and currently resides in Thousand Oaks, California with his wife, Susan, and their daughters who live in the area. Professionally, Bridge provides Sales and Marketing strategic services to startup companies that provide high technology products and/or services.

ELCO PT-103 series bridge console

Photo of the PT-157 model by Bridgeman Carney

Made in the USA
Columbia, SC
16 June 2019